WI

CW01653385

o. I. APPLETONS' POPU

THE CRUIS
CACHALOT
FRANK T. BULLEN - FIRST MATE

[redacted]

THE "CACHALOT." (*See page 3.*)

THE CRUISE OF THE CACHALOT

ROUND THE WORLD AFTER SPERM WHALES

BY

FRANK T. BULLEN

First Mate

With Illustrations

NEW YORK

D. APPLETON AND COMPANY

1899

Authorized Edition.

TO

MISS EMILY HENSLEY

IN GRATEFUL REMEMBRANCE OF

THIRTY YEARS' CONSTANT FRIENDSHIP AND PRACTICAL HELP

THIS WORK IS AFFECTIONATELY DEDICATED

BY HER HUMBLE PUPIL.

LETTER received by the Author from Mr. RUDYARD KIPLING, as the book was passing through the Press.

DEAR MR. BULLEN,—

It is immense—there is no other word. I've never read anything that equals it in its deep-sea wonder and mystery; nor do I think that any book before has so completely covered the whole business of whale-fishing, and at the same time given such real and new sea pictures. You have thrown away material enough to make five books, and I congratulate you most heartily. It's a new world that you've opened the door to.

Very sincerely,

RUDYARD KIPLING.

ROTTINGDEAN, *Nov.* 22, 1898.

PREFACE.

In the following pages an attempt has been made—it is believed for the first time—to give an account of the cruise of a South Sea whaler from the seaman's standpoint. Two very useful books * have been published—both of them over half a century ago—on the same subject; but, being written by the surgeons of whale-ships for scientific purposes, neither of them was interesting to the general reader. They have both been long out of print; but their value to the student of natural history has been, and still is, very great, Dr. Beale's book, in particular, being still *the* authority on the sperm whale.

This book does not pretend to compete with either of the above valuable works. Its aim is to present to the general reader a simple account of the methods employed, and the dangers met with, in a calling about which the great mass of the public knows absolutely nothing. Pending the advent of some great writer who shall see the wonderful possibilities for literature contained in the world-wide wanderings of the South Sea whale-fishers, the author has endeavoured

* "Narrative of a Whaling Voyage round the Globe," by F. Debell Bennett, F.R.C.S. (2 vols.). Bentley, London (1840). "The Sperm Whale Fishery," by Thomas Beale, M.R.C.S. London (1835).

to summarize his experiences so that they may be read without weariness, and, it is hoped, with profit.

The manifold shortcomings of the work will not, it is trusted, be laid to the account of the subject, than which none more interesting could well be imagined, but to the limitations of the writer, whose long experience of sea life has done little to foster the literary faculty.

One claim may be made with perfect confidence—that if the manner be not all that could be wished, the matter is entirely trustworthy, being compiled from actual observation and experience, and in no case at second-hand. An endeavour has also been made to exclude such matter as is easily obtainable elsewhere—matters of common knowledge and "padding" of any sort—the object not being simply the making of a book, but the record of little-known facts.

Great care has been taken to use no names either of ships or persons, which could, by being identified, give annoyance or pain to any one, as in many cases strong language has been necessary for the expression of opinions.

Finally, the author hopes that, although in no sense exclusively a book for boys, the coming generation may find this volume readable and interesting; and with that desire he offers it confidently, though in all humility, to that great impartial jury, the public.

F. T. B.

DULWICH, *July*, 1897.

CONTENTS.

CHAPTER I.

OUTWARD BOUND.

CHAPTER II.

PREPARING FOR ACTION.

CHAPTER III.

FISHING BEGINS.

CHAPTER IV.

BAD WEATHER.

CHAPTER V.

ACTUAL WARFARE. OUR FIRST WHALE.

CHAPTER VI.

"DIRTY WORK FOR CLEAN MONEY."

CHAPTER VII.

GETTING SOUTHWARD.

CHAPTER VIII.

ABNER'S WHALE.

CHAPTER IX.

OUR FIRST CALLING-PLACE.

CHAPTER X.

A VISIT TO SOME STRANGE PLACES.

CHAPTER XI.

ROUND THE COCOS AMD SEYCHELLES.

CHAPTER XII.

WHICH TREATS OF THE KRAKEN.

CHAPTER XIII.

OFF TO THE JAPAN GROUNDS.

CHAPTER XIV.

LIBERTY DAY—AND AFTER.

CHAPTER XX.

"HUMPBACKING" AT VAU VAU.

CHAPTER XXI.

PROGRESS OF THE "HUMPBACK" SEASON.

CHAPTER XXII.

FAREWELL TO VAU VAU.

CHAPTER XXIII.

AT FUTUNA, RECRUITING.

CHAPTER XXIV.

THE BAY OF ISLANDS AND NEW ZEALAND COAST.

CHAPTER XXV.

ON THE SOLANDER GROUNDS.

CHAPTER XXVI.

PADDY'S LATEST EXPLOIT.

CHAPTER XXVII.

PORT PEGASUS.

CHAPTER XXVIII.

TO THE BLUFF, AND HOME.

LIST OF ILLUSTRATIONS.

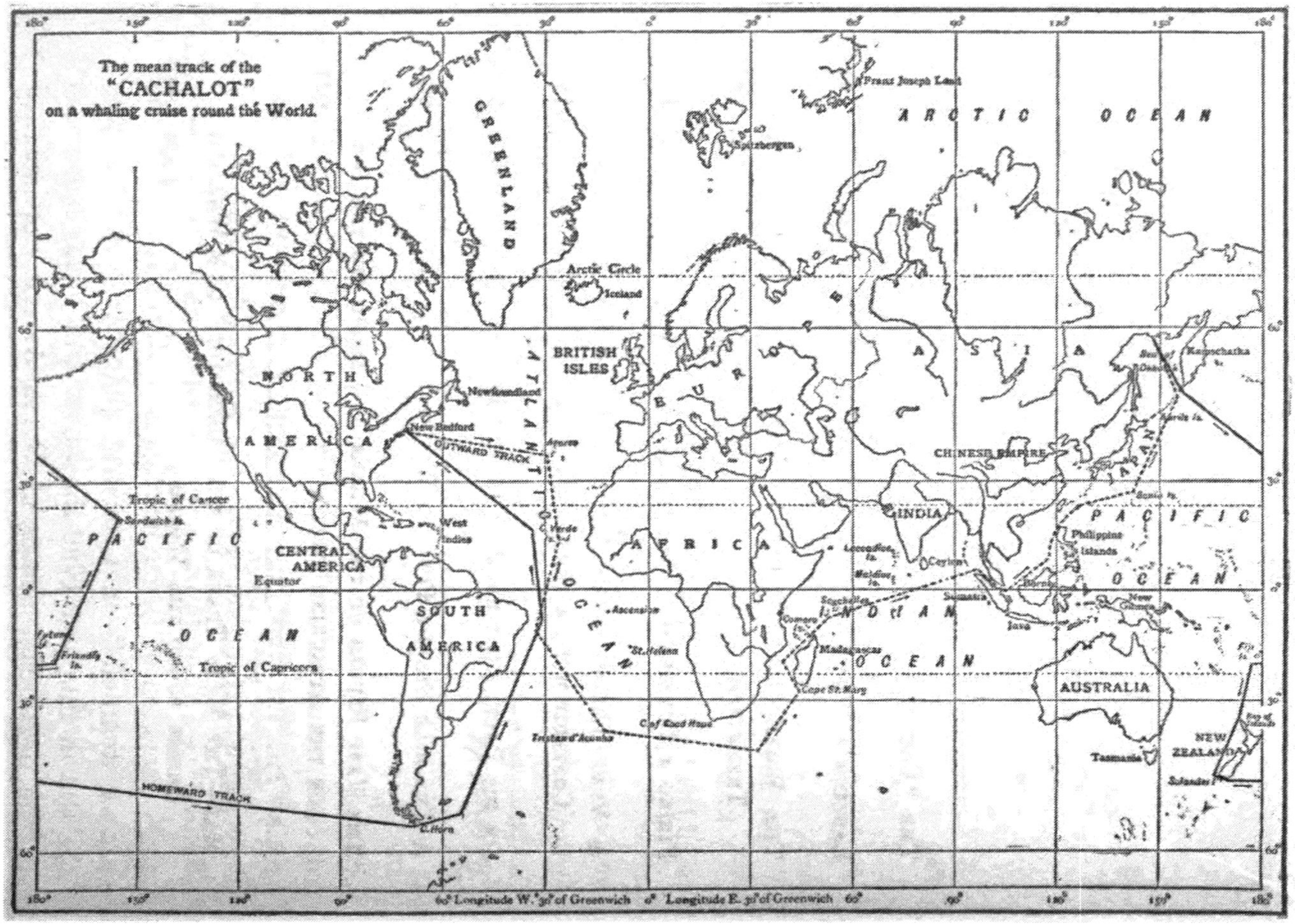
The mean track of the
"CACHALOT"
on a whaling cruise round the World.
GREENLAND
ARCTIC OCEAN
Franz Joseph Land
Spitzbergen
Arctic Circle
Iceland
BRITISH ISLES
NORTH AMERICA
EUROPE
ASIA
Newfoundland
New Bedford
OUTWARD TRACK
ATLANTIC OCEAN
Azores
Tropic of Cancer
PACIFIC OCEAN
West Indies
CENTRAL AMERICA
Equator
AFRICA
CHINESE EMPIRE
JAPAN
INDIA
Ceylon
Philippine Islands
SOUTH AMERICA
Ascension
St. Helena
Madagascar
INDIAN OCEAN
Tropic of Capricorn
AUSTRALIA
Cape St. Mary
Tristan d'Acunha
Tasmania
NEW ZEALAND
HOMEWARD TRACK
C. Horn
Longitude W. of Greenwich
Longitude E. of Greenwich

INTRODUCTION.

Without attempting the ambitious task of presenting a comprehensive sketch of the origin, rise, and fall of whale-fishing as a whole, it seems necessary to give a brief outline of that portion of the subject bearing upon the theme of the present book before plunging into the first chapter.

This preliminary is the more needed for the reason alluded to in the Preface—the want of knowledge of the subject that is apparent everywhere. The Greenland whale fishery has been so popularized that most people know something about it; the sperm whale fishery still awaits its Scoresby and a like train of imitators and borrowers.

Cachalots, or sperm whales, must have been captured on the coasts of Europe in a desultory way from a very early date, by the incidental allusions to the prime products spermaceti and ambergris which are found in so many ancient writers. Shakespeare's reference—"The sovereign'st thing on earth was parmaceti for an inward bruise"—will be familiar to most people, as well as Milton's mention of the delicacies at Satan's feast—"Gris-amber steamed"—not to carry quotation any further.

But in the year 1690 the brave and hardy fishermen of the north-east coasts of North America established that systematic pursuit of the cachalot which has thriven so wonderfully ever since, although it must be confessed that the last few years have witnessed a serious decline in this great branch of trade.

For many years the American colonists completely engrossed this branch of the whale fishery, contentedly leaving to Great Britain and the continental nations the monopoly of the northern or Arctic fisheries, while they cruised the stormy, if milder, seas around their own shores.

For the resultant products, their best customer was the mother country, and a lucrative commerce steadily grew up between the two countries. But when the march of events brought the unfortunate and wholly unnecessary War of Independence, this flourishing trade was the first to suffer, and many of the daring fishermen became our fiercest foes on board their own men-of-war.

The total stoppage of the importation of sperm oil and spermaceti was naturally severely felt in England, for time had not permitted the invention of substitutes. In consequence of this, ten ships were equipped and sent out to the sperm whale fishery from England in 1775, most of them owned by one London firm, the Messrs. Enderby. The next year, in order to encourage the infant enterprise, a Government bounty, graduated from £500 to £1000 per ship, was granted. Under this fostering care the number of ships engaged in the sperm whale fishery progressively increased until 1791, when it attained its maximum.

This method of whaling being quite new to our whalemen, it was necessary, at great cost, to hire

American officers and harpooners to instruct them in the ways of dealing with these highly active and dangerous cetacea. Naturally, it was by-and-by found possible to dispense with the services of these auxiliaries; but it must be confessed that the business never seems to have found such favour, or to have been prosecuted with such smartness, among our whalemen as it has by the Americans.

Something of an exotic the trade always was among us, although it did attain considerable proportions at one time. At first the fishing was confined to the Atlantic Ocean; nor for many years was it necessary to go farther afield, as abundance of whales could easily be found.

As, however, the number of ships engaged increased, it was inevitable that the known grounds should become exhausted, and in 1788 Messrs. Enderby's ship, the *Emilia*, first ventured round Cape Horn, as the pioneer of a greater trade than ever. The way once pointed out, other ships were not slow to follow, until, in 1819, the British whale-ship *Syren* opened up the till then unexplored tract of ocean in the western part of the North Pacific, afterwards familiarly known as the "Coast of Japan." From these teeming waters alone, for many years an average annual catch of 40,000 barrels of oil was taken, which, at the average price of £8 per barrel, will give some idea of the value of the trade generally.

The Australian colonists, early in their career, found the sperm whale fishery easy of access from all their coasts, and especially lucrative. At one-time they bade fair to establish a whale fishery that should rival the splendid trade of the Americans; but, like the mother country, they permitted the fishery to decline, so that even bounties could not keep it alive.

Meanwhile, the Americans added to their fleet continually, prospering amazingly. But suddenly the advent of the civil war let loose among those peaceable cruisers the devastating *Alabama*, whose course was marked in some parts of the world by the fires of blazing whale-ships. A great part of the Geneva award was on this account, although it must be acknowledged that many pseudo-owners were enriched who never owned aught but brazen impudence and influential friends to push their fictitious claims. The real sufferers, seamen especially, in most cases never received any redress whatever.

From this crushing blow the American sperm whale fishery has never fully recovered. When the writer was in the trade, some twenty-two years ago, it was credited with a fleet of between three and four hundred sail; now it may be doubted whether the numbers reach an eighth of that amount. A rigid conservatism of method hinders any revival of the industry, which is practically conducted to-day as it was fifty, or even a hundred years ago; and it is probable that another decade will witness the final extinction of what was once one of the most important maritime industries in the world.

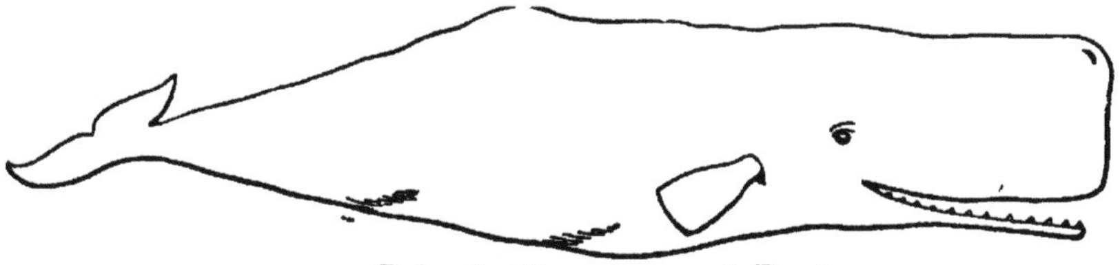

Colnett, Huggins, and Beale.

SPERM WHALE, OR CACHALOT (*Physeter Macrocephalus*).

THE CRUISE OF THE "CACHALOT."

CHAPTER I.

OUTWARD BOUND.

AT the age of eighteen, after a sea-experience of six years from the time when I dodged about London streets, a ragged Arab, with wits sharpened by the constant fight for food, I found myself roaming the streets of New Bedford, Massachusetts. How I came to be there, of all places in the world, does not concern this story at all, so I am not going to trouble my readers with it; enough to say that I *was* there, and mighty anxious to get away. Sailor Jack is always hankering for shore when he is at sea, but when he is "outward bound"—that is, when his money is all gone—he is like a cat in the rain there.

So as *my* money was all gone, I was hungry for a ship; and when a long, keen-looking man with a goat-like beard, and mouth stained with dry tobacco-juice, hailed me one afternoon at the street corner, I answered very promptly, scenting a berth. "Lookin' fer a ship, stranger?" said he. "Yes; do you want a hand?" said I, anxiously. He made a funny little sound something like a pony's whinny, then answered, "Wall, I should surmise that I want between fifty and sixty hands, ef yew kin lay me onto 'em; but, kem along, every dreep's a drop, an' yew seem likely enough." With that he turned and led the way until we reached a building, around which were gathered one of the most nondescript crowds I had ever seen. There certainly did not appear to be a sailor among them. Not so much by their rig, though that is not a great deal to go by, but by their actions and speech. One thing they all had in common, tobacco chewing; but as nearly every male I met with in America did that, it was not much to be noticed. I had hardly done reckoning them up when two or three bustling men came out and shepherded us all energetically into a long, low room, where some form of agreement was read out to us. Sailors are naturally and usually careless about the nature of the "articles" they sign, their chief anxiety being to get to sea, and under somebody's charge. But had I been ever so anxious to know what I was going to sign this time, I could not, for the language might as well have been Chinese for all I understood of it. However, I signed and passed on, engaged to go I knew not where, in some ship I did not know even the name of, in which I was to receive I did not know how much, or how little, for my labour, nor how long I was going to be away. "What a young fool!" I hear somebody say. I quite agree, but there were a good many more in that ship, as in most ships that I have ever sailed in.

From the time we signed the articles, we were never left to ourselves. Truculent-looking men accompanied us to our several boarding-houses, paid our debts for us, finally bringing us by boat to a ship lying out in the bay. As we passed under her stern, I read the name *Cachalot*, of New Bedford; but as soon as we ranged alongside, I realized that I was booked for the sailor's horror—a cruise in a whaler. Badly as I wanted to get to sea, I had not bargained for this, and would have run some risks to get ashore again; but they took no chances, so we were all soon aboard. Before going forward, I took a comprehensive glance around, and saw that I was on board of a vessel belonging to a type which has almost disappeared off the face of the waters. A more perfect contrast to the trim-built English clipper-ships that I had been accustomed to I could hardly imagine. She was one of a class characterized by sailors as "built by the mile, and cut off in lengths as you want 'em," bow and stern almost alike, masts standing straight as broomsticks, and bowsprit soaring upwards at an angle of about forty-five degrees. She was as old-fashioned in her rig as in her hull; but I must not go into the technical differences between rigs, for fear of making myself tedious. Right in the centre of the deck, occupying a space of about ten feet by eight, was a square erection of brickwork, upon which my wondering gaze rested longest, for I had not the slightest idea what it could be. But I was rudely roused from my meditations by the harsh voice of one of the officers, who shouted, "Naow then, git below an' stow yer dunnage, 'n look lively up agin." I took the broad hint, and shouldering my traps, hurried forward to the fo'lk'sle, which was below deck. Tumbling down the steep ladder, I entered the gloomy den which was to be for so long my home, finding it fairly packed with my shipmates. A motley crowd they were. I had been used in English ships to considerable variety of nationality; but here were gathered, not only the representatives of five or six nations, but 'long-shoremen of all kinds, half of whom had hardly ever set eyes on a ship before! The whole space was undivided by partition, but I saw at once that black men and white had separated themselves, the blacks taking the port side and the whites the starboard. Finding a vacant bunk by the dim glimmer of the ancient teapot lamp that hung amidships, giving out as much smoke as light, I hurriedly shifted my coat for a "jumper" or blouse, put on an old cap, and climbed into the fresh air again. For a double reason, even *my* seasoned head was feeling bad with the villainous reek of the place, and I did not want any of those hard-featured officers on deck to have any cause to complain of my "hanging back." On board ship, especially American ships, the first requisite for a sailor who wants to be treated properly is to "show willing," any suspicion of slackness being noted immediately, and the backward one marked accordingly. I had hardly reached the deck when I was confronted by a negro, the biggest I ever saw in my life. He looked me up and down for a moment, then opening his ebony features in a wide smile, he said, "Great snakes! why, here's a sailor man for sure! Guess thet's so, ain't it, Johnny?" I said "yes" very curtly, for I hardly liked his patronizing air; but he snapped me up short with "yes, *sir*, when yew speak to me, yew blank limejuicer. I'se de fourf mate ob dis yar ship, en my name's Mistah Jones, 'n yew jest freeze on to dat ar, ef yew want ter lib long 'n die happy. See, sonny." I *saw*, and answered promptly, "I beg your pardon, sir, I didn't know." "Ob cawse yew didn't know, dat's all right, little Britisher; naow jest skip aloft 'n loose dat fore-taupsle." "Aye, aye, sir," I answered cheerily, springing at once into the fore-rigging and up the ratlines like a monkey, but not too fast to hear him chuckle, "Dat's a smart kiddy, I bet." I had the big sail loose in double quick time, and sung out "All gone, the fore-taupsle," before any of the other sails were adrift. "Loose the to-gantsle and staysles" came up from below in a voice like thunder, and I bounded up higher to my task. On deck I could see a crowd at the windlass heaving up anchor. I said to myself, "They don't waste any time getting this packet away." Evidently they were not anxious to test any of the crew's swimming powers. They were wise, for had she remained at anchor that night I verily believe some of the poor wretches would have tried to escape.

The anchor came aweigh, the sails were sheeted home, and I returned on deck to find the ship gathering way for the heads, fairly started on her long voyage.

What a bear-garden the deck was, to be sure! The black portion of the crew—Portuguese natives from the Western and Canary Islands—were doing their work all right in a clumsy fashion; but the farmers, and bakers, and draymen were being driven about mercilessly amid a perfect hurricane of profanity and blows. And right here I must say that, accustomed as I had always been to bad language all my life, what I now heard was a revelation to me. I would not, if I could, attempt to give a sample of it, but it must be understood that it was incessant throughout the voyage. No order could be given without it, under the impression, apparently, that the more curses the more speed.

Before nightfall we were fairly out to sea, and the ceremony of dividing the crew into watches was gone through. I found myself in the chief mate's or "port" watch (they called it "larboard," a term I had never heard used before, it having long been obsolete in merchant ships), though the huge negro fourth mate seemed none too well pleased that I was not under his command, his being the starboard watch under the second mate.

As night fell, the condition of the "greenies," or non-sailor portion of the crew, was pitiable. Helpless from sea-sickness, not knowing where to go or what to do, bullied relentlessly by the ruthless petty officers—well, I never felt so sorry for a lot of men in my life. Glad enough I was to get below into the fo'lk'sle for supper, and a brief rest and respite from that cruelty on deck. A bit of salt junk and a piece of bread, *i.e.* biscuit, flinty as a pantile, with a pot of something sweetened with "longlick" (molasses), made an apology for a meal, and I turned in. In a very few minutes oblivion came, making me as happy as any man can be in this world.

CHAPTER II.

PREPARING FOR ACTION.

The hideous noise always considered necessary in those ships when calling the watch, roused me effectively at midnight, "eight bells." I hurried on deck, fully aware that no leisurely ten minutes would be allowed here. "Lay aft the watch," saluted me as I emerged into the keen, strong air, quickening my pace accordingly to where the mate stood waiting to muster his men. As soon as he saw me, he said, "Can you steer?" in a mocking tone; but when I quietly answered, "Yes, sir," his look of astonishment was delightful to see. He choked it down, however, and merely telling me to take the wheel, turned forrard roaring frantically for his watch. I had no time to chuckle over what I knew was in store for him, getting those poor greenies collected from their several holes and corners, for on taking the wheel I found a machine under my hands such as I never even heard of before.

The wheel was fixed upon the tiller in such a manner that the whole concern travelled backwards and forwards across the deck in the maddest kind of way. For the first quarter of an hour, in spite of the September chill, the sweat poured off me in streams. And the course—

well, it was not steering, it was sculling; the old bum-boat was wobbling all around like a drunken tailor with two left legs. I fairly shook with apprehension lest the mate should come and look in the compass. I had been accustomed to hard words if I did not steer within half a point each way; but here was a "gadget" that worked me to death, the result being a wake like a letter S. Gradually I got the hang of the thing, becoming easier in my mind on my own account. Even that was not an unmixed blessing, for I had now some leisure to listen to the goings-on around the deck.

Such brutality I never witnessed before. On board of English ships (except men-of-war) there is practically no discipline, which is bad, but this sort of thing was maddening. I knew how desperately ill all those poor wretches were, how helpless and awkward they would be if quite hale and hearty; but there was absolutely no pity for them, the officers seemed to be incapable of any feelings of compassion whatever. My heart sank within me as I thought of what lay before me, although I did not fear that their treatment would also be mine, since I was at least able to do my duty, and willing to work hard to keep out of trouble. Then I began to wonder what sort of voyage I was in for, how long it would last, and what my earnings were likely to be, none of which things I had the faintest idea of.

Fortunately, I was alone in the world. No one, as far as I knew, cared a straw what became of me; so that I was spared any worry on that head. And I had also a very definite and well-established trust in God, which I can now look back and see was as fully justified as I then believed it to be. So, as I could not shut my ears to the cruelties being carried on, nor banish thought by hard work, I looked up to the stately stars, thinking of things not to be talked about without being suspected of cant. So swiftly passed the time that when four bells struck (two o'clock) I could hardly believe my ears.

I was relieved by one of the Portuguese, and went forward to witness a curious scene. Seven stalwart men were being compelled to march up and down on that tumbling deck, men who had never before trodden anything less solid than the earth.

The third mate, a waspish, spiteful little Yankee with a face like an angry cat, strolled about among them, a strand of rope-yarns in his hand, which he wielded constantly, regardless where he struck a man. They fell about, sometimes four or five at once, and his blows flew thick and fast, yet he never seemed to weary of his ill-doing. It made me quite sick, and I longed to be aft at the wheel again. Catching sight of me standing irresolute as to what I had better do, he ordered me on the "look-out," a tiny platform between the "knight heads," just where the bowsprit joins the ship. Gladly I obeyed him, and perched up there looking over the wide sea, the time passed quickly away until eight bells (four o'clock) terminated my watch. I must pass rapidly over the condition of things in the fo'lk'sle, where all the greenies that were allowed below, were groaning in misery from the stifling atmosphere which made their sickness so much worse, while even that dreadful place was preferable to what awaited them on deck. There was a rainbow-coloured halo round the flame of the lamp, showing how very bad the air was; but in spite of that I turned in and slept soundly till seven bells (7.20 a.m.) roused us to breakfast.

American ships generally have an excellent name for

the way they feed their crews, but the whalers are a notable exception to that good rule. The food was really worse than that on board any English ship I have ever sailed in, so scanty also in quantity that it kept all the foremast hands at starvation point. But grumbling was dangerous, so I gulped down the dirty mixture mis-named coffee, ate a few fragments of biscuit, and filled up (?) with a smoke, as many better men are doing this morning. As the bell struck I hurried on deck—not one moment too soon—for as I stepped out of the scuttle I saw the third mate coming forward with a glitter in his eye that boded no good to laggards.

Before going any farther I must apologize for using so many capital I's, but up till the present I had been the only available white member of the crew forrard.

The decks were scrubbed spotlessly clean, and everything was neat and tidy as on board a man-of-war, contrary to all usual notions of the condition of a whaler. The mate was in a state of high activity, so I soon found myself very busily engaged in getting up whale-lines, harpoons, and all the varied equipment for the pursuit of whales. The number of officers carried would have been a good crew for the ship, the complete afterguard comprising captain, four mates, four harpooners or boat-steerers, carpenter, cooper, steward and cook. All these worthies were on deck and working with might and main at the preparations, so that the incompetence of the crowd forrard was little hindrance. I was pounced upon by "Mistah" Jones, the fourth mate, whom I heard addressed familiarly as "Goliath" and "Anak" by his brother officers, and ordered to assist him in rigging the "crow's-nest" at the main royal-mast head. It was a simple affair. There were a pair of cross-trees fitted to the mast, upon which was secured a tiny platform about a foot wide on each side of the mast, while above this foothold a couple of padded hoops like a pair of giant spectacles were secured at a little higher than a man's waist. When all was fast one could creep up on the platform, through the hoop, and resting his arms upon the latter, stand comfortably and gaze around, no matter how vigorously the old barky plunged and kicked beneath him. From that lofty eerie I had a comprehensive view of the vessel. She was about 350 tons and full ship-rigged, that is to say, she carried square sails on all three masts. Her deck was flush fore and aft, the only obstructions being the brick-built "try-works" in the waist, the galley, and cabin skylight right aft by the taff-rail. Her bulwarks were set thickly round with clumsy looking wooden cranes, from which depended five boats. Two more boats were secured bottom up upon a gallows aft, so she seemed to be well supplied in that direction. Mistah Jones, finding I did not presume upon his condescension, gradually unbent and furnished me with many interesting facts about the officers. Captain Slocum, he said, was "de debbil hisself, so jess yew keep yer lamps trim' fer him, sonny, taint helthy ter rile him." The first officer, or *the* mate as he is always called *par excellence*, was an older man than the captain, but a good seaman, a good whaleman, *and* a gentleman. Which combination I found to be a fact, although hard to believe possible at the time. The second mate was a Portuguese about forty years of age, with a face like one of Vandyke's cavaliers, but as I now learned, a perfect fiend when angered. He also was a first-class whaleman, but an indifferent seaman. The third mate was nothing much but bad temper—not much sailor, nor much whaler, generally in hot water with the skipper, who hated him because he was an "owner's man." "An de fourf mate," wound up the narrator, straightening his huge bulk, "am de bes' man in de ship, and de bigges'. Dey aint no whalemen in Noö Bedford caynt teach *me* nuffin, en ef it comes ter man-handlin'; w'y I jes' pick em two't a time 'n crack 'em togerrer like so, see!" and he smote the palms of his great paws against each other, while I nodded complete assent.

The weather being fine, with a steady N.E. wind blowing, so that the sails required no attention, work proceeded steadily all the morning. The oars were sorted, examined for flaws, and placed in the boats; the whale-line, manilla rope like yellow silk, 1½ inch round, was brought on deck, stretched and coiled down with the greatest care into tubs, holding, some 200 fathoms, and others 100 fathoms each. New harpoons were fitted to poles of rough but heavy wood, without any attempt at neatness, but every attention to strength. The shape of these weapons was not, as is generally thought, that of an arrow, but rather like an arrow with one huge barb, the upper part of which curved out from the shaft. The whole of the barb turned on a stout pivot of steel, but was kept in line with the shaft by a tiny wooden peg which passed through barb and shaft, being then cut off smoothly on both sides. The point of the harpoon had at one side a wedge-shaped edge, ground to razor keenness, the other side was flat. The shaft, about thirty inches long, was of the best malleable iron, so soft that it would tie into a knot and straighten out again without fracture. Three harpoons, or "irons" as they were always called, were placed in each boat, fitted one above the other in the starboard bow, the first for use being always one unused before. Opposite to them in the boat were fitted three lances for the purpose of *killing* whales, the harpoons being only the means by which the boat was attached to a fish, and quite useless to inflict a fatal wound. These lances were slender spears of malleable iron about four feet long, with oval or heart-shaped points of fine steel about two inches broad, their edges kept keen as a surgeon's lancet. By means of a socket at the other end they were attached to neat handles, or "lance-poles," about as long again, the whole weapon being thus about eight feet in length, and furnished with a light line, or "lance-warp," for the purpose of drawing it back again when it had been darted at a whale.

Each boat was fitted with a centre-board, or sliding keel, which was drawn up, when not in use, into a case standing in the boat's middle, very much in the way. But the American whalemen regard these clumsy contrivances as indispensable, so there's an end on't. The other furniture of a boat comprised five oars of varying lengths from sixteen to nine feet, one great steering oar of nineteen feet, a mast and two sails of great area for so small a craft, spritsail shape; two tubs of whale-line containing together 1800 feet, a keg of drinking water, and another long narrow one with a few biscuits, a lantern, candles and matches therein; a bucket and "piggin" for baling, a small spade, a flag or "wheft," a shoulder bomb-gun and ammunition, two knives and two small axes. A rudder hung outside by the stern.

With all this gear, although snugly stowed, a boat looked so loaded that I could not help wondering how six men would be able to work in her; but like most "deep-water" sailors, I knew very little about boating. I was going to learn.

All this work and bustle of preparation was so rapidly carried on, and so interesting, that before supper-time everything was in readiness to commence operations, the time having gone so swiftly that I could hardly believe the bell when it sounded four times, six o'clock.

CHAPTER III.

FISHING BEGINS.

During all the bustle of warlike preparation that had been going on, the greenhorns had not suffered from inattention on the part of those appointed to look after them. Happily for them, the wind blew steadily, and the weather, thanks to the balmy influence of the Gulf Stream, was quite mild and genial. The ship was undoubtedly lively, as all good sea-boats are, but her motions were by no means so detestable to a sea-sick man as those of a driving steamer. So, in spite of their treatment, perhaps because of it, some of the poor fellows were beginning to take hold of things "man-fashion," although of course sea legs they had none, their getting about being indeed a pilgrimage of pain. Some of them were beginning to try the dreadful "grub" (I cannot libel "food" by using it in such a connection), thereby showing that their interest in life, even such a life as was now before them, was returning. They had all been allotted places in the various boats, intermixed with the seasoned Portuguese in such a way that the officer and harpooner in charge would not be dependant upon them entirely in case of a sudden emergency. Every endeavour was undoubtedly made to instruct them in their duties, albeit the teachers were all too apt to beat their information in with anything that came to hand, and persuasion found no place in their methods.

The reports I had always heard of the laziness prevailing on board whale-ships were now abundantly falsified. From dawn to dark work went on without cessation. Everything was rubbed and scrubbed and scoured until no speck or soil could be found; indeed, no gentleman's yacht or man-of-war is kept more spotlessly clean than was the *Cachalot*.

A regular and severe routine of labour was kept up; and, what was most galling to me, instead of a regular four hours watch on and off, night and day, all hands were kept on deck the whole day long, doing quite unnecessary tasks, apparently with the object of preventing too much leisure and consequent brooding over their unhappy lot. One result of this continual drive and tear was that all these landsmen became rapidly imbued with the virtues of cleanliness, which was extended to the den in which we lived, or I verily believe sickness would have soon thinned us out.

On the fourth day after leaving port we were all busy as usual except the four men in the "crow's-nests," when a sudden cry of "Porps! porps!" brought everything to a standstill. A large school of porpoises had just joined us, in their usual clownish fashion, rolling and tumbling around the bows as the old barky wallowed along, surrounded by a wide ellipse of snowy foam. All work was instantly suspended, and active preparations made for securing a few of these frolicsome fellows. A "block," or pulley, was hung out at the bowsprit end, a whale-line passed through it and "bent" (fastened) on to a harpoon. Another line with a running "bowline," or slip-noose, was also passed out to the bowsprit end, being held there by one man in readiness. Then one of the harpooners ran out along the back-ropes, which keep the jib-boom down, taking his stand beneath the bowsprit with the harpoon ready. Presently he raised his iron and followed the track of a rising porpoise with its point until the creature broke water. At the same instant the weapon left his grasp, apparently without any force behind it; but we on deck, holding the line, soon found that our excited hauling lifted a big vibrating body clean out of the smother beneath. "'Vast hauling!" shouted the mate, while as the porpoise hung dangling, the harpooner slipped the ready bowline over his body, gently closing its grip round the "small" by the broad tail. Then we hauled on the noose-line, slacking away the harpoon, and in a minute had our prize on deck. He was dragged away at once and the operation repeated. Again and again we hauled them in, until the fore part of the deck was alive with the kicking, writhing sea-pigs, at least twenty of them. I had seen an occasional porpoise caught at sea before, but never more than one at a time. Here, however, was a wholesale catch. At last one of the harpooned ones plunged so furiously while being hauled up that he literally tore himself off the iron, falling, streaming with blood, back into the sea.

Away went all the school after him, tearing at him with their long well-toothed jaws, some of them leaping high in the air in their eagerness to get their due share of the cannibal feast. Our fishing was over for that time. Meanwhile one of the harpooners had brought out a number of knives, with which all hands were soon busy skinning the blubber from the bodies. Porpoises have no skin, that is hide, the blubber or coating of lard which encases them being covered by a black substance as thin as tissue paper. The porpoise hide of the boot maker is really leather, made from the skin of the *Beluga*, or "white whale," which is found only in the far north. The cover was removed from the "try-works" amidships, revealing two gigantic pots set in a frame of brickwork side by side, capable of holding 200 gallons each. Such a cooking apparatus as might have graced a Brobdingnagian kitchen. Beneath the pots was the very simplest of furnaces, hardly as elaborate as the familiar copper-hole sacred to washing day. Square funnels of sheet-iron were loosely fitted to the flues, more as a protection against the oil boiling over into the fire than to carry away the smoke, of which from the peculiar nature of the fuel there was very little. At one side of the try-works was a large wooden vessel, or "hopper," to contain the raw blubber; at the other, a copper cistern or cooler of about 300 gallons capacity, into which the prepared oil was baled to cool off, preliminary to its being poured into the casks. Beneath the furnaces was a space as large as the whole area of the try-works, about a foot deep, which, when the fires were lighted, was filled with water to prevent the deck from burning.

It may be imagined that the blubber from our twenty porpoises made but a poor show in one of the pots; nevertheless, we got a barrel of very excellent oil from them. The fires were fed with "scrap," or pieces of blubber from which the oil had been boiled, some of which had been reserved from the previous voyage. They burnt with a fierce and steady blaze, leaving but a trace of ash. I was then informed by one of the harpooners that no other fuel was ever used for boiling blubber at any time, there being always amply sufficient for the purpose.

The most interesting part of the whole business, though, to us poor half-starved wretches, was the plentiful supply of fresh meat. Porpoise beef is, when decently cooked, fairly good eating to a landsman; judge, then, what it must have been to us. Of course the titbits, such as the liver, kidneys, brains, etc., could not possibly fall to our lot; but we did not complain, we were too thankful to get something eatable, and enough of it. Moreover, although few sailors in English ships know it, porpoise beef improves vastly by keeping, getting tenderer every day the longer it hangs, until at last it becomes as tasty a viand as one could wish to dine upon. It was a good job for us that this *was* the case, for while the porpoises lasted the "harness casks," or salt beef receptacles, were kept locked; so if any man had felt unable to eat porpoise—well, there was no compulsion, he could go hungry.

We were now in the haunts of the Sperm Whale, or "Cachalot," a brilliant look-out being continually kept for any signs of their appearing. One officer and a foremast hand were continually on watch during the day in the main crow's-nest, one harpooner and a seaman in the fore one. A bounty of ten pounds of tobacco was offered to whoever should first report a whale, should it be secured, consequently there were no sleepy eyes up there. Of course none of those who were inexperienced stood much chance against the eagle-eyed Portuguese; but all tried their best, in the hope of perhaps winning some little favour from their hard taskmasters. Every evening at sunset it was "all hands shorten sail," the constant drill rapidly teaching even these clumsy landsmen how to find their way aloft, and do something else besides hold on to anything like grim death when they got there.

At last, one beautiful day, the boats were lowered and manned, and away went the greenies on their first practical lesson in the business of the voyage. As before noticed, there were two greenies in each boat, they being so arranged that whenever one of them "caught a crab," which of course was about every other stroke, his failure made little difference to the boat's progress. They learned very fast under the terrible imprecations and storm of blows from the iron-fisted and iron-hearted officers, so that before the day was out the skipper was satisfied of our ability to deal with a "fish" should he be lucky enough to "raise" one. I was, in virtue of my experience, placed at the after-oar in the mate's boat, where it was my duty to attend to the "main sheet" when the sail was set, where also I had the benefit of the lightest oar except the small one used by the harpooner in the bow.

The very next day after our first exhaustive boat drill, a school of "Black Fish" was reported from aloft, and with great glee the officers prepared for what they considered a rattling day's fun.

The Black Fish (*Phocæna Sp.*) is a small toothed whale, not at all unlike a miniature cachalot, except that its head is rounded at the front, while its jaw is not long and straight, but bowed. It is as frolicsome as the porpoise, gambolling about in schools of from twenty to fifty or more, as if really delighted to be alive. Its average size is from ten to twenty feet long, and seven or eight feet in girth, weight from one to three tons.

Blubber about three inches thick, while the head is almost all oil, so that a good rich specimen will make between one and two barrels of oil of medium quality.

The school we were now in sight of was of middling size and about average weight of individuals, and the officers esteemed it a fortunate circumstance that we should happen across them as a sort of preliminary to our tackling the monarchs of the deep.

All the new harpoons were unshipped from the boats, and a couple of extra "second" irons, as those that have been used are called, were put into each boat for use if wanted. The sails were also left on board. We lowered and left the ship, pulling right towards the school, the noise they were making in their fun effectually preventing them from hearing our approach. It is etiquette to allow the mate's boat first place, unless his crew is so weak as to be unable to hold their own; but as the mate always has first pick of the men this seldom happens. So, as usual, we were first, and soon I heard the order given, "Stand up, Louey, and let 'em have it!" Sure enough, here we were right among them. Louis let drive, "fastening" a whopper about twenty feet long. The injured animal plunged madly forward, accompanied by his fellows, while Louis calmly bent another iron to a "short warp," or piece of whale-line, the loose end of which he made a bowline with round the main line which was fast to the "fish." Then he fastened another "fish," and the queer sight was seen of these two monsters each trying to flee in opposite directions, while the second one ranged about alarmingly as his "bridle" ran along the main line. Another one was secured in the same way, then the game was indeed great. The school had by this time taken the alarm and cleared out, but the other boats were all fast to fish, so that didn't matter. Now, at the rate our "game" were going, it would evidently be a long while before they died, although, being so much smaller than a whale proper, a harpoon will often kill them at a stroke. Yet they were now so tangled or "snarled erp," as the mate said, that it was no easy matter to lance them without great danger of cutting the line. However, we hauled up as close to them as we dared, and the harpooner got a good blow in, which gave the biggest of the three "Jesse," as he said, though why "Jesse" was a stumper. Anyhow, it killed him promptly, while almost directly after another one saved further trouble by passing in his own checks. But he sank at the same time, drawing the first one down with him, so that we were in considerable danger of having to cut them adrift or be swamped. The "wheft" was waved thrice as an urgent signal to the ship to come to our assistance with all speed, but in the meantime our interest lay in the surviving Black Fish keeping alive. Should *he* die, and, as was most probable, sink, we should certainly have to cut and lose the lot, tools included.

We waited in grim silence while the ship came up, so slowly, apparently, that she hardly seemed to move, but really at a good pace of about four knots an hour, which for her was not at all bad. She got alongside of us at last, and we passed up the bight of our line, our fish all safe, very much pleased with ourselves, especially when we found that the other boats had only five between the three of them.

The fish secured to the ship, all the boats were hoisted except one, which remained alongside to sling the bodies. During our absence the ship-keepers had been busy rigging one of the cutting falls, an immense four-fold tackle from the main lowermast-head, of four-inch rope through great double blocks, large as those used at dockyards for lifting ships' masts and boilers. Chain-slings were passed around the carcases, which gripped the animal at the "small," being prevented from slipping off by the broad spread of the tail. The end of the "fall," or tackle-rope, was then taken to the windlass, and we hove away cheerily, lifting the monsters right on deck. A mountainous pile they made. A short spell was allowed, when the whole eight were on board, for dinner; then all hands turned to again to "flench" the blubber, and prepare for trying-out. This was a heavy job, keeping all hands busy until it was quite dark, the latter part of the work being carried on by the light of a "cresset," the flames of which were fed with "scrap," which blazed brilliantly, throwing a big glare over all the ship. The last of the carcases was launched overboard by about eight o'clock that evening, but not before some vast junks of beef had been cut off and hung up in the rigging for our food supply.

The try-works were started again, "trying-out" going on busily all night, watch and watch taking their turn at keeping the pots supplied with minced blubber. The work was heavy, while the energetic way in which it was carried on made us all glad to take what rest was allowed us, which was scanty enough, as usual.

By nightfall the next day the ship had resumed her normal appearance, and we were a tun and a quarter of oil to the good. Black Fish oil is of medium quality, but I learned that, according to the rule of "roguery in all trades," it was the custom to mix quantities such as we had just obtained with better class whale-oil, and thus get a much higher price than it was really worth.

Up till this time we had no sort of an idea as to where our first objective might be, but from scraps of conversation I had overheard among the harpooners, I gathered that we were making for the Cape Verde Islands or the Açores, in the vicinity of which a good number of moderate-sized sperm whales are often to be found. In fact, these islands have long been a nursery for whale-fishers, because the cachalot loves their steep-to shores, and the hardy natives, whenever and wherever they can muster a boat and a little gear, are always ready to sally forth and attack the unwary whale that ventures within their ken. Consequently more than half of the total crews of the American whaling fleet are composed of these islanders. Many of them have risen to the position of captain, and still more are officers and harpooners; but though undoubtedly brave and enterprising, they are cruel and treacherous, and in positions of authority over men of Teutonic or Anglo-Saxon origin, are apt to treat their subordinates with great cruelty.

CHAPTER IV.

BAD WEATHER.

Nautical routine in its essential details is much the same in all ships, whether naval, merchant, or whaling vessels. But while in the ordinary merchantman there are decidedly "no more cats than can catch mice," hardly, indeed, sufficient for all the mousing that should be done, in men-of-war and whaleships the number of hands carried, being far more than are wanted for everyday work, must needs be kept at unnecessary duties in order that they may not grow lazy and discontented.

For instance, in the *Cachalot* we carried a crew of thirty-seven all told, of which twenty-four were men before the mast, or common seamen, our tonnage being under 400 tons. Many a splendid clipper-ship carrying an enormous spread of canvas on four masts, and not overloaded with 2500 tons of cargo on board, carries twenty-eight or thirty all told, or even less than that. As far as we were concerned, the result of this was that our landsmen got so thoroughly drilled, that within a week of leaving port they hardly knew themselves for the clumsy clodhoppers they at first appeared to be.

We had now been eight days out, and in our

leisurely way were making fair progress across the Atlantic, having had nothing, so far, but steady breezes and fine weather. As it was late autumn—the first week in October—I rather wondered at this, for even in my brief experience I had learned to dread a "fall" voyage across the "Western Ocean."

Gradually the face of the sky changed, and the feel of the air, from balmy and genial, became raw and cheerless. The little wave tops broke short off and blew backwards, apparently against the wind, while the old vessel had an uneasy, unnatural motion, caused by a long, new swell rolling athwart the existing set of the sea. Then the wind became fitful and changeable, backing half round the compass, and veering forward again as much in an hour, until at last in one tremendous squall it settled in the N.W. for a business-like blow. Unlike the hurried merchantman who must needs "hang on" till the last minute, only shortening the sail when absolutely compelled to do so, and at the first sign of the gales relenting, piling it on again, we were all snug long before the storm burst upon us, and now rode comfortably under the tiniest of storm staysails.

We were evidently in for a fair specimen of Western Ocean weather, but the clumsy-looking, old-fashioned *Cachalot* made no more fuss over it than one of the long-winged sea-birds that floated around, intent only upon snapping up any stray scraps that might escape from us. Higher rose the wind, heavier rolled the sea, yet never a drop of water did we ship, nor did anything about the deck betoken what a heavy gale was blowing. During the worst of the weather, and just after the wind had shifted back into the N.E., making an uglier cross sea than ever get up, along comes an immense four-masted iron ship homeward bound. She was staggering under a veritable mountain of canvas, fairly burying her bows in the foam at every forward drive, and actually wetting the clews of the upper topsails in the smothering masses of spray, that every few minutes almost hid her hull from sight.

It was a splendid picture; but—for the time—I felt glad I was not on board of her. In a very few minutes she was out of our ken, followed by the admiration of all. Then came, from the other direction, a huge steamship, taking no more notice of the gale than as if it were calm. Straight through the sea she rushed, dividing the mighty rollers to the heart, and often bestriding three seas at once, the centre one spreading its many tons of foaming water fore and aft, so that from every orifice spouted the seething brine. Compared with these greyhounds of the wave, we resembled nothing so much as some old lightship bobbing serenely around, as if part and parcel of the mid-Atlantic.

Our greenies were getting so well seasoned by this time that even this rough weather did not knock any of them over, and from that time forward they had no more trouble from sea-sickness.

The gale gradually blew itself out, leaving behind only a long and very heavy swell to denote the deep-reaching disturbance that the ocean had endured. And now we were within the range of the Sargasso Weed, that mysterious *fucus* that makes the ocean look like some vast hayfield, and keeps the sea from rising, no matter how high the wind. It fell a dead calm, and the harpooners amused themselves by dredging up great masses of the weed, and turning out the many strange creatures abiding therein. What a world of wonderful life the weed is, to be sure! In it the flying fish spawn and the tiny cuttle-fish breed, both of them preparing bounteous provision for the larger denizens of the deep that have no other food. Myriads of tiny crabs and innumerable specimens of less-known shell-fish, small fish of species as yet unclassified in any work on natural history, with jelly-fish of every conceivable and inconceivable shape, form part of this great and populous country in the sea. At one haul there was brought on board a mass of flying-fish spawn, about ten pounds in weight, looking like nothing so much as a pile of ripe white currants, and clinging together in a very similar manner.

Such masses of ova I had often seen cast up among the outlying rocks on the shores of the Caribbean Sea, when as a shipwrecked lad I wandered idly about unburying turtle eggs from their snug beds in the warm sand, and chasing the many-hued coral fish from one hiding place to another.

While loitering in these smooth waters, waiting for the laggard wind, up came a shoal of dolphin, ready as at all times to attach themselves for awhile to the ship. Nothing is more singular than the manner in which deep-sea fish will accompany a vessel that is not going too fast—sometimes for days at a time. Most convenient too, and providing hungry Jack with many a fresh mess he would otherwise have missed. Of all these friendly fish, none is better known than the "dolphin," as from long usage sailors persist in calling them, and will doubtless do so until the end of the chapter. For the true dolphin (*Delphinidæ*) is not a fish at all, but a mammal —a warm-blooded creature that suckles its young, and in its most familiar form is known to most people as the porpoise. The sailor's "dolphin," on the other hand, is a veritable fish, with vertical tail fin instead of the horizontal one which distinguishes all the whale family, scales and gills.

It is well known to literature, under its sea-name, for its marvellous brilliancy of colour, and there are few objects more dazzling than a dolphin leaping out of a calm sea into the sunshine. The beauty of a dying dolphin, however, though sanctioned by many generations of writers, is a delusion, all the glory of the fish departing as soon as he is withdrawn from his native element.

But this habit of digression grows upon one, and I must do my best to check it, or I shall never get through my task.

To resume then: when this school of dolphin (I can't for the life of me call them *Coryphæna hippuris*) came alongside, a rush was made for the "granes"—a sort of five-pronged trident, if I may be allowed a baby bull. It was universally agreed among the fishermen that trying a hook and line was only waste of time and provocative of profanity! since every sailor knows that all the deep-water big fish require a living or apparently living bait. The fish, however, sheered off, and would not be tempted within reach of that deadly fork by any lure. Then did I cover myself with glory. For he who can fish cleverly and luckily may be sure of fairly good times in a whaler, although he may be no great things at any other work. I had a line of my own, and begging one of the small fish that had been hauled up in the Gulf weed, I got permission to go aft and fish over the tafrail. The little fish was carefully secured on the hook, the point of which just protruded near his tail. Then I lowered him into the calm blue waters beneath, and paid out line very gently, until my bait was a silvery spot about a hundred feet astern. Only a very short time, and my hopes rose as I saw one bright gleam after another glide past the keel, heading aft. Then came a gentle drawing at the line, which I suffered to slip slowly through my fingers until I judged it time to try whether I was right or wrong. A long hard pull, and my heart beat fast as I felt the thrill along the line that fishermen love. None of your high art here, but haul in hand over hand, the line being strong enough to land a 250 pound fish. Up he came, the beauty, all silver and scarlet and blue, five feet long if an inch, and weighing 35 pounds. Well, such a lot of astonished men I never saw. They could hardly believe their eyes. That such a daring innovation should be successful was hardly to be believed, even with the vigorous evidence before them. Even grim Captain Slocum came to look, and turned upon me as I thought a less lowering brow than usual, while Mr. Count, the mate, fairly chuckled again at the thought of how the little Britisher had wiped the eyes of these veteran fishermen. The captive was cut open, and two recent flying-fish found in his maw, which were utilized for new bait, with the result that there was a cheerful noise of hissing and spluttering in the galley soon after, and a mess of fish for all hands.

Shortly afterwards a fresh breeze sprang up, which proved to be the beginning of the N.E. trades, and fairly guaranteed us against any very bad weather for some time to come.

Somehow or other it had leaked out that we were to cruise the Cape Verd Islands for a spell before working south, and the knowledge seemed to have quite an enlivening effect upon our Portuguese shipmates.

Most of them belonged there, and although there was but the faintest prospect of their getting ashore upon any pretext whatever, the possibility of seeing their island homes again seemed to quite transform them. Hitherto they had been very moody and exclusive, never associating with us on the white side, or attempting to be at all familiar. A mutual atmosphere of suspicion, in fact, seemed to pervade our quarters, making things already uncomfortable enough, still more so. Now, however, they fraternized with us, and in a variety of uncouth ways made havoc of the English tongue, as they tried to impress us with the beauty, fertility and general incomparability of their beloved Cape Verds. Of the eleven white men besides myself in the forecastle, there were a middle-aged German baker, who had bolted from Buffalo; two Hungarians, who looked like noblemen disguised—in dirt; two slab-sided Yankees of about 22 from farms in Vermont; a drayman from New York; a French Canadian from the neighbourhood of Quebec; two Italians from Genoa; and two nondescripts that I never found out the origin of. Imagine, then, the babel of sound, and think—but no, it is impossible to think, what sort of a jargon was compounded of all these varying elements of language.

One fortunate thing, there was peace below. Indeed, the spirit seemed completely taken out of all of them, and by some devilish ingenuity the afterguard had been able to sow distrust between them all, while treating them like dogs, so that the miseries of their life were never openly discussed. My position among them gave me at times some uneasiness. Though I tried to be helpful to all, and was full of sympathy for their undeserved sufferings, I could not but feel that they would have been more than human had they not envied me my immunity from the kicks and blows they all shared so impartially. However, there was no help for it, so I went on as cheerily as I could.

A peculiarity of all these vessels, as I afterwards learned, was that no stated allowance of anything was made. Even the water was not served out to us, but was kept in a great scuttle-butt by the cabin door, to which every one who needed a drink had to go, and from which none might be carried away. No water was allowed for washing except from the sea; and every one knows, or should know, that neither flesh nor clothes can be cleansed with that. But a cask with a perforated top was lashed by the bowsprit and kept filled with urine, which I was solemnly assured by Goliath was the finest dirt-extractor in the world for clothes. The officers did not avail themselves of its virtues though, but were content with ley, which was furnished in plenty by the ashes from the galley fire, where nothing but wood was used as fuel. Of course when rain fell we might have a good wash, if it was night and no other work was toward; but we were not allowed to store any for washing purposes. Another curious but absolutely necessary custom prevailed in consequence of the short commons under which we lived. When the portion of meat was brought down in its wooden kid, or tub, at dinner-time, it was duly divided as fairly as possible into as many parts as there were mouths. Then one man turned his back upon the carver, who, holding up each portion, called out, "Who's this for?" Whatever name was mentioned by the arbitrator, that man owning it received the piece, and had perforce to be satisfied therewith. Thus justice was done to all in the only way possible, and without any friction whatever.

As some of us were without clothes except what we stood upright in, when we joined, the "slop chest" was opened, and every applicant received from the steward what Captain Slocum thought fit to let him have, being debited with the cost against such wages as he might afterwards earn. The clothes were certainly of fairly good quality, if the price was high, and exactly suited to our requirements. Soap, matches, and tobacco were likewise supplied on the same terms, but at higher prices than I had ever heard of before for these necessaries. After much careful inquiry I ascertained what, in the event of a successful voyage, we were likely to earn. Each of us were on the two hundredth "lay" or share at $200 per tun, which meant that for every two hundred barrels of oil taken on board, we were entitled to one, which we must sell to the ship at the rate of £40 per tun or £4 per barrel. Truly a magnificent outlook for young men bound to such a business for three or four years.

CHAPTER V.

ACTUAL WARFARE. OUR FIRST WHALE.

SIMULTANEOUS ideas occurring to several people, or thought transference, whatever one likes to call the phenomenon, is too frequent an occurrence in most of our experience to occasion much surprise. Yet on the occasion to which I am about to refer, the matter was so very marked that few of us who took part in the day's proceedings are ever likely to forget it.

We were all gathered about the fo'lk'sle scuttle one evening, a few days after the gale referred to in the previous chapter, and the question of whale-fishing came up for discussion. Until that time, strange as it may seem, no word of this, the central idea of all our minds, had been mooted. Every man seemed to shun the subject, although we were in daily expectation of being called upon to take an active part in whale-fighting. Once the ice was broken, nearly all had something to say about it, and very nearly as many addle-headed opinions were ventilated as at a Colney Hatch debating society. For we none of us *knew* anything about it. I was appealed to continually to support this or that theory, but as far as whaling went I could only, like the rest of them, draw upon my imagination for details. How did a whale act, what were the first steps taken, what chance was there of being saved if your boat got smashed, and so on unto infinity. At last, getting very tired of this "Portugee Parliament" of all talkers and no listeners, I went aft to get a drink of water before turning in. The harpooners and other petty officers were grouped in the waist, earnestly discussing the pros and cons of attack upon whales. As I passed I heard the mate's harpooner say, "Feels like whale about. I bet a plug (of tobacco) we raise sperm whale to-morrow." Nobody took his bet, for it appeared that they were mostly of the same mind, and while I was drinking I heard the officers in dignified conclave talking over the same thing. It was Saturday evening, and while at home people were looking forward to a day's respite from work and care, I felt that the coming day, though never taken much notice of on board, was big with the probabilities of strife such as I at least had at present no idea of. So firmly was I possessed by the prevailing feeling.

The night was very quiet. A gentle breeze was blowing, and the sky was of the usual "Trade" character, that is, a dome of dark blue fringed at the horizon with peaceful cumulus clouds, almost motionless. I turned in at four a.m. from the middle watch and, as usual, slept like a babe. Suddenly I started wide awake, a long mournful sound sending a thrill to my very heart. As I listened breathlessly other sounds of the same character but in different tones joined in, human voices monotonously intoning in long drawn-out expirations the single word "bl-o-o-o-w." Then came a hurricane of noise overhead, and adjurations in no gentle language to the sleepers to "tumble up lively there, no skulking, sperm whales." At last, then, fulfilling all the presentiments of yesterday, the long dreaded moment had arrived. Happily there was no time for hesitation, in less than two minutes we were all on deck, and hurrying to our respective boats. There was no flurry or confusion, and except that orders were given more quietly than usual, with a manifest air of suppressed excitement, there was nothing to show that we were not going for an ordinary course of boat drill. The skipper was in the main crow's-nest with his binoculars. Presently he shouted, "Naow then, Mr. Count, lower away soon's y'like. Small pod o'cows, an' one 'r two bulls layin' off to west'ard of 'em." Down went the boats into the water quietly enough, we all scrambled in and shoved off. A stroke or two of the oars were given to get clear of the ship, and one another, then oars were shipped and up went the sails. As I took my allotted place at the main-sheet, and the beautiful craft started off like some big bird, Mr. Count leant forward, saying impressively to me, "Y'r a smart youngster, an' I've kinder took t'yer; but don't ye look ahead an' get gallied, 'r I'll knock ye stiff wi' th' tiller; y'hear me? N' don't ye dare to make thet sheet fast, 'r ye'll die so sudden y' won't know whar y'r hurted." I said as cheerfully as I could, "All right, sir," trying to look unconcerned, telling myself not to be a coward, and all sorts of things; but the cold truth is that I was scared almost to death because I didn't know what was coming. However, I did the best thing under the circumstances, obeyed orders and looked steadily astern, or up into the bronzed impassive face of my chief, who towered above me, scanning with eagle eyes the sea ahead. The other boats were coming flying along behind us, spreading wider apart as they came, while in the bows of each stood the harpooner with his right hand on his first iron, which lay ready, pointing over the bow in a raised fork of wood called the "crutch."

All of a sudden, at a motion of the chief's hand, the peak of our mainsail was dropped, and the boat swung up into the wind, laying "hove to," almost stationary. The centre-board was lowered to stop her drifting to leeward, although I cannot say it made much difference that ever I saw. *Now* what's the matter, I thought, when to my amazement the chief addressing me said, "Wonder why we've hauled up, don't ye?" "Yes, sir, I do," said I. "Wall," said he, "the fish hev sounded, an' 'ef we run over 'em, we've seen the last ov'em. So we wait awhile till they rise agin, 'n then we'll prob'ly git thar' 'r thareabouts before they sound agin." With this explanation I had to be content, although if it be no clearer to my readers than it then was to me, I shall have to explain myself more fully later on. Silently we lay, rocking lazily upon the gentle swell, no other word being spoken by any one. At last Louis, the harpooner, gently breathed "blo-o-o-w;" and there, sure enough, not half a mile away on the lee beam, was a little bushy cloud of steam apparently rising from the sea. At almost the same time as we kept away all the other boats did likewise, and just then, catching sight of the ship, the reason for this apparently concerted action was explained. At the main-mast head of the ship was a square blue flag, and the ensign at the peak was being dipped. These were signals well understood and promptly acted upon by those in charge of the boats, who were thus guided from a point of view at least one hundred feet above the sea.

"Stand up, Louey," the mate murmured softly. I

only just stopped myself in time from turning my head to see why the order was given. Suddenly there was a bump, at the same moment the mate yelled, "Give't to him, Louey, give't to him!" and to me, "Haul that main sheet, naow haul, why don't ye?" I hauled it flat aft, and the boat shot up into the wind, rubbing sides as she did so with what to my troubled sight seemed an enormous mass of black india-rubber floating. As we *crawled* up into the wind, the whale went into convulsions befitting his size and energy. He raised a gigantic tail on high, threshing the water with deafening blows, rolling at the same time from side to side until the surrounding sea was white with froth. I felt in an agony lest we should be crushed under one of those fearful strokes, for Mr. Count appeared to be oblivious of possible danger, although we seemed to be now drifting back on to the writhing leviathan. In the agitated condition of the sea, it was a task of no ordinary difficulty to unship the tall mast, which was of course the first thing to be done. After a desperate struggle, and a narrow escape from falling overboard of one of the men, we got the long "stick," with the sail bundled around it, down and "fleeted" aft, where it was secured by the simple means of sticking the "heel" under the after thwart, two-thirds of the mast extending out over the stern. Meanwhile, we had certainly been in a position of the greatest danger, our immunity from damage being unquestionably due to anything but precaution taken to avoid it.

By the time the oars were handled, and the mate had exchanged places with the harpooner, our friend the enemy had "sounded," that is, he had gone below for a change of scene, marvelling no doubt what strange thing had befallen him. Agreeably to the accounts which I, like most boys, had read of the whale fishery, I looked for the rushing of the line round the loggerhead (a stout wooden post built into the boat aft), to raise a cloud of smoke with occasional bursts of flame; so as it began to slowly surge round the post, I timidly asked the harpooner whether I should throw any water on it. "Wot for?" growled he, as he took a couple more turns with it. Not knowing "what for," and hardly liking to quote my authorities here, I said no more, but waited events. "Hold him up, Louey, hold him up, cain't ye?" shouted the mate, and to my horror, down went the nose of the boat almost under water, while at the mate's order everybody scrambled aft into the elevated stern sheets.

The line sang quite a tune as it was grudgingly allowed to surge round the loggerhead, filling one with admiration at the strength shown by such a small rope. This sort of thing went on for about twenty minutes, in which time we quite emptied the large tub and began on the small one. As there was nothing whatever for us to do while this was going on, I had ample leisure for observing the little game that was being played about a quarter of a mile away. Mr. Cruce, the second mate, had got a whale and was doing his best to kill it; but he was severely handicapped by his crew, or rather had been, for two of them were now temporarily incapable of either good or harm. They had gone quite "batchy" with fright, requiring a not too gentle application of the tiller to their heads in order to keep them quiet. The remedy, if rough, was effectual, for "the subsequent proceedings interested them no more." Consequently his manœuvres were not so well or rapidly executed as he, doubtless, could have wished, although his energy in lancing that whale was something to admire and remember. Hatless, his shirt tail out of the waist of his trousers streaming behind him like a banner, he lunged and thrust at the whale alongside of him, as if possessed of a destroying devil, while his half articulate yells of rage and blasphemy were audible even to us.

Suddenly our boat fell backward from her "slantindicular" position with a jerk, and the mate immediately shouted, "Haul line, there! look lively, now! you—so on, etcetera, etcetera" (he seemed to invent new epithets on every occasion). The line came in hand over hand, and was coiled in a wide heap in the stern sheets, for silky as it was, it could not be expected in its wet state to lie very close. As it came flying in the mate kept a close gaze upon the water immediately beneath us, apparently for the first glimpse of our antagonist. When the whale broke water, however, he was some distance off, and apparently as quiet as a lamb. Now, had Mr. Count been a prudent or less ambitious man, our task would doubtless have been an easy one, or comparatively so; but, being a little over-grasping, he got us all into serious trouble. We were hauling up to our whale in order to lance it, and the mate was standing, lance in hand, only waiting to get near enough, when up comes a large whale right alongside of our boat, so close, indeed, that I might have poked my finger in his little eye, if I had chosen. The sight of that whale at liberty, and calmly taking stock of us like that, was too much for the mate. He lifted his lance and hurled it at the visitor, in whose broad flank it sank, like a knife into butter, right up to the pole-hitches. The recipient disappeared like a flash, but before one had time to think, there was an awful crash beneath us, and the mate shot up into the air like a bomb from a mortar. He came down in a sitting posture on the mast-thwart; but as he fell, the whole framework of the boat collapsed like a derelict umbrella. Louis quietly chopped the line and severed our connection with the other whale, while in accordance with our instructions we drew each man his oar across the boat and lashed it firmly down with a piece of line spliced to each thwart for the purpose. This simple operation took but a minute, but before it was completed we were all up to our necks in the sea. Still in the boat, it is true, and therefore not in such danger of drowning as if we were quite adrift; but, considering that the boat was reduced to a mere bundle of loose planks, I, at any rate, was none too comfortable. Now, had he known it, was the whale's golden opportunity; but he, poor wretch, had had quite enough of our company, and cleared off without any delay, wondering, no doubt, what fortunate accident had rid him of our very unpleasant attentions.

I was assured that we were all as safe as if we were on board the ship, to which I answered nothing; but, like Jack's parrot, I did some powerful thinking. Every little wave that came along swept clean over our heads, sometimes coming so suddenly as to cut a breath in half. If the wind should increase—but no—I wouldn't face the possibility of such a disagreeable thing. I was cool enough now in a double sense, for although we were in the tropics, we soon got thoroughly chilled.

By the position of the sun it must have been between ten a.m. and noon, and we, of the crew, had eaten nothing since the previous day at supper, when, as usual, the meal was very light. Therefore, I suppose we felt the chill sooner than the better-nourished mate and harpooner, who looked rather scornfully at our blue faces and chattering teeth.

In spite of all assurances to the contrary, I have not the least doubt in my own mind that a very little longer would have relieved us of *all* our burdens finally. Because the heave of the sea had so loosened the shattered planks upon which we stood that they were on the verge of falling all asunder. Had they done so we must have drowned, for we were cramped and stiff with cold and our constrained position. However, unknown to us, a bright look-out upon our movements had been kept from the crow's-nest the whole time. We should have been relieved long before, but that the whale killed by the second mate was being secured, and another boat, the fourth mate's, being picked up, having a hole in her bilge you could put your head through. With all these hindrances, especially securing the whale, we were fortunate to be rescued as soon as we were, since it is well known that whales are of much higher commercial value than men.

However, help came at last, and we were hauled alongside. Long exposure had weakened us to such an extent that it was necessary to hoist us on board, especially the mate, whose "sudden stop," when he returned to us after his little aerial excursion, had shaken his sturdy frame considerably, a state of body which the subsequent soaking had by no means improved. In my innocence I imagined that we should be commiserated for our misfortunes by Captain Slocum, and certainly be relieved from further duties until we were a little recovered from the rough treatment we had just undergone. But I never made a greater mistake.

The skipper cursed us all (except the mate, whose sole fault the accident undoubtedly was) with a fluency and vigour that was, to put it mildly, discouraging. Moreover, we were informed that he "wouldn't have no adjective skulking;" we must "turn to" and do something after wasting the ship's time and property in such a blank manner. There was a limit, however, to our obedience, so although we could not move at all for awhile, his threats were not proceeded with farther than theory.

A couple of slings were passed around the boat, by means of which she was carefully hoisted on board, a mere dilapidated bundle of sticks and raffle of gear. She was at once removed aft out of the way, the business of cutting in the whale claiming precedence over everything else just then. The preliminary proceedings consisted of rigging the "cutting stage." This was composed of two stout planks a foot wide and ten feet long, the inner ends of which were suspended by strong ropes over the ship's side about four feet from the water, while the outer extremities were upheld by tackles from the main rigging, and a small crane abreast the try-works.

These planks were about thirty feet apart, their two outer ends being connected by a massive plank which was securely bolted to them. A handrail about as high as a man's waist, supported by light iron stanchions, ran the full length of this plank on the side nearest the ship, the whole fabric forming an admirable standing-place from whence the officers might, standing in comparative comfort, cut and carve at the great mass below to their hearts' content.

So far the prize had been simply held alongside by

the whale-line, which at death had been "rove" through a hole cut in the solid gristle of the tail; but now it became necessary to secure the carcase to the ship in some more permanent fashion. Therefore, a massive chain like a small ship's cable was brought forward, and in a very ingenious way, by means of a tiny buoy and a hand-lead, passed round the body, one end brought through a ring in the other, and hauled upon until it fitted tight round the "small" or part of the whale next the broad spread of the tail. The free end of the fluke-chain was then passed in through a mooring-pipe forward, firmly secured to a massive bitt at the heel of the bowsprit (the fluke-chain-bitt), and all was ready.

But the subsequent proceedings were sufficiently complicated to demand a fresh chapter.

CHAPTER VI.

"DIRTY WORK FOR CLEAN MONEY."

If in the preceding chapter too much stress has been laid upon the smashing of our own boat and consequent sufferings, while little or no notice was taken of the kindred disaster to Mistah Jones' vessel, my excuse must be that the experience "filled me right up to the chin," as the mate concisely, if inelegantly, put it. Poor Goliath was indeed to be pitied, for his well-known luck and capacity as a whaleman seemed on this occasion to have quite deserted him. Not only had his boat been stove upon first getting on to the whale, but he hadn't even had a run for his money. It appeared that upon striking his whale, a small, lively cow, she had at once "settled," allowing the boat to run over her; but just as they were passing, she rose, gently enough, her pointed hump piercing the thin skin of half-inch cedar as if it had been cardboard. She settled again immediately, leaving a hole behind her a foot long by six inches wide, which effectually put a stop to all further fishing operations on the part of Goliath and his merry men for that day, at any rate. It was all *so* quiet, and so tame and so stupid, no wonder Mistah Jones felt savage. When Captain Slocum's fluent profanity flickered around him, including vehemently all he might be supposed to have any respect for, he did not even *look* as if he would like to talk back; he only looked sick and tired of being himself.

The third mate, again, was of a different category altogether. He had distinguished himself by missing every opportunity of getting near a whale while there was a "loose" one about, and then "saving" the crew of Goliath's boat, who were really in no danger whatever. His iniquity was too great to be dealt with by mere bad language. He crept about like a homeless dog—much, I am afraid, to my secret glee, for I couldn't help remembering his untiring cruelty to the green hands on first leaving port.

In consequence of these little drawbacks we were not a very jovial crowd forrard or aft. Not that hilarity was ever particularly noticeable among us, but just now there was a very decided sense of wrong-doing over us all, and a general fear that each of us was about to pay the penalty due to some other delinquent. But fortunately there was work to be done. Oh, blessed work! how many awkward situations you have extricated people from! How many distracted brains have you soothed and restored, by your steady irresistible pressure of duty to be done and brooking of no delay!

The first thing to be done was to cut the whale's head off. This operation, involving the greatest amount of labour in the whole of the cutting in, was taken in hand by the first and second mates, who, armed with twelve-feet spades, took their station upon the stage, leaned over the handrail to steady themselves, and plunged their weapons vigorously down through the massive neck of the animal—if neck it could be said to have—

LANCING A WHALE.

following a well-defined crease in the blubber. At the same time the other officers passed a heavy chain sling around the long, narrow lower jaw, hooking one of the big cutting tackles into it, the "fall" of which was then taken to the windlass and hove tight, turning the whale on her back. A deep cut was then made on both sides of the rising jaw, the windlass was kept going, and gradually the whole of the throat was raised high enough for a hole to be cut through its mass, into which the strap of the second cutting tackle was inserted and secured by passing a huge toggle of oak through its eye. The second tackle was then hove taut, and the jaw, with a large piece of blubber attached, was cut off from the body with a boarding-knife, a tool not unlike a cutlass blade set into a three-foot-long wooden handle.

Upon being severed the whole piece swung easily inboard and was lowered on deck. The fast tackle was now hove upon while the third mate on the stage cut down diagonally into the blubber on the body, which the purchase ripped off in a broad strip or "blanket" about five feet wide and a foot thick. Meanwhile the other two officers carved away vigorously at the head, varying their labours by cutting a hole right through the snout. This when completed received a heavy chain for the purpose of securing the head. When the blubber had been about half stripped off the body, a halt was called in order that the work of cutting off the head might be finished, for it was a task of incredible difficulty. It was accomplished at last, and the mass floated astern by a stout rope, after which the windlass pawls clattered merrily, the "blankets" rose in quick succession, and were cut off and lowered into the square of the main hatch or "blubber-room." A short time sufficed to strip off the whole of the body-blubber, and when at last the tail was reached, the backbone was cut through, the huge mass of flesh floating away to feed the innumerable scavengers of the sea. No sooner was the last of the blubber lowered into the hold than the hatches were put on and the head hauled up alongside. Both tackles were secured to it and all hands took to the windlass levers. This was a small cow whale of about thirty barrels, that is, yielding that amount of oil, so it was just possible to lift the entire head on board; but as it weighed as much as three full-grown elephants, it was indeed a heavy lift for even our united forces, trying our tackle to the utmost. The weather was very fine, and the ship rolled but little; even then, the strain upon the mast was terrific, and right glad was I when at last the immense cube of fat, flesh, and bone was eased inboard and gently lowered on deck.

As soon as it was secured the work of dividing it began. From the snout a triangular mass was cut, which was more than half pure spermaceti. This substance was contained in spongy cells held together by layers of dense white fibre, exceedingly tough and elastic, and called by the whalers "white-horse." The whole mass, or "junk" as it is called, was hauled away to the ship's side and firmly lashed to the bulwarks for the time being, so that it might not "take charge" of the deck during the rest of the operations.

The upper part of the head was now slit open lengthwise, disclosing an oblong cistern or "case" full of liquid spermaceti, clear as water. This was baled out with buckets into a tank, concreting as it cooled into a wax-like substance, bland and tasteless. There being now nothing more remaining about the skull of any value, the lashings were loosed, and the first lee-ward roll sent the great mass plunging overboard with a mighty splash. It sank like a stone, eagerly followed by a few small sharks that were hovering near.

As may be imagined, much oil was running about the deck, for so saturated was every part of the creature with it that it really gushed like water during the cutting-up process. None of it was allowed to run to waste, though, for the scupper-holes which drain the deck were all carefully plugged, and as soon as the "junk" had been dissected all the oil was carefully "squeegeed" up and poured into the try-pots.

Two men were now told off as "blubber-room men," whose duty it became to go below, and squeezing them-selves in as best they could between the greasy masses of fat, cut it up into "horse-pieces" about eighteen inches long and six inches square. Doing this they became perfectly saturated with oil, as if they had taken a bath in a tank of it; for as the vessel rolled it was impossible to maintain a footing, and every fall was upon blubber running with oil. A machine of wonderful construction had been erected on deck in a kind of shallow trough about six feet long by four feet wide and a foot deep. At some remote period of time it had no doubt been looked upon as a triumph of ingenuity, a patent mincing machine. Its action was somewhat like that of a chaff-cutter, except that the knife was not attached to the wheel, and only rose and fell, since it was not required to cut right through the "horse-pieces" with which it was fed. It will be readily understood that in order to get the oil quickly out of the blubber, it needs to be sliced as thin as possible, but for convenience in handling the refuse (which is the only fuel used) it is not chopped up in small pieces, but every "horse-piece" is very deeply scored as it were, leaving a thin strip to hold the slices together. This then was the order of work. Two harpooners attended the try-pots, replenishing them with minced blubber from the hopper at the port side, and baling out the sufficiently boiled oil into the great cooling tank on the starboard. One officer superintended the mincing, another exercised a general supervision over all. There was no man at the wheel and no look-out, for the vessel was "hove-to" under two close-reefed topsails and fore-topmast-staysail, with the wheel lashed hard down. A look-out man was unnecessary, since we could not run anybody down, and if anybody ran us down, it would only be because all hands were asleep, for the glare of our try-works fire, to say nothing of the blazing cresset before mentioned, could have been seen for many miles. So we toiled watch and watch, six hours on and six off, the work never ceasing for an instant night or day. Though the work was hard and dirty, and the discomfort of being so continually wet through with oil great, there was only one thing dangerous about the whole business. That was the job of filling and shifting the huge casks of oil. Some of these were of enormous size, containing 350 gallons when full, and the work of moving them about the greasy deck of a rolling ship was attended with a terrible amount of risk. For only four men at most could get fair hold of a cask, and when she took it into her silly old hull to start rolling, just as we had got one half-way across the deck, with nothing to grip your feet, and the knowledge that one stumbling man would mean a sudden slide of the ton and a half weight, and a little heap of mangled corpses somewhere in the lee scuppers—well one always wanted to be very thankful when the lashings were safely passed.

The whale being a small one, as before noted, the whole business was over within three days, and the decks scrubbed and re-scrubbed until they had quite regained their normal whiteness. The oil was poured by means of a funnel and long canvas hose into the casks stowed in the ground tier at the bottom of the ship, and the gear, all carefully cleaned and neatly "stopped up," stowed snugly away below again.

This long and elaborate process is quite different from that followed on board the Arctic whaleships, whose voyages are of short duration, and who content themselves with merely cutting the blubber up small and bringing it home to have the oil expressed. But the awful putrid mass discharged from a Greenlander's hold is of very different quality and value, apart from the nature of the substance, to the clear and sweet oil, which after three years in cask is landed from a south-seaman as inoffensive in smell and flavour as the day it was shipped. No attempt is made to separate the oil and spermaceti beyond boiling the "head matter," as it is called, by itself first, and putting it into casks which are not filled up with the body oil. Spermaceti exists in all the oil, especially that from the dorsal hump; but it is left for the refiners ashore to extract and leave the oil quite free from any admixture of the wax-like substance, which causes it to become solid at temperatures considerably above the freezing-point.

Uninteresting as the preceding description may be,

it is impossible to understand anything of the economy of a south-sea whaler without giving it, and I have felt it the more necessary because of the scanty notice given to it in the only two works published on the subject, both of them highly technical, and written for scientific purposes by medical men. Therefore I hope to be forgiven if I have tried the patience of my readers by any prolixity.

It will not, of course, have escaped the reader's notice that I have not hitherto attempted to give any details concerning the structure of the whale just dealt with. The omission is intentional. During this, our first attempt at real whaling, my mind was far too disturbed by the novelty and danger of the position in which I found myself for the first time, for me to pay any intelligent attention to the party of the second part.

But I may safely promise that from the workman's point of view, the habits, manners, and build of the whales shall be faithfully described as I saw them during my long acquaintance with them, earnestly hoping that if my story be not as technical or scientific as that of Drs. Bennett and Beale, it may be found fully as accurate and reliable; and perhaps the reader, being like myself a mere layman, so to speak, may be better able to appreciate description free from scientific formula and nine-jointed words.

Two things I did notice on this occasion which I will briefly allude to before closing this chapter. One was the peculiar skin of the whale. It was a bluish-black, and as thin as gold-beater's skin. So thin, indeed, and tender, that it was easily scraped off with the finger-nail. Immediately beneath it, upon the surface of the blubber, was a layer or coating of what for want of a better simile I must call fine short fur, although unlike fur it had no roots or apparently any hold upon the blubber Neither was it attached to the skin which covered it; in fact, it seemed merely a sort of packing between the skin and the surface of the thick layer of solid fat which covered the whole area of the whale's body. The other matter which impressed me was the peculiarity of the teeth. For up till that time I had held, in common with most seamen, and landsmen, too, for that matter, the prevailing idea that a "whale" lived by "suction" (although I did not at all know what that meant), and that it was impossible for him to swallow a herring. Yet here was a mouth manifestly intended for greater things in the way of gastronomy than herrings; nor did it require more than the most casual glances to satisfy one of so obvious a fact. Then the teeth were heroic in size, protruding some four or five inches from the gum, and solidly set more than that into its firm and compact substance. They were certainly not intended for mastication, being, where thickest, three inches apart, and tapering to a short point, curving slightly backwards. In this specimen, a female, and therefore small as I have said, there were twenty of them on each side, the last three or four near the gullet being barely visible above the gum.

Another most convincing reason why no mastication could have been possible was that there were no teeth visible in the upper jaw. Opposed to each of the teeth was a socket where a tooth should apparently have been, and this was conclusive evidence of the soft and yielding nature of the great creature's food. But there were signs that at some period of the development of the whale it had possessed a double row of teeth, because at the bottom of these upper sockets we found in a few cases what seemed to be an abortive tooth, not one that was growing, because they had no roots, but a survival of teeth that had once been perfect and useful, but from disuse, or lack of necessity for them, had gradually ceased to come to maturity. The interior of the mouth and throat was of a livid white, and the tongue was quite small for so large an animal. It was almost incapable of movement, being somewhat like a fowl's. Certainly it could not have been protruded even from the angle of the mouth, much less have extended along the parapet of that lower mandible, which reminded one of the beak of some mighty albatross or stork.

CHAPTER VII.

GETTING SOUTHWARD.

Whether our recent experience had altered the captain's plans or not I do not know, but much to the dismay of the Portuguese portion of the crew, we did but sight, dimly and afar off, the outline of the Cape Verde Islands before our course was altered, and we bore away for the southward like any other outward-bounder. That is, as far as our course went; but as to the speed, we still retained the leisurely tactics hitherto pursued, shortening sail every night, and, if the weather was very fine, setting it all again at daybreak.

The morose and sullen temper of the captain had been, if anything, made worse by recent events, and we were worked as hard as if the success of the voyage depended upon our ceaseless toil of scrubbing, scraping, and polishing. Discipline was indeed maintained at a high pitch of perfection, no man daring to look awry, much less complain of any hardship, however great. Even this humble submissiveness did not satisfy our tyrant, and at last his cruelty took a more active shape. One of the long Yankee farmers from Vermont, Abner Cushing by name, with the ingenuity which seems inbred in his 'cute countrymen, must needs try his hand at making a villainous decoction which he called "beer," the principal ingredients in which were potatoes and molasses. Now potatoes formed no part of our dietary, so Abner set his wits to work to steal sufficient for his purpose, and succeeded so far that he obtained half a dozen. I have very little doubt that one of the Portuguese in the forecastle conveyed the information aft for some reason best known to himself, any more than we white men all had that in a similar manner all our sayings and doings, however trivial, became at once known to the officers. However, the fact that the theft was discovered soon became painfully evident, for we had a visit from the afterguard in force one afternoon, and Abner with his brewage was haled to the quarter-deck. There, in the presence of all hands, he was arraigned, found guilty of stealing the ship's stores, and sentence passed upon him. By means of two small pieces of fishing line he was suspended by his thumbs in the weather rigging, in such a manner that when the ship was upright his toes touched the deck, but when she rolled his whole weight hung from his thumbs. This of itself one would have thought sufficient torture for almost any offence, but in addition to it he received two dozen lashes with an improvised cat-o'-nine-tails, laid on by the brawny arm of one of the harpooners. We were all compelled to witness this, and our feelings may be imagined. When, after what seemed a terribly long time to me (Heaven knows what it must have been to him!), he fainted, although no chicken I nearly fainted too, from conflicting emotions of sympathy and impotent rage.

He was then released in leisurely fashion, and we were permitted to take him forward and revive him. As soon as he was able to stand on his feet, he was called on deck again, and not allowed to go below till his watch was over. Meanwhile Captain Slocum improved the occasion by giving us a short harangue, the burden of which was that we had now seen a *little* of what any of us might expect if we played any "dogs' tricks" on him. But you can get used to anything, I suppose; so after the first shock of the atrocity was over, things went on again pretty much as usual.

For the first and only time in my experience, we sighted St. Paul's Rocks, a tiny group of jagged peaks protruding from the Atlantic nearly on the Equator. Stupendous mountains they must be, rising almost sheer for about four and a half miles from the ocean bed. Although they appear quite insignificant specks upon the vast expanse of water, one could not help thinking how sublime their appearance would be were they visible from the plateau whence they spring. Their chief interest to us at the time arose from the fact that, when within about three miles of them, we were suddenly surrounded by a vast school of bonito. These fish, so-named by the Spaniards from their handsome appearance, are a species of mackerel, a branch of the *Scombridæ* family, and attain a size of about two feet long and forty pounds weight, though their average dimensions are somewhat less than half that. They feed entirely upon flying-fish and the small leaping squid or cuttle-fish, but love to follow a ship, playing around her, if her pace be not too great, for days together. Their flesh resembles beef in appearance, and they are warm-blooded; but, from their habitat being mid-ocean, nothing is known with any certainty of their habits of breeding.

The orthodox method of catching them on board ship is to cover a suitable hook with a piece of white rag a couple of inches long, and attach it to a stout line. The fisherman then takes his seat upon the jibboom end, having first, if he is prudent, secured a sack to the jib-stay in such a manner that its mouth gapes wide. Then he unrolls his line, and as the ship forges ahead the line, blowing out, describes a curve, at the end of which the bait, dipping to the water occasionally, roughly represents a flying-fish. Of course, the faster the ship is going, the better the chance of deceiving the fish, since they have less time to study the appearance of the bait. It is really an exaggerated and clumsy form of fly-fishing, and, as with that elegant pastime, much is due to the skill of the fisherman.

As the bait leaps from crest to crest of the wavelets thrust aside by the advancing ship, a fish more adventurous or hungrier than the rest will leap at it, and in an instant there is a dead, dangling weight of from ten to forty pounds hanging at the end of your line thirty feet below. You haul frantically, for he may be poorly hooked, and you cannot play him. In a minute or two, if all goes well, he is plunged in the sack, and safe. But woe unto you if you have allowed the jeers of your shipmates to dissuade you from taking a sack out with you.

The struggles of these fish are marvellous, and a man runs great risk of being shaken off the boom, unless his legs are firmly locked in between the guys. Such is the tremendous vibration that a twenty-pound bonito makes in a man's grip, that it can be felt in the cabin at the other end of the ship; and I have often come in triumphantly with one, having lost all feeling in my arms and a goodly portion of skin off my breast and side, where I have embraced the prize in a grim determination to hold him at all hazards, besides being literally drenched with his blood.

Like all our fishing operations on board the *Cachalot*, this day's fishing was conducted on scientific principles, and resulted in twenty-five fine fish being shipped, which were a welcome addition to our scanty allowance. Happily for us, they would not take the salt in that sultry latitude soon enough to preserve them; for, when they can be salted, they become like brine itself, and are quite unfit for food. Yet we should have been compelled to eat salt bonito, or go without meat altogether, if it had been possible to cure them.

We were now fairly in the "horse latitudes," and, much to our relief, the rain came down in occasional deluges, permitting us to wash well and often. I suppose the rains of the tropics have been often enough described to need no meagre attempts of mine to convey an idea of them; yet I have often wished I could make home-keeping friends understand how far short what they often speak of as a "tropical shower" falls of the genuine article. The nearest I can get to it is the idea of an ocean suspended overhead, out of which the bottom occasionally falls. Nothing is visible or audible but the glare and roar of falling water, and a ship's deck, despite the many outlets, is full enough to swim about in in a very few minutes. At such times the whole celestial machinery of rain-making may be seen in full working order. Five or six mighty water-spouts in various stages of development were often within easy distance of us; once, indeed, we watched the birth, growth, and death of one less than a mile away. First, a big, black cloud, even among that great assemblage of *nimbi*, began to belly downward, until the centre of it tapered into a stem, and the whole mass looked like a vast, irregularly-moulded funnel. Lower and lower it reached, as if feeling for a soil in which to grow, until the sea beneath was agitated sympathetically, rising at last in a sort of pointed mound to meet the descending column. Our nearness enabled us to see that both descending and rising parts were whirling violently in obedience to some invisible force; and when they had joined each other, although the spiral motion did not appear to continue, the upward rush of the water through what was now a long elastic tube was very plainly to be seen. The cloud overhead grew blacker and bigger, until its gloom was terrible. The pipe, or stem, got thinner gradually, until it became a mere thread; nor, although watching closely, could we determine when the connection between sea and sky ceased —one could not call it severed. The point rising from the sea settled almost immediately amidst a small commotion, as of a whirlpool. The tail depending from the cloud slowly shortened, and the mighty reservoir lost the vast bulge which had hung so threateningly above. Just before the final disappearance of the last portion of the tube, a fragment of cloud appeared to break off. It fell near enough to show by its thundering roar what a body of water it must have been, although it looked like a saturated piece of dirty rag in its descent.

For whole days and nights together we sometimes lay almost "as idle as a painted ship upon a painted ocean," when the deep blue dome above matched the deep blue plain below, and never a fleck of white appeared in sky or sea. This perfect stop to our progress troubled none, although it aggravates a merchant skipper terribly. As for the objects of our search, they had apparently all migrated other-whither, for never a sign of them did we see. Finbacks, a species of rorqual, were always pretty numerous, and, as if they knew how useless they were to us, came and played around like exaggerated porpoises. One in particular kept us company for several days and nights. We knew him well, from a great triangular scar on his right side, near the dorsal fin. Sometimes he would remain motionless by the side of the ship, a few feet below the surface, as distinctly in our sight as a gold-fish in a parlour globe; or he would go under the keel, and gently chafe his broad back to and fro along it, making queer tremors run through the vessel, as if she were scraping over a reef. Whether from superstition or not I cannot tell, but I never saw any creature injured out of pure wantonness, except sharks, while I was on board the *Cachalot*. Of course, injuries to men do not count. Had that finback attempted to play about a passenger ship in such a fashion, all the loungers on board would have been popping at him with their revolvers and rifles without ever a thought of compunction; yet here, in a vessel whose errand was whale-fishing, a whale enjoyed perfect immunity. It was very puzzling. At last my curiosity became too great to bear any longer, and I sought my friend Mistah Jones at what I considered a favourable opportunity. I found him very gracious and communicative, and I got such a lecture on the natural history of the cetacea as I have never forgotten—the outcome of a quarter-century's experience of them, and afterwards proved by me to be correct in every detail, which latter is a great deal more than can be said of any written natural history that ever I came across. But I will not go into that now. Leaning over the rail, with the great rorqual laying perfectly still a few feet below, I was told to mark how slender and elegant were his proportions. "Clipper-built," my Mentor termed him. He was full seventy feet long, but his greatest diameter would not reach ten feet. His snout was long and pointed, while both top and bottom of his head were nearly flat. When he came up to breathe, which he did out of the top of his head, he showed us that, instead of teeth, he had a narrow fringe of baleen (whalebone) all around his upper jaws, although "I kaint see whyfor, kase he lib on all sort er fish, s'long's dey ain't too big. I serpose w'en he kaint get nary fish he do de same ez de 'bowhead'—go er siftin eout dem little tings we calls whale-feed wiv dat ar 'rangement he carry in his mouf." "But why don't we harpoon him?" I asked. Goliath turned on me a pitying look, as he replied, "Sonny, ef yew wuz ter go en stick iron inter dat ar fish, yew'd fink de hole bottom fell eout kerblunk. W'en I uz young 'n foolish, a finback range 'longside me one day, off de Seychelles. I just done gone miss' a spam whale, and I was kiender mad,—muss ha' bin. Wall, I let him hab it blam 'tween de ribs. If I lib ten tousan year, ain't gwine ter fergit dat ar. Wa'nt no time ter spit, tell ye; eberybody hang ober de side ob de boat. Wiz—poof!—de line all gone. Clar to glory, *I* neber see it go. Ef it hab ketch anywhar, nobody eber see *us* too. Fus, I t'ought I jump ober de side—neber face de skipper any mo'. But he uz er good ole man, en he only say, 'Don't be sech blame jackass any more.' En I don't." From which lucid narration I gathered that the finback had himself to thank for his immunity from pursuit. "'Sides," persisted Goliath, "wa' yew gwine do wiv' him?

Ain't six inch uv blubber anywhere 'bout his long ugly carkiss; en dat dirty lill' rag 'er whalebone he got in his mouf, 'taint worf fifty cents. En mor'n dat, we pick up a dead one when I uz in de ole *Rainbow*—done choke hisself, I spec, en we cut him in. He stink fit ter pison de debbil, en, after all, we get eighteen bar'l ob dirty oil out ob him. Wa'nt worf de clean sparm scrap we use ter bile him. G' 'way!" Which emphatic adjuration, addressed not to me, but to the unconscious monster below, closed the lesson for the time.

The calm still persisted, and, as usual, fish began to abound, especially flying-fish. At times, disturbed by some hungry bonito or dolphin, a shoal of them would rise—a great wave of silver—and skim through the air, rising and falling for perhaps a couple of hundred yards before they again took to the water; or a solitary one of larger size than usual would suddenly soar into the air, a heavy splash behind him showing by how few inches he had missed the jaws of his pursuer. Away he would go in a long, long curve, and, meeting the ship in his flight, would rise in the air, turn off at right angles to his former direction, and spin away again, the whir of his wing-fins distinctly visible as well as audible. At last he would incline to the water, but just as he was about to enter it there would be an eddy—the enemy was there waiting—and he would rise twenty, thirty feet, almost perpendicularly, and dart away fully a hundred yards on a fresh course before the drying of his wing membranes compelled him to drop. In the face of such a sight as this, which is of everyday occurrence in these latitudes, how trivial and misleading the statements made by the natural history books seem.

They tell their readers that the *Exocetus Volitans* "does not fly; does not flutter its wings; can only take a prolonged leap," and so on. The misfortune attendant upon such books seems, to an unlearned sailor like myself, to be that, although posing as authorities, most of the authors are content to take their facts not simply at second-hand, but even unto twenty-second-hand. So the old fables get repeated, and brought up to date, and it is nobody's business to take the trouble to correct them.

The weather continued calm and clear, and as the flying-fish were about in such immense numbers, I ventured to suggest to Goliath that we might have a try for some of them. I verily believe he thought I was mad. He stared at me for a minute, and then, with an indescribable intonation, said, "How de ol' Satan yew fink yew gwain ter get 'm, hey? Ef yew spects ter fool dis chile wiv any dem lime-juice yarns, 'bout lanterns 'n boats at night-time, yew's 'way off." I guessed he meant the fable current among English sailors, that if you hoist a sail on a calm night in a boat where flying-fish abound, and hang a lantern in the middle of it, the fish will fly in shoals at the lantern, strike against the sail, and fall in heaps in the boat. It *may* be true, but I never spoke to anybody who has seen it done, nor is it the method practised in the only place in the world where flying-fishing is followed for a living. So I told Mr. Jones that if we had some circular nets of small mesh made and stretched on wooden hoops, I was sure we should be able to catch some. He caught at the idea, and mentioned it to the mate, who readily gave his permission to use a boat. A couple of "Guineamen" (a very large kind of flying-fish, having four wings) flew on board that night, as if purposely to provide us with the necessary bait.

Next morning, about four bells, the sea being like a mirror, unruffled by a breath of wind, we lowered and paddled off from the ship about a mile. When far enough away, we commenced operations by squeezing in the water some pieces of fish that had been kept for the purpose until they were rather high-flavoured. The exuding oil from this fish spread a thin film for some distance around the boat, through which, as through a sheet of glass, we could see a long way down. Minute specks of the bait sank slowly through the limpid blue, but for at least an hour there was no sign of life. I was beginning to fear that I should be called to account for misleading all hands, when, to my unbounded delight, an immense shoal of flying-fish came swimming round the boat, eagerly picking up the savoury morsels. We grasped our nets, and, leaning over the gunwale, placed them silently in the water, pressing them downward and in towards the boat at the same time. Our success was great and immediate. We lifted the wanderers by scores, while I whispered imploringly, "Be careful not to scare them; don't make a sound." All hands entered into the spirit of the thing with great eagerness. As for Mistah Jones, his delight was almost more than he could bear. Suddenly one of the men, in lifting his net, slipped on the smooth bottom of the boat, jolting one of the oars. There was a gleam of light below as the school turned—they had all disappeared instanter. We had been so busy that we had not noticed the dimensions of our catch; but now, to our great joy, we found that we had at least eight hundred fish nearly as large as herrings. We at once returned to the ship, having been absent only two hours, during which we had caught sufficient to provide all hands with three good meals. Not one of the crew had ever seen or heard of such fishing before, so my pride and pleasure may be imagined. A little learning may be a dangerous thing at times, but it certainly is often handy to have about you. The habit of taking notice and remembering has often been the means of saving many lives in suddenly-met situations of emergency, at sea perhaps more than anywhere else, and nothing can be more useful to a sailor than the practice of keeping his weather-eye open.

In Barbadoes there is established the only regular flying-fishery in the world, and in just the manner I have described, except that the boats are considerably larger, is the whole town supplied with delicious fish at so trifling a cost as to make it a staple food among all classes.

But I find that I am letting this chapter run to an unconscionable length, and it does not appear as if we were getting at the southward very fast either. Truth to tell, our progress was mighty slow; but we gradually crept across the belt of calms, and a week after our never-to-be-forgotten haul of flying-fish we got the first of the south-east trades, and went away south at a good pace—for us. We made the Island of Trinidada with its strange conical-topped pillar, the Ninepin Rock, but did not make a call, as the skipper was beginning to get fidgety at not seeing any whales, and anxious to get down to where he felt reasonably certain of falling in with them. Life had been very monotonous of late, and much as we dreaded still the prospect of whale-fighting (by "we," of course, I mean the chaps forward), it began to lose much of its terror for us, so greatly did we long for a little change. Keeping, as we did, out of the ordinary track of ships, we hardly ever saw a sail. We had no recreations; fun was out of the question; and had it not been for a Bible, a copy of Shakespeare, and a couple of cheap copies of "David Copperfield" and "Bleak House," all of which were mine, we should have had no books.

CHAPTER VIII.

ABNER'S WHALE.

In a previous chapter I have referred to the fact of a bounty being offered to whoever should first sight a useful whale, payable only in the event of the prize being secured by the ship. In consequence of our ill-success, and to stimulate the watchfulness of all, that bounty was now increased from ten pounds of tobacco to twenty, or fifteen dollars, whichever the winner chose to have. Most of us whites regarded this as quite out of the question for us, whose untrained vision was as the naked eye to a telescope when pitted against the eagle-like sight of the Portuguese. Nevertheless, we all did our little best, and I know, for one, that when I descended from my lofty perch, after a two hours' vigil, my eyes often ached and burned for an hour afterwards from the intensity of my gaze across the shining waste of waters.

Judge, then, of the surprise of everybody, when one forenoon watch, three days after we had lost sight of Trinidada, a most extraordinary sound was heard from the fore crow's-nest. I was, at the time, up at the main, in company with Louis, the mate's harpooner, and we stared across to see whatever was the matter. The watchman was unfortunate Abner Cushing, whose trivial offence had been so severely punished a short time before, and he was gesticulating and howling like a madman. Up from below came the deep growl of the skipper, "Foremast head, there, what d'ye say?" "B-b-b-blow, s-s-sir," stammered Abner; "a big whale right in the way of the sun, sir." "See anythin', Louey?" roared the skipper to my companion, just as we had both "raised" the spout almost in the glare cast by the sun. "Yessir," answered Louis; "but I kaint make him eout yet, sir." "All right; keep yer eye on him, and lemme know sharp;" and away he went aft for his glasses.

The course was slightly altered, so that we headed direct for the whale, and in less than a minute afterwards we saw distinctly the great black column of a sperm whale's head rise well above the sea, scattering a circuit of foam before it, and emitting a bushy, tufted burst of vapour into the clear air. "There she white-waters! Ah bl-o-o-o-o-o-w, blow, blow!" sang Louis; and then, in another tone, "Sperm whale, sir; big, 'lone fish, headin' 'beout east-by-nothe." "All right. 'Way down from aloft," answered the skipper, who was already half-way up the main-rigging; and like squirrels we slipped out of our hoops and down the backstays, passing the skipper like a flash as he toiled upwards, bellowing orders as he went. Short as our journey down had been, when we arrived on deck we found all ready for a start. But as the whale was at least seven miles away, and we had a fair wind for him, there was no hurry to lower, so we all stood at attention by our respective boats, waiting for the signal. I found, to my surprise, that, although I was conscious of a much more rapid heart-beat than usual, I was not half so scared as I expected to be—that the excitement was rather pleasant than otherwise. There were a few traces of funk about some of the others still; but as for Abner, he was fairly transformed; I hardly knew the man. He was one of Goliath's boat's crew, and the big darkey was quite proud of him. His eyes sparkled, and he chuckled and smiled constantly, as one who is conscious of having done a grand stroke of business, not only for himself, but for all hands. "Lower away boats!" came pealing down from the skipper's lofty perch, succeeded instantly by the rattle of the patent blocks as the falls flew through them, while the four beautiful craft took the water with an almost simultaneous splash. The ship-keepers had trimmed the yards to the wind and hauled up the courses, so that simply putting the helm down deadened our way, and allowed the boats to run clear without danger of fouling one another. To shove off and hoist sail was the work of a few moments, and with a fine working breeze away we went. As before, our boat, being the chief's, had the post of honour; but there was now only one whale, and I rather wondered why we had all left the ship. According to expectations, down he went when we were within a couple of miles of him, but quietly and with great dignity, elevating his tail perpendicularly in the air, and sinking slowly from our view. Again I found Mr. Count talkative.

"Thet whale 'll stay down fifty minutes, I guess," said he, "fer he's every gill ov a hundred en twenty bar'l; and don't yew fergit it." "Do the big whales give much more trouble than the little ones?" I asked, seeing him thus chatty. "Wall, it's jest ez it happens, boy—just ez it happens. I've seen a fifty-bar'l bull make the purtiest fight I ever hearn tell ov—a fight thet lasted twenty hours, stove three boats, 'n killed two men. Then, again, I've seen a hundred 'n fifty bar'l whale lay 'n take his grooel 'thout hardly wunkin 'n eyelid—never moved ten fathom from fust iron till fin eout. So yew may say, boy, that they're like peepul—got thair individooal pekyewlyarities, an' thars no countin' on 'em for sartin nary time." I was in great hopes of getting some useful information while his mood lasted; but it was over, and silence reigned. Nor did I dare to ask any more questions; he looked so stern and fierce. The scene was very striking. Overhead, a bright blue sky just fringed with fleecy little clouds; beneath, a deep blue sea with innumerable tiny wavelets dancing and glittering in the blaze of the sun; but all swayed in one direction by a great, solemn swell that slowly rolled from east to west, like the measured breathing of some world-supporting monster. Four little craft in a group, with twenty-four men in them, silently waiting for battle with one of the mightiest of God's creatures—one that was indeed a terrible foe to encounter were he but wise enough to make the best use of his opportunities. Against him we came with our puny weapons, of which I could not help reminding myself that "he laugheth at the shaking of a spear." But when the man's brain was thrown into the scale against the instinct of the brute, the contest looked less unequal than at first sight, for *there* is the secret of success. My musings were very suddenly interrupted. Whether we had overrun our distance, or the whale, who was not "making a passage," but feeding, had changed his course, I do not know; but, anyhow, he broke water close ahead, coming straight for our boat. His great black head, like the broad bow of a dumb barge, driving the waves before it, loomed high and menacing to me, for I was not forbidden to look ahead now. But coolly, as if coming alongside the ship, the mate bent to the big steer-oar, and swung the boat off at right angles to her course, bringing her back again with another broad sheer as the whale passed foaming. This manœuvre brought us side by side with him before he had time to realize that we were there. Up till that instant he had evidently not seen us, and his surprise was correspondingly great. To see Louis raise his harpoon high above his head, and with a hoarse grunt of satisfaction plunge it into the black, shining mass beside him up to the hitches, was indeed a sight to be remembered. Quick as thought he snatched up a second harpoon, and as the whale rolled from us it flew from his hands, burying itself like the former one, but lower down the body. The great impetus we had when we reached the whale carried us a long way past him, out of all danger from his struggles. No hindrance was experienced from the line by which we were connected with the whale, for it was loosely coiled in a space for the purpose in the boat's bow to the extent of two hundred feet, and this was cast overboard by the harpooner as soon as the fish was fast. He made a fearful to-do over it, rolling completely over several times backward and forward, at the same time smiting the sea with his mighty tail, making an almost deafening noise and pother. But we were comfortable enough, while we unshipped the mast and made ready for action, being sufficiently far away from him to escape the full effect of his gambols. It was impossible to avoid reflecting, however, upon what *would* happen if, in our unprepared and so far helpless state, he were, instead of simply tumbling about in an aimless, blind sort of fury, to rush at the boat and try to destroy it. Very few indeed would survive such an attack, unless the tactics were radically altered. No doubt they would be, for practices grow up in consequence of the circumstances with which they have to deal.

After the usual time spent in furious attempts to free himself from our annoyance, he betook himself below, leaving us to await his return, and hasten it as much as possible by keeping a severe strain upon the line. Our efforts in this direction, however, did not seem to have any effect upon him at all. Flake after flake ran out of the tubs, until we were compelled to hand the end of our line to the second mate to splice his own on to. Still it slipped away, and at last it was handed to the third mate, whose two tubs met the same fate. It was now Mistah Jones' turn to "bend on," which he did with many chuckles as of a man who was the last resource of the unfortunate. But his face grew longer and longer as the never-resting line continued to disappear. Soon he signalled us that he was nearly out of line, and two or three minutes after he bent on his "drogue" (a square piece of plank with a rope tail spliced into its centre, and considered to hinder a whale's progress at least as much as four boats), and let go the end. We had each bent on our drogues in the same way, when we passed our ends to one another. So now our friend was getting along somewhere below with 7200 feet of 1½-inch rope, and weight additional equal to the drag of sixteen 30-feet boats.

Of course we knew that, unless he were dead and sinking, he could not possibly remain much longer beneath the surface. The exhibition of endurance we had just been favoured with was a very unusual one, I was told, it being a rare thing for a cachalot to take out two boats' lines before returning to the surface to spout.

Therefore, we separated as widely as was thought necessary, in order to be near him on his arrival. It was, as might be imagined, some time before we saw the light of his countenance; but when we did, we had no difficulty in getting alongside of him again. My friend Goliath, much to my delight, got there first, and succeeded in picking up the bight of the line. But having done so, his chance of distinguishing himself was gone. Hampered by the immense quantity of sunken line which was attached to the whale, he could do nothing, and soon received orders to cut the bight of the line and pass the whale's end to us. He had hardly obeyed, with a very bad grace, when the whale started off to windward with us at a tremendous rate. The other boats, having no line, could do nothing to help, so away we went alone, with barely a hundred fathoms of line, in case he should take it into his head to sound again. The speed at which he went made it appear as if a gale of wind was blowing, and we flew along the sea surface, leaping from crest to crest of the waves with an incessant succession of cracks like pistol-shots. The flying spray drenched us and prevented us from seeing him, but I fully realized that it was nothing to what we should have to put up with if the wind freshened much. One hand was kept baling the water out which came so freely over the bows, but all the rest hauled with all their might upon the line, hoping to get a little closer to the flying monster. Inch by inch we gained on him, encouraged by the hoarse objurgations of the mate, whose excitement was intense. After what seemed a terribly long chase, we found his speed slackening, and we redoubled our efforts. Now we were close upon him; now, in obedience to the steersman, the boat sheered out a bit, and we were abreast of his labouring flukes; now the mate hurls his quivering lance with such hearty good-will that every inch of its slender shaft disappears within the huge body. "Lay off! Off with her, Louey!" screamed the mate; and she gave a wide sheer away from the whale, not a second too soon. Up flew that awful tail, descending with a crash upon the water not two feet from us. "Out oars! Pull, two! starn, three!" shouted the mate; and as we obeyed our foe turned to fight. Then might one see how courage and skill were such mighty factors in the apparently unequal contest. The whale's great length made it no easy job for him to turn, while our boat, with two oars a-side, and the great leverage at the stern supplied by the nineteen-foot steer-oar, circled, backed, and darted ahead like a living thing animated by the mind of our commander. When the leviathan settled, we gave a wide berth to his probable place of ascent; when he rushed at us, we dodged him; when he paused, if only momentarily, in we flew, and got home a fearful thrust of the deadly lance.

All fear was forgotten now—I panted, thirsted for his life. Once, indeed, in a sort of frenzy, when for an instant we lay side by side with him, I drew my sheath-knife, and plunged it repeatedly into the blubber, as if I were assisting in his destruction. Suddenly the mate gave a howl: "Starn all—starn all! oh, starn!" and the oars bent like canes as we obeyed. There was an upheaval of the sea just ahead; then slowly, majestically, the vast body of our foe rose into the air. Up, up it went, while my heart stood still, until the whole of that immense creature hung on high, apparently motionless, and then fell—a hundred tons of solid flesh—back into the sea. On either side of that mountainous mass the waters rose in shining towers of snowy foam, which fell in their turn, whirling and eddying around us as we tossed and fell like a chip in a whirlpool. Blinded by the flying spray, baling for very life to free the boat from the water with which she was nearly full, it was some minutes before I was able to decide whether we were still uninjured or not. Then I saw, at a little distance, the whale lying quietly. As I looked he spouted, and the vapour was red with his blood. "Starn all!" again cried our chief, and we retreated to a considerable distance. The old warrior's practised eye had detected the coming climax of our efforts, the dying agony or "flurry" of the great mammal. Turning upon his side, he began to move in a circular direction, slowly at first, then faster and faster, until he was rushing round at tremendous speed, his great head raised quite out of water at times, clashing his enormous jaws. Torrents of blood poured from his spout-hole, accompanied by hoarse bellowings, as of some gigantic bull, but really caused by the labouring breath trying to pass through the clogged air passages. The utmost caution and rapidity of manipulation of the boat was necessary to avoid his maddened rush, but this gigantic energy was short-lived. In a few minutes he subsided slowly in death, his mighty body reclined on one side, the fin uppermost waving limply as he rolled to the swell, while the small waves broke gently over the carcass in a low, monotonous surf, intensifying the profound silence that had succeeded the tumult of our conflict with the late monarch of the deep. Hardly had the flurry ceased, when we hauled up alongside of our hard-won prize, in order to secure a line to him in a better manner than at present for hauling him to the ship. This was effected by cutting a hole through the tough, gristly substance of the flukes with the short "boat-spade," carried for the purpose. The end of the line, cut off from the faithful harpoon that had held it so long, was then passed through this hole and made fast. This done, it was "Smoke-oh!" The luxury of that rest and refreshment was something to be grateful for, coming, as it did, in such complete contrast to our recent violent exertions.

The ship was some three or four miles off to leeward, so we reckoned she would take at least an hour and a half to work up to us. Meanwhile, our part of the performance being over, and well over, we thoroughly enjoyed ourselves, lazily rocking on the gentle swell by the side of a catch worth at least £800. During the conflict I had not noticed what now claimed attention—several great masses of white, semi-transparent-looking substance floating about, of huge size and irregular shape. But one of these curious lumps came floating by as we lay, tugged at by several fish, and I immediately asked the mate if he could tell me what it was and where it came from. He told me that, when dying, the cachalot always ejected the contents of his stomach, which were invariably composed of such masses as we saw before us; that he believed the stuff to be portions of big cuttle-fish, bitten off by the whale for the purpose of swallowing, but he wasn't sure. Anyhow, I could haul this piece alongside now, if I liked, and see. Secretly wondering at the indifference shown by this officer of forty years' whaling experience to such a wonderful fact as appeared to be here presented, I thanked him, and, sticking the boat-hook into the lump, drew it alongside. It was at once evident that it was a massive fragment of cuttle-fish—tentacle or arm—as thick as a stout man's body, and with six or seven sucking-discs or *acetabula* on it. These were about as large as a saucer, and on their inner edge were thickly set with hooks or claws all round the rim, sharp as needles, and almost the shape and size of a tiger's.

To what manner of awful monster this portion of limb belonged, I could only faintly imagine; but of course I remembered, as any sailor would, that from my earliest sea-going I had been told that the cuttle-fish was the biggest in the sea, although I never even began to think it might be true until now. I asked the mate if he had ever seen such creatures as this piece belonged to alive and kicking. He answered, languidly, "Wall, I guess so; but I don't take any stock in fish, 'cept for provisions er ile—en thet's a fact." It will be readily believed that I vividly recalled this conversation when, many years after, I read an account by the Prince of Monaco of *his* discovery of a gigantic squid, to which his naturalist gave the name of *Lepidoteuthis Grimaldii!* Truly the indifference and apathy manifested by whalers generally to everything except commercial matters is wonderful—hardly to be credited. However, this was a mighty revelation to me. For the first time, it was possible to understand that, contrary to the usual notion of a whale's being unable to swallow a herring, here was a kind of whale that could swallow—well, a block four or five feet square apparently; who lived upon creatures as large as himself, if one might judge of their bulk by the sample to hand; but being unable, from only possessing teeth in one jaw, to

THE WHALE STARTED OFF TO WINDWARD WITH US AT A TREMENDOUS RATE.

masticate his food, was compelled to tear it in sizable pieces, bolt it whole, and leave his commissariat department to do the rest.

While thus ruminating, the mate and Louis began a desultory conversation concerning what they termed "ambergrease." I had never even heard the word before, although I had a notion that Milton, in "Paradise Regained," describing the Satanic banquet, had spoken of something being "gris-amber steamed." They could by no means agree as to what this mysterious substance was, how it was produced, or under what conditions. They knew that it was sometimes found floating near the dead body of a sperm whale—the mate, in fact, stated that he had taken it once from the rectum of a cachalot —and they were certain that it was of great value—from one to three guineas per ounce. When I got to know more of the natural history of the sperm whale, and had studied the literature of the subject, I was no longer surprised at their want of agreement, since the learned doctors who have written upon the subject do not seem to have come to definite conclusions either.

By some it is supposed to be the product of a diseased condition of the creature; others consider that it is merely the excreta, which, normally fluid, has by some means become concreted. It is nearly always found with cuttle-fish beaks imbedded in its substance, showing that these indigestible portions of the sperm whale's food have in some manner become mixed with it during its formation in the bowel. Chemists have analyzed it with scanty results. Its great value is due to its property of intensifying the power of perfumes, although, strange to say, it has little or no odour of its own, a faint trace of musk being perhaps detectable in some cases.

The Turks are said to use it for a truly Turkish purpose, which need not be explained here, while the Moors are credited with a taste for it in their cookery. About both these latter statements there is considerable doubt; I only give them for what they are worth, without committing myself to any definite belief in them.

The ship now neared us fast, and as soon as she rounded-to, we left the whale and pulled towards her, paying out line as we went. Arriving alongside, the line was handed on board, and in a short time the prize was hauled to the gangway. We met with a very different reception this time. The skipper's grim face actually looked almost pleasant as he contemplated the colossal proportions of the latest addition to our stock. He was indeed a fine catch, being at least seventy feet long, and in splendid condition. As soon as he was secured alongside in the orthodox fashion, all hands were sent to dinner, with an intimation to look sharp over it. Judging from our slight previous experience, there was some heavy labour before us, for this whale was nearly four times as large as the one caught off the Cape Verds. And it was so. Verily those officers toiled like Titans to get that tremendous head off, even the skipper taking a hand. In spite of their efforts, it was dark before the heavy job was done. As we were in no danger of bad weather, the head was dropped astern by a hawser until morning, when it would be safer to dissect it. All that night we worked incessantly, ready to drop with fatigue, but not daring to suggest the possibility of such a thing. Several of the officers and harpooners were allowed a few hours off, as their special duty of dealing with the head at daylight would be so arduous as to need all their energies. When day dawned we were allowed a short rest, while the work of cutting up the head was undertaken by the rested men aft. At seven bells (7.30) it was "turn to" all hands again. The "junk" was hooked on to both cutting tackles, and the windlass manned by everybody who could get hold. Slowly the enormous mass rose, canting the ship heavily as it came, while every stick and rope aloft complained of the great strain upon them. When at last it was safely shipped, and the tackles cast off, the size of this small portion of a full-grown cachalot's body could be realized, not before.

It was hauled from the gangway by tackles, and securely lashed to the rail running round beneath the top of the bulwarks for that purpose—the "lash-rail" —where the top of it towered up as high as the third ratline of the main-rigging. Then there was another spell, while the "case" was separated from the skull. This was too large to get on board, so it was lifted half-way out of water by the tackles, one hooked on each side; then they were made fast, and a spar rigged across them at a good height above the top of the case. A small block was lashed to this spar, through which a line was rove. A long, narrow bucket was attached to one end of this rope; the other end on deck was attended by two men. One unfortunate beggar was perched aloft on the above-mentioned spar, where his position, like the main-yard of Marryatt's verboso carpenter was "precarious and not at all permanent." He was provided with a pole, with which he pushed the bucket down through a hole cut in the upper end of the "case," whence it was drawn out by the chaps on deck full of spermaceti. It was a weary, unsatisfactory process, wasting a great deal of the substance being baled out; but no other way was apparently possible. The grease blew about, drenching most of us engaged in an altogether unpleasant fashion, while, to mend matters, the old barky began to roll and tumble about in an aimless, drunken sort of way, the result of a new cross swell rolling up from the south-westward. As the stuff was gained, it was poured into large tanks in the blubber-room, the quantity being too great to be held by the try-pots at once. Twenty-five barrels of this clear, wax-like substance were baled from that case; and when at last it was lowered a little, and cut away from its supports, it was impossible to help thinking that much was still remaining within which we, with such rude means, were unable to save. Then came the task of cutting up the junk. Layer after layer, eight to ten inches thick, was sliced off, cut into suitable pieces, and passed into the tanks. So full was the matter of spermaceti that one could take a piece as large as one's head in the hands, and squeeze it like a sponge, expressing the spermaceti in showers, until nothing remained but a tiny ball of fibre. All this soft, pulpy mass was held together by walls of exceedingly tough, gristly integument ("white horse"), which was as difficult to cut as gutta-percha, and, but for the peculiar texture, not at all unlike it.

When we had finished separating the junk, there was nearly a foot of oil on deck in the waist, and uproarious was the laughter when some hapless individual, losing his balance, slid across the deck and sat down with a loud splash in the deepest part of the accumulation.

The lower jaw of this whale measured exactly nineteen feet in length from the opening of the mouth, or, say the last of the teeth, to the point, and carried twenty-eight teeth on each side. For the time, it was hauled aft out of the way, and secured to the lash-rail. The subsequent proceedings were just the same as before described, only more so. For a whole week our labours continued, and when they were over we had stowed below a hundred and forty-six barrels of mingled oil and spermaceti, or fourteen and a half tuns.

It was really a pleasant sight to see Abner receiving, as if being invested with an order of merit, the twenty pounds of tobacco to which he was entitled. Poor fellow! he felt as if at last he were going to be thought a little of, and treated a little better. He brought his bounty forrard, and shared it out as far as it would go with the greatest delight and good nature possible. Whatever he might have been thought of aft, certainly, for the time, he was a very important personage forrard; even the Portuguese, who were inclined to be jealous of what they considered an infringement of their rights, were mollified by the generosity shown.

After every sign of the operations had been cleared away, the jaw was brought out, and the teeth extracted with a small tackle. They were set solidly into a hard white gum, which had to be cut away all around them before they would come out. When cleaned of the gum, they were headed up in a small barrel of brine. The great jaw-pans were sawn off, and placed at the disposal of anybody who wanted pieces of bone for "scrimshaw," or carved work. This is a very favourite pastime on board whalers, though, in ships such as ours, the crew have little opportunity for doing anything, hardly any leisure during daylight being allowed. But our carpenter was a famous workman at "scrimshaw," and he started half a dozen walking-sticks forthwith. A favourite design is to carve the bone into the similitude of a rope, with "worming" of smaller line along its lays. A handle is carved out of a whale's tooth, and insets of baleen, silver, cocoa-tree, or ebony, give variety and finish. The tools used are of the roughest. Some old files, softened in the fire, and filed into grooves something like saw-teeth, are most used; but old knives, sail-needles, and chisels are pressed into service. The work turned out would, in many cases, take a very high place in an exhibition of turnery, though never a lathe was near it. Of course, a long time is taken over it, especially the polishing, which is done with oil and whiting, if it can be got—powdered pumice if it cannot. I once had an elaborate pastry-cutter carved out of six whale's teeth, which I purchased for a pound of tobacco from a seaman of the *Coral* whaler, and afterwards sold in Dunedin, New Zealand, for £2 10*s*., the purchaser being decidedly of opinion that he had a bargain.

CHAPTER IX.

OUR FIRST CALLING-PLACE.

PERHAPS it may hastily be assumed, from the large space already devoted to fishing operations of various kinds, that the subject will not bear much more dealing with, if my story is to avoid being monotonous. But I beg to assure you, dear reader, that while of course I have most to say in connection with the business of the voyage, nothing is farther from my plan than to neglect the very interesting portion of our cruise which relates to visiting strange, out-of-the-way corners of the world. If—which I earnestly deprecate—the description hitherto given of sperm whale-fishing and its adjuncts be found not so interesting as could be wished, I cry you mercy. I have been induced to give more space to it because it has been systematically avoided in the works upon whale-fishing before mentioned, which, as I have said, were not intended for popular reading. True, neither may my humble tome become popular either; but, if it does not, no one will be so disappointed as the author.

We had made but little progress during the week of oil manufacture, very little attention being paid to the sails while that work was about; but, as the south-east trades blew steadily, we did not remain stationary altogether. So that the following week saw us on the south side of the tropic of Capricorn, the south-east trade done, and the dirty weather and variable squalls, which nearly always precede the "westerlies," making our lives a burden to us. Here, however, we were better off than in an ordinary merchantman, where doldrums are enough to drive you mad. The one object being to get along, it is incessant "pully-hauly," setting and taking in sail, in order, on the one hand, to lose no time, and, on the other, to lose no sails. Now, with us, whenever the weather was doubtful or squally-looking, we shortened sail, and kept it fast till better weather came along, being quite careless whether we made one mile a day or one hundred. But just because nobody took any notice of our progress as the days passed, we were occasionally startled to find how far we had really got. This was certainly the case with all of us forward, even to me who had some experience, so well used had I now become to the leisurely way of getting along. To the laziest of ships, however, there comes occasionally a time when the bustling, hurrying wind will take no denial, and you've got to "git up an' git," as the Yanks put it. Such a time succeeded our "batterfanging" about, after losing the trades. We got hold of a westerly wind that, commencing quietly, gently, steadily, taking two or three days before it gathered force and volume, strengthened at last into a stern, settled gale that would brook no denial, to face which would have been misery indeed. To vessels bound east it came as a boon and blessing, for it would be a crawler that could not reel off her two hundred and fifty miles a day before the push of such a breeze. Even the *Cachalot* did her one hundred and fifty, pounding and bruising the ill-used sea in her path, and spreading before her broad bows a far-reaching area of snowy foam, while her wake was as wide as any two ordinary ships ought to make. Five or six times a day the flying East India or colonial-bound English ships, under every stitch of square sail, would appear as tiny specks on the horizon astern, come up with us, pass like a flash, and fade away ahead, going at least two knots to our one. I could not help feeling a bit home-sick and tired of my present surroundings, in spite of their interest, when I saw those beautiful ocean-flyers devouring the distance which lay before them, and reflected that in little more than one month most of them would be discharging in Melbourne, Sydney, Calcutta, or some other equally distant port, while we should probably be dodging about in our present latitude a little farther east.

After a few days of our present furious rate of speed, I came on deck one morning, and instantly recognized an old acquaintance. Right ahead, looking nearer than I had ever seen it before, rose the towering mass of Tristan d'Acunha, while farther away, but still visible, lay Nightingale and Inaccessible Islands. Their aspect was familiar, for I had sighted them on nearly every voyage I had made round the Cape, but I had never seen them so near as this. There was a good deal of excitement among us, and no wonder. Such a break in the monotony of our lives as we were about to have was enough to turn our heads. Afterwards, we learned to view these matters in a more philosophic light; but now, being new and galled by the yoke, it was a different thing. Near as the island seemed, it was six hours before we got near enough to distinguish objects on shore. I have seen the top of Tristan peeping through a cloud nearly a hundred miles away, for its height is tremendous. St. Helena looks a towering, scowling mass when you approach it closely; but Tristan d'Acunha is far more imposing, its savage-looking cliffs seeming to sternly forbid the venturesome voyager any nearer familiarity with their frowning fastnesses. Long before we came within working distance of the settlement, we were continually passing broad patches of kelp (*fucus gigantea*), whose great leaves and cable-laid stems made quite reef-like breaks in the heaving waste of restless sea. Very different indeed were these patches of marine growth from the elegant wreaths of the Gulf-weed with which parts of the North Atlantic are so thickly covered. Their colour was deep brown, almost black in some cases, and the size of many of the leaves amazing, being four to five feet long, by a foot wide, with stalks as thick as one's arm. They have their origin around these storm-beaten rocks, which lie scattered thinly over the immense area of the Southern Ocean, whence they are torn, in masses like those we saw, by every gale, and sent wandering round the world.

When we arrived within about three miles of the landing-place, we saw a boat coming off, so we immediately hove-to and awaited her arrival. There was no question of anchoring; indeed, there seldom is in these vessels, unless they are going to make a long stay, for they are past masters in the art of "standing off and on." The boat came alongside—a big, substantially-built craft of the whale-boat type, but twice the size—manned by ten sturdy-looking fellows, as unkempt and wild-looking as any pirates. They were evidently put to great straits for clothes, many curious makeshifts being noticeable in their rig, while it was so patched with every conceivable kind of material that it was impossible to say which was the original or "standing part." They brought with them potatoes, onions, a few stunted cabbages, some fowls, and a couple of good-sized pigs, at the sight of which good things our eyes glistened and our mouths watered. Alas! none of the cargo of that boat ever reached *our* hungry stomachs. We were not surprised, having anticipated that every bit of provision would be monopolized by our masters; but of course we had no means of altering such a state of things.

The visitors had the same tale to tell that seems universal—bad trade, hard times, nothing doing. How very familiar it seemed, to be sure. Nevertheless, it could not be denied that their sole means of communication with the outer world, as well as market for their goods, the calling whale-ships, were getting fewer and fewer every year; so that their outlook was not, it must be confessed, particularly bright. But their wants are few, beyond such as they can themselves supply. Groceries and clothes, the latter especially, as the winters are very severe, are almost the only needs they require to be supplied with from without. They spoke of the "Cape" as if it were only across the way, the distance separating them from that wonderful place being over thirteen hundred miles in reality. Very occasionally a schooner from Capetown does visit them; but, as the seals are almost exterminated, there is less and less inducement to make the voyage.

Like almost all the southern islets, this group has been in its time the scene of a wonderfully productive seal-fishery. It used to be customary for whaling and sealing vessels to land a portion of their crews, and leave them to accumulate a store of seal-skins and oil, while the ships cruised the surrounding seas for whales, which were exceedingly numerous, both "right" and sperm varieties. In those days there was no monotony of existence in these islands, ships were continually coming and going, and the islanders prospered exceedingly. When they increased beyond the capacity of the islands to entertain them, a portion migrated to the Cape, while many of the men took service in the whale-ships, for which they were eminently suited.

They are, as might be expected, a hybrid lot, the women all mulattoes, but intensely English in their views and loyalty. Since the visit of H.M.S. *Galatea*, in August, 1867, with the Duke of Edinburgh on board, this sentiment had been intensified, and the little collection of thatched cottages, nameless till then, was called Edinburgh, in honour of the illustrious voyager. They breed cattle, a few sheep, and pigs, although the sheep thrive but indifferently for some reason or another. Poultry they have in large numbers, so that, could they command a market, they would do very well.

The steep cliffs, rising from the sea for nearly a thousand feet, often keep their vicinity in absolute calm, although a heavy gale may be raging on the other side of the island, and it would be highly dangerous for any navigator not accustomed to such a neighbourhood to get too near them. The immense rollers setting in-shore, and the absence of wind combined, would soon carry a vessel up against the beetling crags, and letting go an anchor would not be of the slightest use, since the bottom, being of massive boulders, affords no holding ground at all. All round the island the kelp grows thickly, so thickly indeed as to make a boat's progress through it difficult. This, however, is very useful in one way here, as we found. Wanting more supplies, which were to be had cheap, we lowered a couple of boats, and went ashore after them. On approaching the black, pebbly beach which formed the only landing-place, it appeared as if getting ashore would be a task of no ordinary danger and difficulty. The swell seemed to culminate as we neared the beach, lifting the boats at one moment high in air, and at the next lowering them into a green valley, from whence nothing could be seen but the surrounding watery summits. Suddenly we entered the belt of kelp, which extended for perhaps a quarter of a mile seaward, and, lo! a transformation indeed. Those loose, waving fronds of flexible weed, though swayed hither and thither by every ripple, were able to arrest the devastating rush of the gigantic swell, so that the task of landing, which had looked so terrible, was one of the easiest. Once in among the kelp, although we could hardly use the oars, the water was quite smooth and tranquil. The islanders collected on the beach, and guided us to the best spot for landing, the huge boulders, heaped in many places, being ugly impediments to a boat.

We were as warmly welcomed as if we had been old friends, and hospitable attentions were showered upon us from every side. The people were noticeably well-behaved, and, although there was something Crusoe-like in their way of living, their manners and conversation were distinctly good. A rude plenty was evident, there being no lack of good food—fish, fowl, and vegetables. The grassy plateau on which the village stands is a sort of shelf jutting out from the mountain-side, the mountain being really the whole island. Steep roads were hewn out of the solid rock, leading, as we were told, to the cultivated terraces above. These reached an elevation of about a thousand feet. Above all towered the great, dominating peak, the summit lost in the clouds eight or nine thousand feet above. The rock-hewn roads and cultivated land certainly gave the settlement an old-established appearance, which was not surprising, seeing that it has been inhabited for more than a hundred years. I shall always bear a grateful recollection of the place, because my host gave me what I had long been a stranger to—a good, old-fashioned English dinner of roast beef and baked potatoes. He apologized for having no plum-pudding to crown the feast. "But, you see," he said, "we kaint grow no corn hyar, and we'm clean run out ov flour; hev ter make out on taters 's best we kin." I sincerely sympathized with him on the lack of bread-stuff among them, and wondered no longer at the avidity with which they had munched our flinty biscuits on first coming aboard. His wife, a buxom, motherly woman of about fifty, of dark, olive complexion, but good features, was kindness itself; and their three youngest children, who were at home, could not, in spite of repeated warnings and threats, keep their eyes off me, as if I had been some strange animal dropped from the moon. I felt very unwilling to leave them so soon, but time was pressing, the stores we had come for were all ready to ship, and I had to tear myself away from these kindly entertainers. I declare, it seemed like parting with old friends; yet our acquaintance might have been measured by minutes, so brief it had been. The mate had purchased a fine bullock, which had been slaughtered and cut up for us with great celerity, four or five dozen fowls (alive), four or five sacks of potatoes, eggs, etc., so that we were heavily laden for the return journey to the ship. My friend had kindly given me a large piece of splendid cheese, for which I was unable to make him any return, being simply clad in a shirt and pair of trousers, neither of which necessary garments could be spared.

With hearty cheers from the whole population, we shoved off and ploughed through the kelp seaward again. When we got clear of it, we found the swell heavier than when we had come, and a rough journey back to the ship was the result. But, to such boatmen as we were, that was a trifle hardly worth mentioning, and after an hour's hard pull we got alongside again, and transhipped our precious cargo. The weather being threatening, we at once hauled off the land and out to sea, as night was falling and we did not wish to be in so dangerous a vicinity any longer than could be helped in stormy weather. Altogether, a most enjoyable day, and one that I have ever since had a pleasant recollection of.

By daybreak next morning the islands were out of sight, for the wind had risen to a gale, which, although we carried little sail, drove us along before it some seven or eight knots an hour.

Two days afterwards we caught another whale of medium size, making us fifty-four barrels of oil. As nothing out of the ordinary course marked the capture, it is unnecessary to do more than allude to it in passing, except to note that the honours were all with Goliath. He happened to be close to the whale when it rose, and immediately got fast. So dexterous and swift were his actions that before any of the other boats could "chip in" he had his fish "fin out," the whole affair from start to finish only occupying a couple of hours. We were now in the chosen haunts of the great albatross, Cape pigeons, and Cape hens, but never in my life had I imagined such a concourse of them as now gathered around us. When we lowered there might have been perhaps a couple of dozen birds in sight, but no sooner was the whale dead than from out of the great void around they began to drift towards us. Before we had got him fast alongside, the numbers of that feathered host were incalculable. They surrounded us until the sea surface was like a plain of snow, and their discordant cries were deafening. With the exception of one peculiar-looking bird, which has received from whalemen the inelegant name of "stinker," none of them attempted to alight upon the body of the dead monster. This bird, however, somewhat like a small albatross, but of dirty-grey colour, and with a peculiar excrescence on his beak, boldly took his precarious place upon the carcass, and at once began to dig into the blubber. He did not seem to make much impression, but he certainly tried hard.

It was dark before we got our prize secured by the fluke-chain, so that we could not commence operations before morning. That night it blew hard, and we got an idea of the strain these vessels are sometimes subjected to. Sometimes the ship rolled one way and the whale another, being divided by a big sea, the wrench at the fluke-chain, as the two masses fell apart down different hollows, making the vessel quiver from truck to keelson as if she was being torn asunder. Then we would come together again with a crash and a shock that almost threw everybody out of their bunks. Many an earnest prayer did I breathe that the chain would prove staunch, for what sort of a job it would be to go after that whale during the night, should he break loose, I could only faintly imagine. But all our gear was of the very best;

no thieving ship-chandler had any hand in supplying our outfit with shoddy rope and faulty chain, only made to sell, and ready at the first call made upon it to carry away and destroy half a dozen valuable lives. There was one coil of rope on board which the skipper had bought for cordage on the previous voyage from a homeward-bound English ship, and it was the butt of all the officers' scurrilous remarks about Britishers and their gear. It was never used but for rope-yarns, being cut up in lengths, and untwisted for the ignominious purpose of tying things up—"hardly good enough for that," was the verdict upon it.

Tired as we all were, very little sleep came to us that night—we were barely seasoned yet to the exigencies of a whaler's life—but afterwards I believe nothing short of dismasting or running the ship ashore would wake us, once we got to sleep. In the morning we commenced operations in a howling gale of wind, which placed the lives of the officers on the "cutting in" stage in great danger. The wonderful seaworthy qualities of our old ship shone brilliantly now. When an ordinary modern-built sailing-ship would have been making such weather of it as not only to drown anybody about the deck, but making it impossible to keep your footing anywhere without holding on, we were enabled to cut in this whale. True, the work was terribly exhausting and decidedly dangerous, but it was not impossible, for it was done. By great care and constant attention, the whole work of cutting in and trying out was got through without a single accident; but had another whale turned up to continue the trying time, I am fully persuaded that some of us would have gone under from sheer fatigue. For there was no mercy shown. All that I have ever read of "putting the slaves through for all they were worth" on the plantations was fully realized here, and our worthy skipper must have been a lineal descendant of the doughty Simon Legree.

The men were afraid to go on to the sick-list. Nothing short of total inability to continue would have prevented them from working, such was the terror with which that man had inspired us all. It may be said that we were a pack of cowards, who, without the courage to demand better treatment, deserved all we got. While admitting that such a conclusion is quite a natural one at which to arrive, I must deny its truth. There were men in that forecastle as good citizens and as brave fellows as you would wish to meet—men who in their own sphere would have commanded and obtained respect. But under the painful and abnormal circumstances in which they found themselves—beaten and driven like dogs while in the throes of sea-sickness, half starved and hopeless, their spirit had been so broken, and they were so kept down to that sad level by the display of force, aided by deadly weapons aft, that no other condition could be expected for them but that of broken-hearted slaves. My own case was many degrees better than that of the other whites, as I have before noted; but I was perfectly well aware that the slightest attempt on my part to show that I resented our common treatment would meet with the most brutal repression, and, in addition, I might look for a dreadful time of it for the rest of the voyage.

The memory of that week of misery is so strong upon me even now that my hand trembles almost to preventing me from writing about it. Weak and feeble do the words seem as I look at them, making me wish for the fire and force of Carlyle or Macaulay to portray our unnecessary sufferings.

Like all other earthly ills, however, they came to an end, at least for a time, and I was delighted to note that we were getting to the northward again. In making the outward passage round the Cape, it is necessary to go well south, in order to avoid the great westerly set of the Agulhas current, which for ever sweeps steadily round the southern extremity of the African continent at an average rate of three or four miles an hour. To homeward-bound ships this is a great boon. No matter what the weather may be—a stark calm or a gale of wind right on end in your teeth—that vast, silent river in the sea steadily bears you on at the same rate in the direction of home. It is perfectly true that with a gale blowing across the set of this great current, one of the very ugliest combinations of broken waves is raised; but who cares for that, when he knows that, as long as the ship holds together, some seventy or eighty miles per day nearer home must be placed to her credit? In like manner, it is of the deepest comfort to know that, storm or calm, fair or foul, the current of time, unhasting, unresting, bears us on to the goal that we shall surely reach—the haven of unbroken rest.

Not the least of the minor troubles on board the *Cachalot* was the uncertainty of our destination; we never knew where we were going. It may seem a small point, but it is really not so unimportant as a landsman might imagine. On an ordinary passage, certain well-known signs are as easily read by the seaman as if the ship's position were given out to him every day. Every alteration of the course signifies some point of the journey reached, some well-known track entered upon, and every landfall made becomes a new departure from whence to base one's calculations, which, rough as they are, rarely err more than a few days.

Say, for instance, you are bound for Calcutta. The first of the north-east trades will give a fair idea of your latitude being about the edge of the tropics somewhere, or say from 20° to 25° N., whether you have sighted any of the islands or not. Then away you go before the wind down towards the Equator, the approach to which is notified by the loss of the trade and the dirty, changeable weather of the "doldrums." That weary bit of work over, along come the south-east trades, making you brace "sharp up," and sometimes driving you uncomfortably near the Brazilian coast. Presently more "doldrums," with a good deal more wind in them than in the "wariables" of the line latitude. The brave "westerly" will come along by-and-by and release you, and, with a staggering press of sail carried to the reliable gale, away you go for the long stretch of a hundred degrees or so eastward. You will very likely sight Tristan d'Acunha or Gough Island; but, if not, the course will keep you fairly well informed of your longitude, since most ships make more or less of a great circle track. Instead of steering due East for the whole distance, they make for some southerly latitude by running along the arc of a great circle, *then* run due east for a thousand miles or so before gradually working north again. These alterations in the courses tell the foremast hand nearly all he wants to know, slight as they are. You will most probably sight Amsterdam Island or St. Paul's in about 77° E.; but whether you do or not, the big change made in the course, to say nothing of the difference in the weather and temperature, say loudly that your long easterly run is over, and you are bound to the northward again. Soon the south-east trades will take you gently in hand, and waft you pleasurably upward to the line again, unless you should be so unfortunate as to meet one of the devastating meteors known as "cyclones" in its gyration across the Indian Ocean. After losing the trade, which signals your approach to the line once more, your guides fluctuate muchly with the time of year. But it may be broadly put that the change of the monsoon in the Bay of Bengal is beastliness unadulterated, and the south-west monsoon itself, though a fair wind for getting to your destination, is worse, if possible. Still, having got that far, you are able to judge pretty nearly when, in the ordinary course of events, you will arrive at Saugor, and get a tug for the rest of the journey.

But on this strange voyage I was quite as much in the dark concerning our approximate position as any of the chaps who had never seen salt water before they viewed it from the bad eminence of the *Cachalot's* deck. Of course, it was evident that we were bound eastward, but whether to the Indian seas or to the South Pacific, none knew but the skipper, and perhaps the mate. I say "perhaps" advisedly. In any well-regulated merchant ship there is an invariable routine of observations performed by both captain and chief officer, except in very big vessels, where the second mate is appointed navigating officer. The two men work out their reckoning independently of each other, and compare the result, so that an excellent check upon the accuracy of the positions found is thereby afforded. Here, however, there might not have been, as far as appearances went, a navigator in the ship except the captain, if it be not a misuse of terms to call him a navigator. If the test be ability to take a ship round the world, poking into every undescribed, out-of-the-way corner you can think of, and return home again without damage to the ship of any kind except by the unavoidable perils of the sea, then doubtless he *was* a navigator, and a ripe, good one. But anything cruder than the "rule-of-thumb" way in which he found his positions, or more out of date than his "hog-yoke," or quadrant, I have never seen. I suppose we carried a chronometer, though I never saw it or heard the cry of "stop," which usually accompanies a.m. or p.m. "sights" taken for longitude. He used sometimes to make a deliberate sort of haste below after taking a sight, when he may have been looking at a chronometer perhaps. What I do know about his procedure is, that he always used a very rough method of equal altitudes, which would make a mathematician stare and gasp; that his nautical almanac was a ten-cent one published by some speculative optician in New York; that he never worked up a "dead reckoning;" and that the extreme limit of time that he took to work out his observations was ten minutes. In fact, all our operations in seamanship or navigation were run on the same happy-go-lucky principle. If it was required tc "tack" ship, there was no formal parade and preparation for the manœuvre, not even as much as would be made in a Goole billy-boy. Without any previous intimation, the helm would be put down, and round she would come, the yards being trimmed by whoever happened to be nearest to the braces. The old tub seemed to like it that way, for she never missed stays or exhibited any of that unwillingness to do what she was required that is such a frequent characteristic of merchantmen. Even getting under way or coming to an anchor was unattended by any of the fuss and bother from which those important evolutions ordinarily appear inseparable.

To my great relief, we saw no more whales of the kind we were after during our passage round the Cape. The weather we were having was splendid for making a passage, but to be dodging about among those immense rollers, or towed athwart them by a wounded whale, in so small a craft as one of our whale-boats, did not have any attractions for me. There was little doubt in any of our minds that, if whales were seen, off we must go while daylight lasted, let the weather be what it might. So when one morning I went to the wheel, to find the course N.N.E. instead of E. by N., it may be taken for granted that the change was a considerable relief to me. It was now manifest that we were bound up into the Indian Ocean, although of course I knew nothing of the position of the districts where whales were to be looked for. Gradually we crept northward, the weather improving every day as we left the "roaring forties" astern. While thus making northing we had several fine catches of porpoises, and saw many rorquals, but sperm whales appeared to have left the locality. However, the "old man" evidently knew what he was about, as we were not now cruising, but making a direct passage for some definite place.

At last we sighted land, which, from the course which we had been steering, might have been somewhere on the east coast of Africa, but for the fact that it was right ahead, while we were pointing at the time about N.N.W. By-and-by I came to the conclusion that it must be the southern extremity of Madagascar, Cape St. Mary, and, by dint of the closest attention to every word I heard uttered while at the wheel by the officers, found that my surmise was correct. We skirted this point pretty closely, heading to the westward, and, when well clear of it, bore up to the northward again for the Mozambique Channel. Another surprise. The very idea of *whaling* in the Mozambique Channel seemed too ridiculous to mention; yet here we were, guided by a commander who, whatever his faults, was certainly most keen in his attention to business, and the unlikeliest man imaginable to take the ship anywhere unless he anticipated a profitable return for his visit.

CHAPTER X.

A VISIT TO SOME STRANGE PLACES.

We had now entered upon what promised to be the most interesting part of our voyage. As a commercial speculation, I have to admit that the voyage was to me a matter of absolute indifference. Never, from the first week of my being on board, had I cherished any illusions upon that score, for it was most forcibly impressed on my mind that, whatever might be the measure of success attending our operations, no one of the crew forward could hope to benefit by it. The share of profits was so small, and the time taken to earn it so long, such a number of clothes were worn out and destroyed by us, only to be replaced from the ship's slop-chest at high prices, that I had quite resigned myself to the prospect of leaving the vessel in debt, whenever that desirable event might happen. Since, therefore, I had never made it a practice to repine at the inevitable, and make myself unhappy by the contemplation of misfortunes I was powerless to prevent, I tried to interest myself as far as was possible in gathering information, although at that time I had no idea, beyond a general thirst for knowledge, that what I was now learning would ever be of any service to me. Yet I had been dull indeed not to have seen how unique were the opportunities I was now enjoying for observation of some of the least known and understood aspects of the ocean world and its wonderful inhabitants, to say nothing of visits to places unvisited, except by such free lances as we were, and about which so little is really known.

The weather of the Mozambique Channel was fairly good, although subject to electric storms of the most terrible aspect, but perfectly harmless. On the second evening after rounding Cape St. Mary, we were proceeding, as usual, under very scanty sail, rather enjoying the mild, balmy air, scent-laden, from Madagascar. The moon was shining in tropical splendour, paling the lustre of the attendant stars, and making the glorious Milky Way but a faint shadow of its usual resplendent road. Gradually from the westward there arose a murky mass of cloud, fringed at its upper edges with curious tinted tufts of violet, orange, and crimson. These colours were not brilliant, but plainly visible against the deep blue sky. Slowly and solemnly the intruding gloom overspread the sweet splendour of the shining sky, creeping like a death-shadow over a dear face, and making the most talkative feel strangely quiet and ill at ease. As the pall of thick darkness blotted out the cool light, it seemed to descend until at last we were completely over-canopied by a dome of velvety black, seemingly low enough to touch the mast-heads. A belated sea-bird's shrill scream but emphasized the deep silence which lent itself befittingly to the solemnity of nature. Presently thin suggestions of light, variously tinted, began to thread the inky mass. These grew brighter and more vivid, until at last, in fantastic contortions, they appeared to rend the swart concave asunder, revealing through the jagged clefts a lurid waste of the most intensely glowing fire. The coming and going of these amazing brightnesses, combined with the Egyptian dark between, was completely blinding. So loaded was the still air with electricity that from every point aloft pale flames streamed upward, giving the ship the appearance of a huge candelabrum with innumerable branches. One of the hands, who had been ordered aloft on some errand of securing a loose end, presented a curious sight. He was bareheaded, and from his hair the all-pervading fluid arose, lighting up his features, which were ghastly beyond description. When he lifted his hand, each separate finger became at once an additional point from which light streamed. There was no thunder, but a low hissing and a crackling which did not amount to noise, although distinctly audible to all. Sensations most unpleasant of pricking and general irritation were felt by every one, according to their degree of susceptibility.

After about an hour of this state of things, a low moaning of thunder was heard, immediately followed by a few drops of rain large as dollars. The mutterings and grumblings increased until, with one peal that made the ship tremble as though she had just struck a rock at full speed, down came the rain. The windows of heaven were opened, and no man might stand against the steaming flood that descended by thousands of tons per minute. How long it continued, I cannot say; probably, in its utmost fierceness, not more than half an hour. Then it slowly abated, clearing away as it did so the accumulation of gloom overhead, until, before midnight had struck, all the heavenly host were shedding their beautiful brilliancy upon us again with apparently increased glory, while the freshness and invigorating feel of the air was inexpressibly delightful.

We did not court danger by hugging too closely any of the ugly reefs and banks that abound in this notably difficult strait, but gave them all a respectfully wide berth. It was a feature of our navigation that, unless we had occasion to go near any island or reef for fishing or landing purposes, we always kept a safe margin of distance away, which probably accounts for our continued immunity from accident while in tortuous waters. Our anchors and cables were, however, always kept ready for use now, in case of an unsuspected current or sudden storm; but beyond that precaution, I could see little or no difference in the manner of our primitive navigation.

We met with no "luck" for some time, and the faces of the harpooners grew daily longer, the great heat of those sultry waters trying all tempers sorely. But Captain Slocum knew his business, and his scowling, impassive face showed no sign of disappointment, or indeed any other emotion, as day by day we crept farther north. At last we sighted the stupendous peak of Comoro mountain, which towers to nearly nine thousand feet from the little island which gives its name to the Comoro group of four. On that same day a school of medium-sized sperm whales were sighted, which appeared to be almost of a different race to those with which we had hitherto had dealings. They were exceedingly fat and lazy, moving with the greatest deliberation, and, when we rushed in among them, appeared utterly bewildered and panic-stricken, knowing not which way to flee. Like a flock of frightened sheep they huddled together, aimlessly wallowing in each other's way, while we harpooned them with the greatest ease and impunity. Even the "old man" himself lowered the fifth boat, leaving the ship to the carpenter, cooper, cook, and steward, and coming on the scene as if determined to make a field-day of the occasion. He was no "slouch" at the business either. Not that there was much occasion or opportunity to exhibit any prowess. The record of the day's proceedings would be as tame as to read of a day's work in a slaughter-house. Suffice it to say, that we actually killed six whales, none of whom were less than fifty barrels, no boat ran out more than one hundred fathoms of line, neither was a bomb-lance used. Not the slightest casualty occurred to any of the boats, and the whole work of destruction was over in less than four hours.

Then came the trouble. The fish were, of course, somewhat widely separated when they died, and the task of collecting all those immense carcasses was one of no ordinary magnitude. Had it not been for the wonderfully skilful handling of the ship, the task would, I should think, have been impossible, but the way in which she was worked compelled the admiration of anybody who knew what handling a ship meant. Still, with all the ability manifested, it was five hours after the last whale died before we had gathered them all alongside, bringing us to four o'clock in the afternoon.

A complete day under that fierce blaze of the tropical sun, without other refreshment than an occasional furtive drink of tepid water, had reduced us to a pitiable condition of weakness, so much so that the skipper judged it prudent, as soon as the fluke-chains were passed, to give us a couple of hours' rest. As soon as the sun had set we were all turned to again, three cressets were prepared, and by their blaze we toiled the whole night through. Truth compels me to state, though, that none of us foremast hands had nearly such heavy work as the officers on the stage. What they had to do demanded special knowledge and skill; but it was also terribly hard work, constant and unremitting, while we at the windlass had many a short spell between the lifting of the pieces. Even the skipper took a hand, for the first time, and right manfully did he do his share.

By the first streak of dawn, three of the whales had been stripped of their blubber, and five heads were bobbing astern at the ends of as many hawsers. The sea all around presented a wonderful sight. There must have been thousands of sharks gathered to the feast, and their incessant incursions through the phosphorescent water wove a dazzling network of brilliant tracks which made the eyes ache to look upon. A short halt was called for breakfast, which was greatly needed, and, thanks to the cook, was a thoroughly good one. He—blessings on him!—had been busy fishing, as we drifted slowly, with savoury pieces of whale-beef for bait, and the result was a mess of fish which would have gladdened the heart of an epicure. Our hunger appeased, it was "turn to" again, for there was now no time to be lost. The fierce heat soon acts upon the carcass of a dead whale, generating an immense volume of gas within it, which, in a wonderfully short space of time, turns the flesh putrid and renders the blubber so rotten that it cannot be lifted, nor, if it could, would it be of any value. So it was no wonder that our haste was great, or that the august arbiter of our destinies himself condescended to take his place among the toilers. By nightfall the whole of our catch was on board, excepting such toll as the hungry hordes of sharks had levied upon it in transit. A goodly number of them had paid the penalty of their rapacity with their lives, for often one would wriggle his way right up on to the reeking carcass, and, seizing a huge fragment of blubber, strive with might and main to tear it away. Then the lethal spade would drop upon his soft crown, cleaving it to the jaws, and with one flap of his big tail he would loose his grip, roll over and over, and sink, surrounded by a writhing crowd of his fellows, by whom he was speedily reduced into digestible fragments.

The condition of the *Cachalot's* deck was now somewhat akin to chaos. From the cabin door to the try-works there was hardly an inch of available space, and the oozing oil kept some of us continually baling it up, lest it should leak out through the interstices in the bulwarks. In order to avoid a breakdown, it became necessary to divide the crew into six-hour watches, as, although the work was exceedingly urgent on account of the weather, there were evident signs that some of the crew were perilously near giving in. So we got rest none too soon, and the good effects of it were soon apparent. The work went on with much more celerity than one would have thought possible, and soon the lumbered-up decks began to resume their normal appearance.

As if to exasperate the "old man" beyond measure, on the third day of our operations a great school of sperm whales appeared, disporting all around the ship, apparently conscious of our helplessness to interfere with them. Notwithstanding our extraordinary haul,

Captain Slocum went black with impotent rage, and, after glowering at the sportive monsters, beat a retreat below, unable to bear the sight any longer. During his absence we had a rare treat. The whole school surrounded the ship, and performed some of the strangest evolutions imaginable. As if instigated by one common impulse, they all elevated their massive heads above the surface of the sea, and remained for some time in that position, solemnly bobbing up and down amid the glittering wavelets like movable boulders of black rock. Then, all suddenly reversed themselves, and, elevating their broad flukes in the air, commenced to beat them slowly and rhythmically upon the water, like so many machines. Being almost a perfect calm, every movement of the great mammals could be plainly seen; some of them even passed so near to us that we could see how the lower jaw hung down, while the animal was swimming in a normal position.

For over an hour they thus paraded around us, and then, as if startled by some hidden danger, suddenly headed off to the westward, and in a few minutes were out of our sight.

We cruised in the vicinity of the Comoro Islands for two months, never quite out of sight of the mountain while the weather was clear. During the whole of that time we were never clear of oil on deck, one catch always succeeding another before there had been time to get cleared up. Eight hundred barrels of oil were added to our cargo, making the undisciplined hearts of all to whom whaling was a novel employment beat high with hopes of a speedy completion of the cargo, and consequent return. Poor innocents that we were! How could we know any better? According to Goliath, with whom I often had a friendly chat, this was quite out of the ordinary run to have such luck in the "Channel."

"'Way back in de dark ages, w'en de whaleships war de pi'neers ob commerce, 'n dey wan't no worryin', poofity-plunkity steamboats a-poundin' along, 'nough ter galley ebery whale clean eout ob dere skin, dey war plenty whaleships fill up in twelve, fifteen, twenty monf' after leabin' home. 'N er man hed his pick er places, too—didn' hab ter go moseyin erroun' like some ol' hobo lookin' fer day's work, 'n prayin de good Lord not ter let um fine it. No, sah; roun yer China Sea, coas' Japan, on de line, off shore, Vasquez, 'mong de islan's, ohmos' anywhar, you couldn' hardly git way from 'em. Neow, I clar ter glory I kaint imagine *war* dey all gone ter, dough we bin eout only six seven monf, 'n got over tousan bar'l below. But I bin two year on er voy'ge and doan hardly *see* a sparm whale, much less catch one. But"—and here he whispered mysteriously—"dish yer ole man's de bery debbil's own chile, 'n his farder lookin' after him well—dat's my 'pinion. Only yew keep yer head tight shut, an' nebber say er word, but keep er lookin', 'n sure's death you'll see." This conversation made a deep and lasting impression upon me, for I had not before heard even so much as a murmur from an officer against the tyranny of the skipper. Some of the harpooners were fluent enough, too.

Yet I had often thought that his treatment of them, considering the strenuous nature of their toil, and the willingness with which they worked as long as they had an ounce of energy left, was worth at least a little kindness and courtesy on his part.

What the period may have been during which whales

were plentiful here, I do not know, but it was now May, and for the last few days we had not seen a solitary spout of any kind. Preparations, very slight it is true, were made for departure; but before we left those parts we made an interesting call for water at Mohilla, one of the Comoro group, which brought out, in unmistakable fashion, the wonderful fund of local knowledge possessed by these men. At the larger ports of Johanna and Mayotte there is a regular tariff of port charges, which are somewhat heavy, and no whaleman would be so reckless as to incur these unless driven thereto by the necessity of obtaining provisions; otherwise, the islands offer great inducements to whaling captains to call, since none but men hopelessly mad would venture to desert in such places. That qualification is the chief one for any port to possess in the eyes of a whaling captain.

Our skipper, however, saw no necessity for entering any port. Running up under the lee of Mohilla, we followed the land along until we came to a tiny bight on the western side of the island, an insignificant inlet which no mariner in charge of a vessel like ours could be expected even to notice, unless he were surveying. The approaches to this tiny harbour (save the mark) were very forbidding. Ugly-looking rocks showed up here and there, the surf over them frequently blinding the whole entry. But we came along, in our usual leisurely fashion, under two topsails, spanker, and fore-topmast staysail, and took that ugly passage like a sailing barge entering the Medway. There was barely room to turn round when we got inside, but all sail had been taken off her except the spanker, so that her way was almost stopped by the time she was fairly within the harbour. Down went the anchor, and she was fast—anchored for the first time since leaving New Bedford seven months before. Here we were shut out entirely from the outer world, for I doubt greatly whether even a passing dhow could have seen us from seaward. We were not here for rest, however, but wood and water; so while one party was supplied with well-sharpened axes, and sent on shore to cut down such small trees as would serve our turn, another party was busily employed getting out a number of big casks for the serious business of watering. The cooper knocked off the second or quarter hoops from each of these casks, and drove them on again with two "beckets" or loops of rope firmly jammed under each of them in such a manner that the loops were in line with each other on each side of the bunghole. They were then lowered overboard, and a long rope rove through all the beckets. When this was done, the whole number of casks floated end to end, upright and secure. We towed them ashore to where, by the skipper's directions, at about fifty yards from high-water mark, a spring of beautiful water bubbled out of the side of a mass of rock, losing itself in a deep crevice below. Lovely ferns, rare orchids, and trailing plants of many kinds surrounded this fairy-like spot in the wildest profusion, making a tangle of greenery that we had considerable trouble to clear away. Having done so, we led a long canvas hose from the spot whence the water flowed down to the shore where the casks floated. The chief officer, with great ingenuity, rigged up an arrangement whereby the hose, which had a square mouth about a foot wide, was held up to the rock, saving us the labour of baling and filling by hand. So we were able to rest and admire at our ease the wonderful variety of beautiful plants which grew here so lavishly, unseen by mortal eye from one year's end to another. I have somewhere read that the Creator has delight in the beautiful work of His will, wherever it may be; and that while our egotism wonders at the waste of beauty, as we call it, there is no waste at all, since the Infinite Intelligence can dwell with complacency upon the glories of His handiwork, perfectly fulfilling their appointed ends.

All too soon the pleasant occupation came to an end. The long row of casks, filled to the brim and tightly bunged, were towed off by us to the ship, and ranged alongside. A tackle and pair of "can-hooks" was overhauled to the water and hooked to a cask. "Hoist away!" And as the cask rose, the beckets that had held it to the mother-rope were cut, setting it quite free to come on board, but leaving all the others still secure. In this way we took in several thousand gallons of water in a few hours, with a small expenditure of labour, free of cost; whereas, had we gone into Mayotte or Johanna, the water would have been bad, the price high, the labour great, with the chances of a bad visitation of fever in the bargain.

The woodmen had a much more arduous task. The only wood they could find, without cutting down big trees, which would have involved far too much labour in cutting up, was a kind of iron-wood, which, besides being very heavy, was so hard as to take pieces clean out of their axe-edges, when a blow was struck directly across the grain. As none of them were experts, the condition of their tools soon made their work very hard. But that they had taken several axes in reserve, it is doubtful whether they would have been able to get sufficient fuel for our purpose. When they pitched the wood off the rocks into the harbour, it sank immediately, giving them a great deal of trouble to fish it up again. Neither could they raft it as intended, but were compelled to load it into the boats and make several journeys to and fro before all they had cut was shipped. Altogether, I was glad that the wooding had not fallen to my share. On board the ship fishing had been going on steadily most of the day by a few hands told off for the purpose. The result of their sport was splendid, over two hundred-weight of fine fish of various sorts, but all eatable, having been gathered in.

We lay snugly anchored all night, keeping a bright look-out for any unwelcome visitors either from land or sea, for the natives are not to be trusted, neither do the Arab mongrels who cruise about those waters in their dhows bear any too good a reputation. We saw none, however, and at daylight we weighed and towed the ship out to sea with the boats, there being no wind. While busy at this uninteresting pastime, one of the boats slipped away, returning presently with a fine turtle, which they had surprised during his morning's nap. One of the amphibious Portuguese slipped over the boat's side as she neared the sleeping *Spharga*, and, diving deep, came up underneath him, seizing with crossed hands the two hind flippers, and, with a sudden, dexterous twist, turned the astonished creature over on his back. Thus rendered helpless, the turtle lay on the surface feebly waving his flippers, while his captor, gently treading water, held him in that position till the boat reached the pair and took them on board. It was a clever feat, neatly executed, as unlike the clumsy efforts I had before seen made with the same object as anything could possibly be.

After an hour's tow, we had got a good offing, and a light air springing up, we returned on board, hoisted the boats, and made sail to the northward again.

With the exception of the numerous native dhows that crept lazily about, we saw no vessels as we gradually drew out of the Mozambique Channel and stood away towards the Line. The part of the Indian Ocean in which we now found ourselves is much dreaded by merchantmen, who give it a wide berth on account of the numerous banks, islets, and dangerous currents with which it abounds. We, however, seemed quite at home here, pursuing the even tenor of our usual way without any special precautions being taken. A bright look-out we always kept, of course—none of your drowsy lolling about such as is all too common on the "fo'lk'sle head" of many a fine ship, when, with lights half trimmed or not shown at all, she is ploughing along blindly at twelve knots or so an hour. No; while we were under way during daylight, four pairs of keen eyes kept incessant vigil a hundred feet above the deck, noting everything, even to a shoal of small fish, that crossed within the range of vision. At night we scarcely moved, but still a vigilant look-out was always kept both fore and aft, so that it would have been difficult for us to drift upon a reef unknowingly.

Creeping steadily northward, we passed the Cosmoledo group of atolls without paying them a visit, which was strange, as, from their appearance, no better fishing-ground would be likely to come in our way. They are little known, except to the wandering fishermen from Réunion and Rodriguez, who roam about these islets and reefs, seeking anything that may be turned into coin, from wrecks to turtle, and in nowise particular as to rights of ownership. When between the Cosmoledos and Astove, the next island to the northward, we sighted a "solitary" cachalot one morning just as the day dawned. It was the first for some time—nearly three weeks—and being all well seasoned to the work now, we obeyed the call to arms with great alacrity. Our friend was making a passage, turning neither to the right hand nor the left as he went. His risings and number of spouts while up, as well as the time he remained below, were as regular as the progress of a clock, and could be counted upon with quite as much certainty.

Bearing in mind, I suppose, the general character of the whales we had recently met with, only two boats were lowered to attack the new-comer, who, all unconscious of our coming, pursued his leisurely course unheeding.

We got a good weather-gage of him, and came flying on as usual, getting two irons planted in fine style. But a surprise awaited us. As we sheered up into the wind away from him, Louis shouted, "Fightin' whale, sir; look out for de rush!" Look out, indeed! Small use in looking out when, hampered as we always were at first with the unshipping of the mast, we could do next to nothing to avoid him. Without any of the desperate flounderings generally indulged in on first feeling the iron, he turned upon us, and had it not been that he caught sight of the second mate's boat, which had just arrived, and turned his attentions to her, there would have been scant chance of any escape for us. Leaping half out of water, he made direct for our comrades with a vigour and ferocity marvellous to see, making it a no easy matter for them to avoid his tremendous rush. Our actions, at no time slow, were considerably hastened by this display of valour, so that before he could turn his attentions in our direction we were ready for him. Then ensued a really big fight, the first, in fact, of my experience, for none of the other whales had shown any serious determination to do us an injury, but had devoted all their energies to attempts at escape. So quick were the evolutions, and so savage the appearance of this fellow, that even our veteran mate looked anxious as to the possible result. Without attempting to "sound," the furious monster kept mostly below the surface; but whenever he rose, it was either to deliver a fearful blow with his tail, or, with jaws widespread, to try and bite one of our boats in half. Well was it for us that he was severely handicapped by a malformation of the lower jaw. At a short distance from the throat it turned off nearly at right angles to his body, the part that thus protruded sideways being deeply fringed with barnacles, and plated with big limpets.

Had it not been for this impediment, I verily believe he would have beaten us altogether. As it was, he worked us nearly to death with his ugly rushes. Once he delivered a sidelong blow with his tail, which, as we spun round, shore off the two oars on that side as if they had been carrots. At last the second mate got fast to him, and then the character of the game changed again. Apparently unwearied by his previous exertions, he now started off to windward at top speed, with the two boats sheering broadly out upon either side of his foaming wake. Doubtless because he himself was much fatigued, the mate allowed him to run at his will, without for the time attempting to haul any closer to him, and very grateful the short rest was to us. But he had not gone a couple of miles before he turned a complete somersault in the water, coming up *behind* us to rush off again in the opposite direction at undiminished speed. This move was a startler. For the moment it seemed as if both boats would be smashed like egg-shells against each other, or else that some of us would be impaled upon the long lances with which each boat's bow bristled. By what looked like a hand-breadth, we cleared each other, and the race continued. Up till now we had not succeeded in getting home a single lance, the foe was becoming warier, while the strain was certainly telling upon our nerves. So Mr. Count got out his bomb-gun, shouting at the same time to Mr. Cruce to do the same. They both hated these weapons, nor ever used them if they could help it; but what was to be done?

Our chief had hardly got his gun ready, before we came to almost a dead stop. All was silent for just a moment; then, with a roar like a cataract, up sprang the huge creature, head out, jaw wide open, coming direct for us. As coolly as if on the quarter-deck, the mate raised his gun, firing the bomb directly down the great livid cavern of a throat fronting him. Down went that mountainous head not six inches from us, but with a perfectly indescribable motion, a tremendous writhe, in fact; up flew the broad tail in air, and a blow which might have sufficed to stave in the side of the ship struck the second mate's boat fairly amidships. It was right before my eyes, not sixty feet away, and the sight will haunt me to my death. The tub oarsman was the poor German baker, about whom I have hitherto said nothing, except to note that he was one of the crew. That awful blow put an end summarily to all his earthly anxieties. As it shore obliquely through the centre of the boat, it drove his poor body right through her timbers—an undistinguishable bundle of what was an instant before a human being. The other members of the crew escaped the blow, and the harpooner managed to cut the line, so that for the present they were safe enough, clinging to the remains of their boat, unless the whale should choose to rush across them.

Happily, his rushing was almost over. The bomb fired by Mr. Count, with such fatal result to poor Bamberger, must have exploded right in the whale's throat. Whether his previous titanic efforts had completely exhausted him, or whether the bomb had broken his massive backbone, I do not know, of course, but he went into no flurry, dying as peacefully as his course had been furious. For the first time in my life, I had been face to face with a violent death, and I was quite stunned with the awfulness of the experience. Mechanically, as it seemed to me, we obeyed such orders as were given, but every man's thoughts were with the shipmate so suddenly dashed from amongst us. We never saw sign of him again.

While the ship was running down to us, another boat had gone to rescue the clinging crew of the shattered boat, for the whole drama had been witnessed from the ship, although they were not aware of the death of the poor German. When the sad news was told on board, there was a deep silence, all work being carried on so quietly that we seemed like a crew of dumb men. With a sentiment for which I should not have given our grim skipper credit, the stars and stripes were hoisted half-mast, telling the silent sky and moaning sea, sole witnesses besides ourselves, of the sudden departure from among us of our poor shipmate.

We got the whale cut in as usual without any incident worth mentioning, except that the peculiar shape of the jaw made it an object of great curiosity to all of us who were new to the whale-fishing. Such malformations are not very rare. They are generally thought to occur when the animal is young, and its bones soft; but whether done in fighting with one another, or in some more mysterious way, nobody knows. Cases have been known, I believe, where the deformed whale does not appear to have suffered from lack of food in consequence of his disability; but in each of the three instances which have come under my own notice, such was certainly not the case. These whales were what is termed by the whalers "dry-skins;" that is, they were in poor condition, the blubber yielding less than half the usual quantity of oil. The absence of oil makes it very hard to cut up, and there is more work in one whale of this kind than in two whose blubber is rich and soft. Another thing which I have also noticed is, that these whales were much more difficult to tackle than others, for each of them gave us something special to remember them by. But I must not get ahead of my yarn.

The end of the week brought us up to the Aldabra Islands, one of the puzzles of the world. For here, in these tiny pieces of earth, surrounded by thousands of miles of sea, the nearest land a group of islets like unto them, is found the gigantic tortoise, and in only one other place in the wide world, the Galapagos group of islands in the South Pacific. How, or by what strange freak of Dame Nature these curious reptiles, sole survivals of another age, should come to be found in this lonely spot, is a deep mystery, and one not likely to be unfolded now. At any rate, there they are, looking as if some of them might be coeval with Noah, so venerable and storm-beaten do they appear.

We made the island early on a Sunday morning, and, with the usual celerity, worked the vessel into the fine harbour, called, from one of the exploring ships, Euphrates Bay or Harbour. The anchor down, and everything made snug below and aloft, we were actually allowed a run ashore free from restraint. I could hardly believe my ears. We had got so accustomed to our slavery that liberty was become a mere name; we hardly knew what to do with it when we got it. However, we soon got used (in a very limited sense) to being our own masters, and, each following the bent of his inclinations, set out for a ramble. My companion and I had not gone far, when we thought we saw one of the boulders, with which the island was liberally besprinkled, on the move. Running up to examine it with all the eagerness of children let out of school, we found it to be one of the inhabitants, a monstrous tortoise. I had seen some big turtle around the cays of the Gulf of Mexico, but this creature dwarfed them all. We had no means of actually measuring him, and had to keep clear of his formidable-looking jaws, but roughly, and within the mark, he was four feet long by two feet six inches wide. Of course he was much more dome-shaped than the turtle are, and consequently looked a great deal bigger than a turtle of the same measurement would, besides being much thicker through. As he was loth to stay with us, we made up our minds to go with him, for he was evidently making for some definite spot, by the tracks he was following, which showed plainly how many years that same road had been used. Well, I mounted on his back, keeping well astern, out of the reach of that serious-looking head, which, having rather a long neck, looked as if it might be able to reach round and take a piece out of a fellow without any trouble. He was perfectly amicable, continuing his journey as if nothing had happened, and really getting over the ground at a good rate, considering the bulk and shape of him. Except for the novelty of the thing, this sort of ride had nothing to recommend it; so I soon tired of it, and let him waddle along in peace. By following the tracks aforesaid, we arrived at a fine stream of water sparkling out of a hillside, and running down a little ravine. The sides of this gully were worn quite smooth by the innumerable feet of the tortoises, about a dozen of which were now quietly crouching at the water's edge, filling themselves up with the cooling fluid. I did not see the patriarch upon whom a sailor once reported that he had read the legend carved, "The Ark, Captain Noah. Ararat for orders"; perhaps he had at last closed his peaceful career. But strange and quaint as this exhibition of ancient reptiles was, we had other and better employment for the limited time at our disposal. There were innumerable curious things to see, and, unless we were to run the risk of going on board again and stopping there, dinner must be obtained. Eggs of various kinds were exceedingly plentiful; in many places the flats were almost impassable for sitting birds, mostly "boobies."

But previous experience of boobies' eggs in other places had not disposed me to seek them where others were to be obtained, and as I had seen many of the well-known frigate or man-o'-war birds hovering about, we set out to the other side of the island in search of the breeding-place.

These peculiar birds are, I think, misnamed. They should be called pirate or buccaneer birds, from their marauding habits. Seldom or never do they condescend to fish for themselves, preferring to hover high in the blue, their tails opening and closing like a pair of scissors as they hang poised above the sea. Presently booby—like some honest housewife who has been a-marketing—comes flapping noisily home, her maw laden with fish for the chicks. Down comes the black watcher from above with a swoop like an eagle. Booby puts all she knows into her flight, but vainly; escape is impossible, so with a despairing shriek she drops her load. Before it has touched the water the graceful thief has intercepted it, and soared slowly aloft again, to repeat the performance as occasion serves.

When we arrived on the outer shore of the island, we found a large breeding-place of these birds, but totally different to the haunt of the boobies. The nests, if they might be so-called, being at best a few twigs, were mostly in the hollows of the rocks, the number of eggs being two to a nest, on an average. The eggs were nearly as large as a turkey's. But I am reminded of the range of size among turkeys' eggs, so I must say they were considerably larger than a small turkey's egg. Their flavour was most delicate, as much so as the eggs of a moor-fed fowl. We saw no birds sitting, but here and there the gaunt skeleton forms of birds, who by reason of sickness or old age were unable to provide for themselves, and so sat waiting for death, appealed most mournfully to us. We went up to some of these poor creatures, and ended their long agony; but there were many of them that we were obliged to leave to Nature.

We saw no animals larger than a rat, but there were a great many of those eerie-looking land-crabs, that seemed as if almost humanly intelligent as they scampered about over the sand or through the undergrowth, busy about goodness knows what. The beautiful cocoa-nut palm was plentiful, so much so that I wondered why there were no settlers to collect "copra," or dried cocoa-nut, for oil. My West Indian experience came in handy now, for I was able to climb a lofty tree in native fashion, and cut down a grand bunch of green nuts, which form one of the most refreshing and nutritious of foods, as well as a cool and delicious drink. We had no line with us, so we took off our belts, which, securely joined together, answered my purpose very well. With them I made a loop round the tree and myself; then as I climbed I pushed the loop up with me, so that whenever I wanted a rest, I had only to lean back in it, keeping my knees against the trunk, and I was almost as comfortable as if on the ground.

After getting the nuts, we made a fire and roasted some of our eggs, which, with a biscuit or two, made a delightful meal. Then we fell asleep under a shady tree, upon some soft moss; nor did we wake again until nearly time to go on board. A most enjoyable swim terminated our day's outing, and we returned to the beach abreast of the ship very pleased with the excursion.

We had no adventures, found no hidden treasure or ferocious animals, but none the less we thoroughly enjoyed ourselves. While we sat waiting for the boat to come and fetch us off, we saw a couple of good-sized turtle come ashore quite close to us. We kept perfectly still until we were sure of being able to intercept them. As soon as they had got far enough away from their native element, we rushed upon them, and captured them both, so that when the boat arrived we were not empty-handed. We had also a "jumper," or blouse, full of eggs, and a couple of immense bunches of cocoa-nuts. When we got on board we felt quite happy, and, for the first time since leaving America, we had a little singing. Shall I be laughed at when I confess that our musical efforts were confined to Sankey's hymns? Maybe, but I do not care. Cheap and clap-trap as the music may be, it tasted "real good," as Abner said, and I am quite sure that that Sunday night was the best that any of us had spent for a very long time.

A long, sound sleep was terminated at dawn, when we weighed and stood out through a narrow passage by East Island, which was quite covered with fine trees—of what kind I do not know, but they presented a beautiful sight. Myriads of birds hovered about, busy fishing from the countless schools that rippled the placid sea. Beneath us, at twenty fathoms, the wonderful architecture of the coral was plainly visible through the brilliantly-clear sea, while, wherever the tiny builders had raised their fairy domain near the surface, an occasional roller would crown it with a snowy garland of foam—a dazzling patch of white against the sapphire sea. Altogether, such a panorama was spread out at our feet, as we stood gazing from the lofty crow's-nest, as was worth a year or two of city life to witness. I could not help pitying my companion, one of the Portuguese harpooners, who stolidly munched his quid with no eyes for any of these glorious pictures, no thought of anything but a possible whale in sight.

My silent rhapsodies were rudely interrupted by something far away on the horizon. Hardly daring to breathe, I strained my eyes, and—yes, it was—"Ah blow-w-w-w!" I bellowed at the top of my lung-power.

Never before had I had the opportunity of thus distinguishing myself, and I felt a bit sore about it.

There was a little obliquity about the direction of the spout that made me hopeful, for the cachalot alone sends his spout diagonally upward, all the others spout vertically. It was but a school of kogia, or "short-headed" cachalots; but as we secured five of them, averaging seven barrels each, with scarcely any trouble, I felt quite pleased with myself. We had quite an exciting bit of sport with them, they were so lively; but as for danger—well, they only seemed like big "black fish" to us now, and we quite enjoyed the fun. They were, in all respects, miniature sperm whales, except that the head was much shorter and smaller in proportion to the body than their big relations.

CHAPTER XI.

ROUND THE COCOS AND SEYCHELLES.

Hitherto, with the exception of a couple of gales in the North and South Atlantic, we had been singularly fortunate in our weather. It does happen so sometimes.

I remember once making a round voyage from Cardiff to Hong Kong and the Philippines, back to London, in ten months, and during the whole of that time we did not have a downright gale. The worst weather we encountered was between Beachy Head and Portland, going round from London to Cardiff.

And I once spoke the barque *Lutterworth*, a companion ship to us from Portland, Oregon to Falmouth, whose mate informed me that they carried their royals from port to port without ever furling them once, except to shift the suit of sails. But now a change was evidently imminent. Of course, we forward had no access to the barometer; not that we should have understood its indications if we had seen it, but we all knew that something was going to be radically wrong with the weather. For instead of the lovely blue of the sky we had been so long accustomed to by day and night, a nasty, greasy shade had come over the heavens, which, reflected in the sea, made that look dirty and stale also. That well-known appearance of the waves before a storm was also very marked, which consists of an undecided sort of break in their tops. Instead of running regularly, they seemed to hunch themselves up in little heaps, and throw off a tiny flutter of spray, which generally fell in the opposite direction to what little wind there was. The pigs and fowls felt the approaching change keenly, and manifested the greatest uneasiness, leaving their food and acting strangely. We were making scarcely any headway, so that the storm was longer making its appearance than it would have been had we been a swift clipper ship running down the Indian Ocean. For two days we were kept in suspense; but on the second night the gloom began to deepen, the wind to moan, and a very uncomfortable "jobble" of a sea got up. Extra "gaskets" were put upon the sails, and everything movable about the decks was made as secure as it could be. Only the two close-reefed topsails and two storm stay-sails were carried, so that we were in excellent trim for fighting the bad weather when it did come. The sky gradually darkened and assumed a livid green tint, the effect of which was most peculiar.

The wind blew fitfully in short gusts, veering continually back and forth over about a quarter of the compass. Although it was still light, it kept up an incessant mournful moan not to be accounted for in any way. Darker and darker grew the heavens, although no clouds were visible, only a general pall of darkness. Glimmering lightnings played continually about the eastern horizon, but not brilliant enough to show us the approaching storm-cloud. And so came the morning of the third day from the beginning of the change. But for the clock we should hardly have known that day had broken, so gloomy and dark was the sky. At last light came in the east, but such a light as no one would wish to see. It was a lurid glare, such as may be seen playing over a cupola of Bessemer steel when the speigeleisen is added, only on such an extensive scale that its brilliancy was dulled into horror. Then, beneath it we saw the mountainous clouds fringed with dull violet and with jagged sabres of lightning darting from their solid black bosoms. The wind began to rise steadily but rapidly, so that by eight a.m. it was blowing a furious gale from E.N.E. In direction it was still unsteady, the ship coming up and falling off to it several points. Now, great masses of torn, ragged cloud hurtled past us above, so low down as almost to touch the mast-heads. Still the wind increased, still the sea rose, till at last the skipper judged it well to haul down the tiny triangle of storm stay-sail still set (the topsail and fore stay-sail had been furled long before), and let her drift under bare poles, except for three square feet of stout canvas in the weather mizen-rigging. The roar of the wind now dominated every sound, so that it might have been thundering furiously, but we should not have heard it. The ship still maintained her splendid character as a sea-boat, hardly shipping a drop of water; but she lay over at a most distressing angle, her deck sloping off fully thirty-five to forty degrees. Fortunately she did not roll to windward. It may have been raining in perfect torrents, but the tempest tore off the surface of the sea, and sent it in massive sheets continually flying over us, so that we could not possibly have distinguished between fresh water and salt.

The chief anxiety was for the safety of the boats. Early on the second day of warning they had been hoisted to the topmost notch of the cranes, and secured as thoroughly as experience could suggest; but at every lee lurch we gave it seemed as if we must dip them under water, while the wind threatened to stave the weather ones in by its actual solid weight. It was now blowing a furious cyclone, the force of which has never been accurately gauged (even by the present elaborate instruments of various kinds in use). That force is, however, not to be imagined by any one who has not witnessed it, except that one notable instance is on record by which mathematicians may get an approximate estimate.

Captain Toynbee, the late highly respected and admired Marine Superintendent of the British Meteorological Office, has told us how, during a cyclone which he rode out in the *Hotspur* at Sandheads, the mouth of the Hooghly, the three naked topgallant-masts of his ship, though of well-tested timber a foot in diameter, and supported by all the usual network of stays, and without the yards, were snapped off and carried away solely by the violence of the wind. It must, of course, have been an extreme gust, which did not last many seconds, for no cable that was ever forged would have held the ship against such a cataclysm as that. This gentleman's integrity is above suspicion, so that no exaggeration could be charged against him, and he had the additional testimony of his officers and men to this otherwise incredible fact.

The terrible day wore on, without any lightening of the tempest, till noon, when the wind suddenly fell to a calm. Until that time the sea, although heavy, was not vicious or irregular, and we had not shipped any heavy water at all. But when the force of the wind was suddenly withdrawn, such a sea arose as I have never seen before or since. Inky mountains of water raised their savage heads in wildest confusion, smashing one another in whirlpools of foam. It was like a picture of the primeval deep out of which arose the new-born world. Suddenly out of the whirling blackness overhead the moon appeared, nearly in the zenith, sending down through the apex of a dome of torn and madly gyrating cloud a flood of brilliant light. Illumined by that startling radiance, our staunch and seaworthy ship was tossed and twirled in the hideous vortex of mad sea until her motion was distracting. It was quite impossible to loose one's hold and attempt to do anything without running the imminent risk of being dashed to pieces. Our decks were full of water now, for it tumbled on board at all points; but as yet no serious weight of a sea had fallen upon us, nor had any damage been done. Such a miracle as that could not be expected to continue for long. Suddenly a warning shout rang out from somewhere—"Hold on all, for your lives!" Out of the hideous turmoil around arose, like some black, fantastic ruin, an awful heap of water. Higher and higher it towered, until it was level with our lower yards, then it broke and fell upon us. All was blank. Beneath that mass every thought, every feeling, fled but one—"How long shall I be able to hold my breath?" After what seemed a never-ending time, we emerged from the wave more dead than alive, but with the good ship still staunch underneath us, and Hope's lamp burning brightly. The moon had been momentarily obscured, but now shone out again, lighting up brilliantly our bravely-battling ship. But, alas for others!—men, like ourselves, whose hopes were gone. Quite near us was the battered remainder of what had been a splendid ship. Her masts were gone, not even the stumps being visible, and it seemed to our eager eyes as if she was settling down. It was even so, for as we looked, unmindful of our own danger, she quietly disappeared—swallowed up with her human freight in a moment, like a pebble dropped into a pond.

While we looked with hardly beating hearts at the place where she had sunk, all was blotted out in thick darkness again. With a roar, as of a thousand thunders, the tempest came once more, but from the opposite direction now. As we were under no sail, we ran little risk of being caught aback; but, even had we, nothing could have been done, the vessel being utterly out of control, besides the impossibility of getting about. It so happened, however, that when the storm burst upon us again, we were stern on to it, and we drove steadily for a few moments until we had time to haul to the wind again. Great heavens! how it blew! Surely, I thought, this cannot last long—just as we sometimes say of the rain when it is extra heavy. It did last, however, for what seemed an interminable time, although any one could see that the sky was getting kindlier. Gradually, imperceptibly, it took off, the sky cleared, and the tumult ceased, until a new day broke in untellable beauty over a revivified world.

Years afterwards I read, in one of the hand-books treating of hurricanes and cyclones, that "in the centre of these revolving storms the sea is so violent that few ships can pass through it and live." That is true talk. I have been there, and bear witness that but for the build and sea-kindliness of the *Cachalot*, she could not have come out of that horrible cauldron again, but would have joined that nameless unfortunate whom we saw succumb, "never again heard of." As it was, we found two of the boats stove in, whether by breaking sea or crushing wind nobody knows. Most of the planking of the bulwarks was also gone, burst outward by the weight of the water on deck. Only the normal quantity of water was found in the well on sounding, and not even a rope-yarn was gone from aloft. Altogether, we came out of the ordeal triumphantly, where many a gallant vessel met her fate, and the behaviour of the grand old tub gave me a positive affection for her, such as I have never felt for a ship before or since.

There was now a big heap of work for the carpenter, so the skipper decided to run in for the Cocos or Keeling Islands, in order to lay quietly and refit. We had now only three boats sound, the one smashed when poor Bamberger died being still unfinished—of course, the repairs had practically amounted to rebuilding. Therefore we kept away for this strange assemblage of reefs and islets, arriving off them early the next day.

They consist of a true "atoll," or basin, whose rim is of coral reefs, culminating occasionally in sandy islands or cays formed by the accumulated *débris* washed up from the reef below, and then clothed upon with all sorts of plants by the agency of birds and waves.

These islands have lately been so fully described in many different journals, that I shall not burden the reader with any twice-told tales about them, but merely chronicle the fact that for a week we lay at anchor off one of the outlying cays, toiling continuously to get the vessel again in fighting trim.

At last the overworked carpenter and his crew got through their heavy task, and the order was given to "man the windlass." Up came the anchor, and away we went again towards what used to be a noted haunt of the sperm whale, the Seychelle Archipelago. Before the French, whose flag flies over these islands, had with their usual short-sighted policy, clapped on prohibitive port charges, Mahè was a specially favoured place of call for the whalers. But when whaleships find that it does not pay to visit a place, being under no compulsion as regards time, they soon find other harbours that serve their turn. We, of course, had no need to visit any port for some time to come, having made such good use of our opportunities at the Cocos.

We found whales scarce and small, so, although we cruised in this vicinity for nearly two months, six small cow cachalots were all we were able to add to our stock, representing less than two hundred barrels of oil. This was hardly good enough for Captain Slocum. Therefore, we gradually drew away from this beautiful cluster of islands, and crept across the Indian Ocean towards the Straits of Malacca. On the way, we one night encountered that strange phenomenon, a "milk" sea. It was a lovely night, with scarcely any wind, the stars trying to make up for the absence of the moon by shining with intense brightness. The water had been more phosphorescent than usual, so that every little fish left a track of light behind him, greatly disproportionate to his size. As the night wore on, the sea grew brighter and brighter, until by midnight we appeared to be sailing on an ocean of lambent flames. Every little wave that broke against the ship's side sent up a shower of diamond-like spray, wonderfully beautiful to see, while a passing school of porpoises fairly set the sea blazing as they leaped and gambolled in its glowing waters. Looking up from sea to sky, the latter seemed quite black instead of blue, and the lustre of the stars was diminished till they only looked like points of polished steel, having quite lost for the time their radiant sparkle. In that shining flood the blackness of the ship stood out in startling contrast, and when we looked over the side our faces were strangely lit up by the brilliant glow.

For several hours this beautiful appearance persisted, fading away at last as gradually as it come. No satisfactory explanation of this curious phenomenon has ever been given, nor does it appear to portend any change of weather. It cannot be called a rare occurrence, although I have only seen it thrice myself—once in the Bay of Cavité, in the Philippine Islands; onco in the Pacific, near the Solomon Islands; and on this occasion of which I now write. But no one who had ever witnessed it could forget so wonderful a sight.

One morning, a week after we had taken our departure from the Seychelles, the officer at the main crow's-nest reported a vessel of some sort about five miles to windward. Something strange in her appearance made the skipper haul up to intercept her. As we drew nearer, we made her out to be a Malay "prahu;" but, by the look of her, she was deserted. The big three-cornered sail that had been set, hung in tattered festoons from the long, slender yard, which, without any gear to steady it, swung heavily to and fro as the vessel rolled to the long swell. We drew closer and closer, but no sign of life was visible on board, so the captain ordered a boat to go and investigate.

In two minutes we were speeding away towards her, and, making a sweep round her stern, prepared to board her. But we were met by a stench so awful that Mr. Count would not proceed, and at once returned to the ship. The boat was quickly hoisted again, and the ship manœuvred to pass close to windward of the derelict. Then, from our mast-head, a horrible sight became visible. Lying about the weather-beaten deck, in various postures, were thirteen corpses, all far advanced in decay, which horrible fact fully accounted for the intolerable stench that had driven us away. It is, perhaps, hardly necessary to say that we promptly hauled our wind, and placed a good distance between us and that awful load of death as soon as possible. Poor wretches! What terrible calamity had befallen them, we could not guess; whatever it was, it had been complete; nor would any sane man falling across them run the risk of closer examination into details than we had done. It was a great pity that we were not able to sink the prahu with her ghastly cargo, and so free the air from that poisonous fœtor that was a deadly danger to any vessel getting under her lee.

Next day, and for a whole week after, we had a stark calm—such a calm as one realizes who reads sympathetically that magical piece of work, the "Ancient Mariner." What an amazing instance of the triumph of the human imagination! For Coleridge certainly never witnessed such a scene as he there describes with an accuracy of detail that is astounding. Very few sailors have noticed the sickening condition of the ocean when the life-giving breeze totally fails for any length of time, or, if they have, they have said but little about it. Of course, some parts of the sea show the evil effects of stagnation much sooner than others; but, generally speaking, want of wind at sea, if long continued, produces a condition of things dangerous to the health of any land near by. Whale-ships, penetrating as they do to parts carefully avoided by ordinary trading vessels, often afford their crews an opportunity of seeing things mostly hidden from the sight of man, when, actuated by some mysterious impulse, the uncanny denizens of the middle depths of the ocean rise to higher levols, and show their weird shapes to the sun.

CHAPTER XII.

WHICH TREATS OF THE KRAKEN.

It has often been a matter for considerable surprise to me, that while the urban population of Great Britain is periodically agitated over the great sea-serpent question, sailors, as a class, have very little to say on the subject. During a considerable sea experience in all classes of vessels, except men-of-war, and in most positions, I have heard a fairly comprehensive catalogue of subjects brought under dog-watch discussion; but the sea-serpent has never, within my recollection, been one of them.

The reasons for this abstinence may vary a great deal, but chief among them is—sailors, as a class, "don't believe in no such a pusson." More than that, they do believe that the mythical sea-serpent is "boomed" at certain periods, in the lack of other subjects, which may not be far from the fact. But there is also another reason, involving a disagreeable, although strictly accurate, statement. Sailors are, again taken as a class, the least observant of men. They will talk by the hour of trivialities about which they know nothing; they will spin interminable "cuffers" of debaucheries ashore all over the world; pick to pieces the reputation of all the officers with whom they have ever sailed; but of the glories, marvels, and mysteries of the mighty deep you will hear not a word. I can never forget when on my first voyage to the West Indies, at the age of twelve, I was one night smitten with awe and wonder at the sight of a vast halo round the moon, some thirty or forty degrees in diameter. Turning to the man at the wheel, I asked him earnestly "what *that* was." He looked up with an uninterested eye for an instant in the direction of my finger, then listlessly informed me, "That's what they call a sarcle." For a long time I wondered what he could mean, but it gradually dawned upon me that it was his Norfolk pronunciation of the word circle. The definition was a typical one, no worse than would be given by the great majority of seamen of most of the natural phenomena they witness daily. Very few seamen could distinguish between one whale and another of a different species, or give an intelligible account of the most ordinary and often-seen denizens of the sea. Whalers are especially to be blamed for their blindness. "Eyes and no Eyes; or the Art of Seeing" has evidently been little heard of among them. To this day I can conceive of no more delightful journey for a naturalist to take than a voyage in a southern whaler, especially if he were allowed to examine at his leisure such creatures as were caught. But on board the *Cachalot* I could get no information at all upon the habits of the strange creatures we met with, except whales, and very little about them.

I have before referred to the great molluscs upon which the sperm whale feeds, portions of which I so frequently saw ejected from the stomach of dying whales. Great as my curiosity naturally was to know more of these immense organisms, all my inquiries on the subject were fruitless. These veterans of the whale-fishery knew that the sperm whale lived on big cuttle-fish; but they neither knew, nor cared to know, anything more about these marvellous molluscs. Yet, from the earliest dawn of history, observant men have been striving to learn something definite about the marine monsters of which all old legends of the sea have something to say.

As I mentioned in the last chapter, we were gradually edging across the Indian Ocean towards Sumatra, but had been checked in our course by a calm lasting a whole week. A light breeze then sprang up, aided by which we crept around Achin Head, the northern point of the great island of Sumatra. Like some gigantic beacon, the enormous mass of the Golden Mountain dominated the peaceful scene. Pulo Way, or Water Island, looked very inviting, and I should have been glad to visit a place so well known to seamen by sight, but so little known by actual touching at. Our recent stay at the Cocos, however, had settled the question of our calling anywhere else for some time decidedly in the negative, unless we might be compelled by accident; moreover, even in these days of law and order, it is not wise to go poking about among the islands of the Malayan seas unless you are prepared to fight. Our mission being to fight whales, we were averse to running any risks, except in the lawful and necessary exercise of our calling.

It would at first sight appear strange that, in view of the enormous traffic of steamships through the Malacca Straits, so easily "gallied" a creature as the cachalot should care to frequent its waters; indeed, I should certainly think that a great reduction in the numbers of whales found there must have taken place. But it must also be remembered, that in modern steam navigation certain well-defined courses are laid down, which vessels follow from point to point with hardly any deviation therefrom, and that consequently little disturbance of the sea by their panting propellers takes place, except upon these marine pathways; as, for instance, in the Red Sea, where the examination of thousands of log-books proved conclusively that, except upon straight lines drawn from point to point between Suez to Perim, the sea is practically unused to-day.

The few Arab dhows and loitering surveying ships hardly count in this connection, of course. At any rate, we had not entered the straits, but were cruising between Car Nicobar and Junkseylon, when we "met up" with a full-grown cachalot, as ugly a customer as one could wish. From nine a.m. till dusk the battle raged—for I have often noticed that unless you kill your whale pretty soon, he gets so wary, as well as fierce, that you stand a gaudy chance of being worn down yourselves before you settle accounts with your adversary. This affair certainly looked at one time as if such would be the case with us; but along about five p.m., to our great joy, we got him killed. The ejected food was in masses of enormous size, larger than any we had yet seen on the voyage, some of them being estimated to be of the size of our hatch-house, viz. 8 feet × 6 feet × 6 feet. The whale having been secured alongside, all hands were sent below, as they were worn out with the day's work. The third mate being ill, I had been invested with the questionable honour of standing his watch, on account of my sea experience and growing favour with the chief. Very bitterly did I resent the privilege at

A VERY LARGE SPERM WHALE WAS LOCKED IN DEADLY CONFLICT WITH A SQUID.

the time, I remember, being so tired and sleepy that I knew not how to keep awake. I did not imagine that anything would happen to make me prize that night's experience for the rest of my life, or I should have taken matters with a far better grace.

At about eleven p.m. I was leaning over the lee rail, gazing steadily at the bright surface of the sea, where the intense radiance of the tropical moon made a broad path like a pavement of burnished silver. Eyes that saw not, mind only confusedly conscious of my surroundings, were mine; but suddenly I started to my feet with an exclamation, and stared with all my might at the strangest sight I ever saw. There was a violent commotion in the sea right where the moon's rays were concentrated, so great that, remembering our position, I was at first inclined to alarm all hands; for I had often heard of volcanic islands suddenly lifting their heads from the depths below, or disappearing in a moment, and, with Sumatra's chain of active volcanoes so near, I felt doubtful indeed of what was now happening. Getting the night-glasses out of the cabin scuttle, where they were always hung in readiness, I focussed them on the troubled spot, perfectly satisfied by a short examination that neither volcano nor earthquake had anything to do with what was going on; yet so vast were the forces engaged that I might well have been excused for my first supposition. A very large sperm whale was locked in deadly conflict with a cuttle-fish, or squid, almost as large as himself, whose interminable tentacles seemed to enlace the whole of his great body. The head of the whale especially seemed a perfect net-work of writhing arms—naturally, I suppose, for it appeared as if the whale had the tail part of the mollusc in his jaws, and, in a business-like, methodical way, was sawing through it. By the side of the black columnar head of the whale appeared the head of the great squid, as awful an object as one could well imagine even in a fevered dream. Judging as carefully as possible, I estimated it to be at least as large as one of our pipes, which contained three hundred and fifty gallons; but it may have been, and probably was, a good deal larger. The eyes were very remarkable from their size and blackness, which, contrasted with the livid whiteness of the head, made their appearance all the more striking. They were, at least, a foot in diameter, and, seen under such conditions, looked decidedly eerie and hobgoblin-like. All around the combatants were numerous sharks, like jackals round a lion, ready to share the feast, and apparently assisting in the destruction of the huge cephalopod. So the titanic struggle went on, in perfect silence as far as we were concerned, because, even had there been any noise, our distance from the scene of conflict would not have permitted us to hear it.

Thinking that such a sight ought not to be missed by the captain, I overcame my dread of him sufficiently to call him, and tell him of what was taking place. He met my remarks with such a furious burst of anger at my daring to disturb him for such a cause, that I fled precipitately on deck again, having the remainder of the vision to myself, for none of the others cared sufficiently for such things to lose five minutes' sleep in witnessing them. The conflict ceased, the sea resumed its placid calm, and nothing remained to tell of the fight but a strong odour of fish, as of a bank of seaweed left by the tide in the blazing sun. Eight bells struck, and I went below to a troubled sleep, wherein all the awful monsters that an over-excited brain could conjure up pursued me through the gloomy caves of ocean, or mocked my pigmy efforts to escape.

The occasions upon which these gigantic cuttle-fish appear at the sea surface must, I think, be very rare. From their construction, they appear fitted only to grope among the rocks at the bottom of the ocean. Their mode of progression is backward, by the forcible ejection of a jet of water from an orifice in the neck, beside the rectum or cloaca. Consequently their normal position is head-downward, and with tentacles spread out like the ribs of an umbrella—eight of them at least; the two long ones, like the antennæ of an insect, rove unceasingly around, seeking prey.

The imagination can hardly picture a more terrible object than one of these huge monsters brooding in the ocean depths, the gloom of his surroundings increased by the inky fluid (sepia) which he secretes in copious quantities, every cup-shaped disc, of the hundreds with which the restless tentacles are furnished, ready at the slightest touch to grip whatever is near, not only by suction, but by the great claws set all round within its circle. And in the centre of this net-work of living traps is the chasm-like mouth, with its enormous parrot-beak, ready to rend piecemeal whatever is held by the tentaculæ. The very thought of it makes one's flesh crawl. Well did Michelet term them "the insatiable nightmares of the sea."

Yet, but for them, how would such great creatures as the sperm whale be fed? Unable, from their bulk, to capture small fish except by accident, and, by the absence of a sieve of baleen, precluded from subsisting upon the tiny crustacea which support the *Mysticetæ*, the cachalots seem to be confined for their diet to cuttle-fish, and, from their point of view, the bigger the latter are the better. How big they may become in the depths of the sea, no man knoweth; but it is unlikely that even the vast specimens seen are full-sized, since they have only come to the surface under abnormal conditions, like the one I have attempted to describe, who had evidently been dragged up by his relentless foe.

Creatures like these, who inhabit deep waters, and do not need to come to the surface by the exigencies of their existence, necessarily present many obstacles to accurate investigation of their structure and habits; but, from the few specimens that have been obtained of late years, fairly comprehensive details have been compiled, and may be studied in various French and German works, of which the Natural History Museum at South Kensington possesses copies. These, through the courtesy of the authorities in charge, are easily accessible to students who wish to prosecute the study of this wonderful branch of the great mollusca family.

When we commenced to cut in our whale next morning, the sea was fairly alive with fish of innumerable kinds, while a vast host of sea-birds, as usual, waited impatiently for the breaking-up of the huge carcass, which they knew would afford them no end of a feast. An untoward accident, which happened soon after the work was started, gave the waiting myriads immense satisfaction, although the unfortunate second mate, whose slip of the spade was responsible, came in for a hurricane of vituperation from the enraged skipper. It was in detaching the case from the head—always a work of difficulty, and requiring great precision of aim. Just as

Mr. Cruce made a powerful thrust with his keen tool, the vessel rolled, and the blow, missing the score in which he was cutting, fell upon the case instead, piercing its side. For a few minutes the result was unnoticed amidst the wash of the ragged edges of the cut, but presently a long streak of white, wax-like pieces floating astern, and a tremendous commotion among the birds, told the story. The liquid spermaceti was leaking rapidly from the case, turning solid as it got into the cool water. Nothing could be done to stop the waste, which, as it was a large whale, was not less than twenty barrels, or about two tuns of pure spermaceti. An accident of this kind never failed to make our skipper almost unbearable in his temper for some days afterwards; and, to do him justice, he did not discriminate very carefully as to who felt his resentment besides its immediate cause.

Therefore we had all a rough time of it while his angry fit lasted, which was a whole week, or until all was shipshape again. Meanwhile we were edging gradually through the Malacca Straits and around the big island of Borneo, never going very near the land on account of the great and numerous dangers attendant upon coasting in those localities to any but those continually engaged in such a business.

Indeed, all navigation in those seas to sailing vessels is dangerous, and requires the greatest care. Often we were obliged at a minute's notice to let go the anchor, although out of sight of land, some rapid current being found carrying us swiftly towards a shoal or race, where we might come to grief. Yet there was no fuss or hurry, the same leisurely old system was continued, and worked as well as ever. But it was not apparent why we were threading the tortuous and difficult waters of the

Indian Archipelago. No whales of any kind were seen for at least a month, although, from our leisurely mode of sailing, it was evident that they were looked for.

An occasional native craft came alongside, desirous of bartering fish, which we did not want, being able to catch all we needed as readily almost as they were. Fruit and vegetables we could not get at such distances from land, for the small canoes that lie in wait for passing ships do not of course venture far from home.

CHAPTER XIII.

OFF TO THE JAPAN GROUNDS.

Very tedious and trying was our passage northward, although every effort was made by the skipper to expedite it. Nothing of advantage to our cargo was seen for a long time, which, although apparently what was to be expected, did not improve Captain Slocum's temper. But, to the surprise of all, when we had arrived off the beautiful island of Hong Kong, to which we approached closely, we "raised" a grand sperm whale.

Many fishing-junks were in sight, busily plying their trade, and at any other time we should have been much interested in the quaint and cunning devices by which the patient, wily Chinaman succeeds so admirably as a fisherman. Our own fishing, for the time being, absorbed all our attention—the more, perhaps, that we had for so long been unable to do anything in that line. After the usual preliminaries, we were successful in getting fast to the great creature, who immediately showed fight. So skilful and wary did he prove that Captain Slocum, growing impatient at our manœuvring with no result, himself took the field, arriving on the scene with the air of one who comes to see and conquer without more delay. He brought with him a weapon which I have not hitherto mentioned, because none of the harpooners could be induced to use it, and consequently it had not been much in evidence. Theoretically, it was an ideal tool for such work, its chief drawback being its cumbrousness. It was known as "Pierce's darting gun," being a combination of bomb-gun and harpoon, capable of being darted at the whale like a plain harpoon. Its construction was simple; indeed, the patent was a very old one. A tube of brass, thickening towards the butt, at which was a square chamber firmly welded to a socket for receiving the pole, formed the gun itself. Within the chamber aforesaid a nipple protruded from the base of the tube, and in line with it. The trigger was simply a flat bit of steel, like a piece of clock spring, which was held down by the hooked end of a steel rod long enough to stick out beyond the muzzle of the gun three or four inches, and held in position by two flanges at the butt and muzzle of the barrel. On the opposite side of the tube were two more flanges, close together, into the holes of which was inserted the end of a specially made harpoon, having an eye twisted in its shank through which the whale line was spliced. The whole machine was fitted to a neat pole, and strongly secured to it by means of a "gun warp," or short piece of thin line, by which it could be hauled back into the boat after being darted at a whale. To prepare this weapon for use, the barrel was loaded with a charge of powder and a bomb similar to those used in the shoulder-guns, the point of which just protruded from the muzzle. An ordinary percussion cap was placed upon the nipple, and the trigger cocked by placing the trigger-rod in position. The harpoon, with the line attached, was firmly set into the socketed flanges prepared for it, and the whole arrangement was then ready to be darted at the whale in the usual way.

Supposing the aim to be good and the force sufficient, the harpoon would penetrate the blubber until the end of the trigger-rod was driven backwards by striking the blubber, releasing the trigger and firing the gun. Thus the whale would be harpooned and bomb-lanced at the same time, and, supposing everything to work satisfactorily, very little more would be needed to finish him. But the weapon was so cumbersome and awkward, and the harpooners stood in such awe of it, that in the majority of cases the whale was either missed altogether or the harpoon got such slight hold that the gun did not go off, the result being generally disastrous.

In the present case, however, the "Pierce" gun was in the hands of a man by no means nervous, and above criticism or blame in case of failure. So when he sailed in to the attack, and delivered his "swashing blow," the report of the gun was immediately heard, proving conclusively that a successful stroke had been made.

It had an instantaneous and astonishing effect. The sorely-wounded monster, with one tremendous expiration, rolled over and over swift as thought towards his aggressor, literally burying the boat beneath his vast bulk. Now, one would have thought surely, upon seeing this, that none of that boat's crew would ever have been seen again. Nevertheless, strange as it may appear, out of that seething lather of foam, all six heads emerged again in an instant, but on the *other* side of the great creature. How any of them escaped instant violent death was, and from the nature of the case must ever remain, an unravelled mystery, for the boat was crumbled into innumerable fragments, and the three hundred fathoms of line, in a perfect maze of entanglement, appeared to be wrapped about the writhing trunk of the whale. Happily, there were two boats disengaged, so that they were able very promptly to rescue the sufferers from their perilous position in the boiling vortex of foam by which they were surrounded. Meanwhile, the remaining boat had an easy task. The shot delivered by the captain had taken deadly effect, the bomb having entered the creature's side low down, directly abaft the pectoral fin. It must have exploded within the cavity of the bowels, from its position, causing such extensive injuries as to make even that vast animal's death but a matter of a few moments. Therefore, we did not run any unnecessary risks, but hauled off to a safe distance and quietly watched the death-throes. They were so brief, that in less than ten minutes from the time of the accident we were busy securing the line through the flukes of our prize.

The vessel was an unusually long time working up to us, so slow, in fact, that Mr. Count remarked, critically, "Shouldn't wonder if th' ole man ain't hurt; they're taking things so all-fired easy." By the time she had reached us, we had a good few visitors around us from the fishing fleet, who caused us no little anxiety. The Chinese have no prejudices; they would just as soon steal a whale as a herring, if the conveyance could be effected without more trouble or risk to their own yellow skins. If it involved the killing of a few foreign devils —well, so much to the good. The ship, however, arrived before the fishermen had decided upon any active steps, and we got our catch alongside without any delay. The truth of Mr. Count's forecast was verified to the hilt, for we found that the captain was so badly bruised about the body that he was unable to move, while one of the hands, a Portuguese, was injured internally, and seemed very bad indeed. Had any one told us that morning that we should be sorry to see Captain Slocum with sore bones, we should have scoffed at the notion, and some of us would probably have said that we should like to have the opportunity of making him smart. But under the present circumstances, with some hundreds of perfectly ruthless wretches hovering around us, looking with longing eyes at the treasure we had alongside, we could not help remembering the courage and resource so often shown by the skipper, and wished with all our hearts that we could have the benefit of them now. As soon as dinner was over, we all "turned to" with a will to get the whale cut in. None of us required to be told that to lay all night with that whale alongside would be extremely unhealthy for us, great doubt existing as to whether any of us would see morning dawn again. There was, too, just a possibility that when the carcass, stripped of its blubber, was cut adrift, those ravenous crowds would fasten upon it, and let us go in peace.

All hands, therefore, worked like Trojans. There was no need to drive us, nor was a single harsh word spoken. Nothing was heard but the almost incessant clatter of the windlass pawls, abrupt monosyllabic orders, and the occasional melancholy wail of a gannet overhead. No word had been spoken on the subject among us, yet somehow we all realized that we were working for a large stake—no less than our lives. What! says somebody, within a few miles of Hong Kong? Oh yes; and even within Hong Kong harbour itself, if opportunity offers. Let any man go down the wharf at Hong Kong after sunset, and hail a sampan from the hundreds there that are waiting to be hired. Hardly will the summons have left his lips before a white policeman will be at his side, note-book in hand, inquiring his name and ship, and taking a note of the sampan's number with the time of his leaving the wharf. Nothing perfunctory about the job either. Let but these precautions be omitted, and the chances that the passenger (if he have aught of value about him) will ever arrive at his destination are almost nil.

So good was the progress made that by five p.m. we were busy at the head, while the last few turns of the windlass were being taken to complete the skinning of the body. With a long pent-up shout that last piece was severed and swung inboard, as the huge mass of reeking flesh floated slowly astern. As it drifted away we saw the patient watchers who had been waiting converging upon it from all quarters, and our hopes rose high. But there was no slackening of our efforts to get in the head. By the time it was dark we managed to get the junk on board, and by the most extraordinary efforts lifted the whole remainder of the head high enough to make sail and stand off to sea. The wind was off the land, the water smooth, and no swell on, so we took no damage from that tremendous weight surging by our side, though, had the worst come to the worst, we could have cut it adrift.

When morning dawned we hove-to, the land being only dimly visible astern, and finished taking on board our "head matter" without further incident. The danger past, we were all well pleased that the captain was below, for the work proceeded quite pleasantly under the genial rule of the mate. Since leaving port we had not felt so comfortable, the work, with all its disagreeables, seeming as nothing now that we could do it without fear and trembling. Alas for poor Jemmy!—as we always persisted in calling him from inability to pronounce his proper name—his case was evidently hopeless. His fellows did their poor best to comfort his fast-fleeting hours, one after another murmuring to him the prayers of the Church, which, although they did not understand them, they evidently believed most firmly to have some marvellous power to open the gates of paradise and cleanse the sinner. Notwithstanding the grim fact that their worship was almost pure superstition, it was far more in accordance with the fitness of things for a dying man's surroundings than such scenes as I have witnessed in the forecastles of merchant ships when poor sailors lay a-dying. I remember well once, when I was second officer of a large passenger ship, going in the forecastle as she lay at anchor at St. Helena, to see a sick man. Half the crew were drunk, and the beastly kennel in which they lived was in a thick fog of tobacco-smoke and the stale stench of rum. Ribald songs, quarrelling, and blasphemy made a veritable pandemonium of the place. I passed quietly through it to the sick man's bunk, and found him—dead! He had passed away in the midst of that, but the horror of it did not seem to impress his bemused shipmates much.

Here, at any rate, there was quiet and decorum, while all that could be done for the poor sufferer (not much, from ignorance of how he was injured) was done. He was released from his pain in the afternoon of the second day after the accident, the end coming suddenly and peacefully. The same evening, at sunset, the body, neatly sewn up in canvas, with a big lump of sandstone secured to the feet, was brought on deck, laid on a hatch at the gangway, and covered with the blue, star-spangled American Jack. Then all hands were mustered in the waist, the ship's bell was tolled, and the ensign run up halfway.

The captain was still too ill to be moved, so the mate stepped forward with a rusty old Common Prayer-book in his hands, whereon my vagrant fancy immediately fastened in frantic endeavour to imagine how it came to be there. The silence of death was over all. True, the man was but a unit of no special note among us, but death had conferred upon him a brevet rank, in virtue of which he dominated every thought. It seemed strange to me that we who faced death so often and variously, until natural fear had become deadened by custom, should, now that one of our number lay a rapidly-corrupting husk before us, be so tremendously impressed by the simple, inevitable fact. I suppose it was because none of us were able to realize the immanence of Death until we saw his handiwork. Mr. Count opened the book, fumbling nervously among the unfamiliar leaves. Then he suddenly looked up, his weather-scarred face glowing a dull brick-red, and said, in a low voice, "This thing's too many fer me; kin any of ye do it? Ef not, I guess we'll hev ter take it as read." There was no response for a moment; then I stepped forward, reaching out my hand for the book. Its contents were familiar enough to me, for in happy pre-arab days I had been a chorister in the old Lock Chapel, Harrow Road, and had borne my part in the service so often that I think even now I could repeat the greater part of it *memoriter*. Mr. Count gave it me without a word, and, trembling like a leaf, I turned to the "Burial Service," and began the majestic sentences, "I am the Resurrection and the Life, saith the Lord." I did not know my own voice as the wonderful words sounded clearly in the still air; but if ever a small body of soul-hardened men *felt* the power of God, it was then. At the words, "We therefore commit his body to the deep," I paused, and, the mate making a sign, two of the harpooners tilted the hatch, from which the remains slid off into the unknown depths with a dull splash. Several of the dead man's compatriots covered their faces, and murmured prayers for the repose of his soul, while the tears trickled through their horny fingers. But matters soon resumed their normal course; the tension over, back came the strings of life into position again, to play the same old tunes and discords once more.

The captured whale made an addition to our cargo of one hundred and ten barrels—a very fair haul indeed. The harpooners were disposed to regard this capture as auspicious upon opening the North Pacific, where, in spite of the time we had spent, and the fair luck we had experienced in the Indian Ocean, we expected to make the chief portion of our cargo.

Our next cruising-ground is known to whalemen as the "Coast of Japan" ground, and has certainly proved in the past the most prolific fishery of sperm whales in the whole world. I am inclined now to believe that there are more and larger cachalots to be found in the Southern Hemisphere, between the parallels of 33° and 50° South; but there the drawback of heavy weather and mountainous seas severely handicaps the fishermen.

It is somewhat of a misnomer to call the Coast of Japan ground by that name, since to be successful you should not sight Japan at all, but keep out of range of the cold current that sweeps right across the Pacific, skirting the Philippines, along the coasts of the Japanese islands as far as the Kuriles, and then returns to the eastward again to the southward of the Aleutian Archipelago. The greatest number of whales are always found in the vicinity of the Bonin and Volcano groups of islands, which lie in the eddy formed by the northward bend of the mighty current before mentioned. This wonderful ground was first cruised by a London whale-ship, the *Syren*, in 1819, when the English branch of the sperm whale-fishery was in its prime, and London skippers were proud of the fact that one of their number, in the *Emilia*, had thirty-one years before first ventured around Cape Horn in pursuit of the cachalot.

After the advent of the *Syren*, the Bonins became the favourite fishing-ground for both Americans and British, and for many years the catch of oil taken from these teeming waters averaged four thousand tuns annually. That the value of the fishery was maintained at so high a level for over a quarter of a century was doubtless due to the fact that there was a long, self-imposed close season, during which the whales were quite unmolested. Nothing in the migratory habits of this whale, so far as has ever been observed, would have prevented a profitable fishing all the year round; but custom, stronger even than profit, ordained that whale-ships should never stay too long upon one fishing-ground, but move on farther until the usual round had been made, unless the vessel were filled in the mean time.

Of course, there are whales whose habits lead them at certain seasons, for breeding purposes, to frequent various groups of islands, but the cachalot seems to be quite impartial in his preferences; if he "uses" around certain waters, he is just as likely to be found there in July as January.

The Bonins, too, form an ideal calling-place, from

the whaling captain's point of view. Peel Island, the principal one of the cluster, has a perfect harbour in Port Lloyd, where a vessel can not only lie in comfort, sheltered from almost every wind that blows, but where provisions, wood, and water are plentiful. There is no inducement, or indeed room, for desertion, and the place is healthy. It is colonized by Japs from the kingdom so easily reached to the westward, and the busy little people, after their manner, make a short stay very agreeable.

Once clear of the southern end of Formosa we had quite a rapid run to the Bonins, carrying a press of sail day and night, as the skipper was anxious to arrive there on account of his recent injuries. He was still very lame, and he feared that some damage might have been done to him of which he was ignorant. Besides, it was easy to see that he did not altogether like anybody else being in charge of his ship, no matter how good they were. Such was the expedition we made that we arrived at Port Lloyd twelve days after clearing up our last whale. Very beautiful indeed the islands appeared, with their bold, steep sides clad in richest green, or, where no vegetation appeared, worn into a thousand fantastic shapes by the sea or the mountain torrents carving away the lava of which they were all composed. For the whole of the islands were volcanic, and Port Lloyd itself is nothing more than the crater of a vast volcano, which in some tremendous convulsion of nature has sunk from its former high estate low enough to become a haven for ships.

I have said that it was a perfect harbour, but there is no doubt that getting in or out requires plenty of nerve as well as seamanship. There was so little room, and the eddying flaws of wind under the high land were so baffling, that at various times during our passage in it appeared as if nothing could prevent us from getting stuck upon some of the adjacent hungry-looking coral reefs. Nothing of the kind happened, however, and we came comfortably to an anchor near three other whale-ships which were already there. They were the *Diego Ramirez*, of Nantucket; the *Coronel*, of Providence, Rhode Island; and the *Grampus*, of New Bedford. These were the first whale-ships we had yet seen, and it may be imagined how anxious we felt to meet men with whom we could compare notes and exchange yarns. It might be, too, that we should get some news of that world which, as far as we were concerned, might as well have been at the other extremity of the solar system for the last year, so completely isolated had we been.

The sails were hardly fast before a boat from each of the ships was alongside with their respective skippers on board. The extra exertion necessary to pilot the ship in had knocked the old man up, in his present weak state, and he had gone below for a short rest; so the three visitors dived down into the stuffy cabin, all anxious to interview the latest comer. Considerate always, Mr. Count allowed us to have the remainder of the day to ourselves, so we set about entertaining our company. It was no joke twelve of them coming upon us all at once, and babel ensued for a short time. They knew the system too well to expect refreshments, so we had not to apologize for having nothing to set before them. They had not come, however, for meat and drink, but for talk. And talk we did, sometimes altogether, sometimes rationally; but I doubt whether any of us had ever enjoyed talking so much before.

CHAPTER XIV.

LIBERTY DAY—AND AFTER.

THERE is generally current among seamen a notion that all masters of ships are bound by law to give their crews twenty-four hours' liberty and a portion of their wages to spend every three months, if they are in port. I have never heard any authority quoted for this, and do not know what foundation there is for such a belief, although the practice is usually adhered to in English ships. But American whale-ships apparently know no law, except the will of their commanders, whose convenience is always the first consideration. Thus, we had now been afloat for well over a year, during which time, except for our foraging excursions at the Cocos and Aldabra, we had certainly known no liberty for a whole day.

Our present port being one where it was impossible to desert without the certainty of prompt recapture, with subsequent suffering altogether disproportionate to the offence, we were told that one watch at a time would be allowed their liberty for a day. So we of the port watch made our simple preparations, received twenty-five cents each, and were turned adrift on the beach to enjoy ourselves. We had our liberty, but we didn't know what to do with it. There was a native town and a couple of low groggeries kept by Chinamen, where some of my shipmates promptly invested a portion of their wealth in some horrible liquor, the smell of which was enough to make an ordinary individual sick. There was no place apparently where one could get a meal, so that the prospect of our stay ashore lasting a day did not seem very great. I was fortunate enough, however, to foregather with a Scotchman who was a beach-comber, and consequently "knew the ropes." I dare say he was an unmitigated blackguard whenever he got the chance, but he was certainly on his best behaviour with me. He took me into the country a bit to see the sights, which were such as most of the Pacific islands afford. Wonderful indeed were the fantastic rocks, twisted into innumerable grotesque shapes, and, along the shores, hollowed out into caverns of all sizes, some large enough to shelter an army. He was quite familiar with the natives, understanding enough of their queer lingo to get along. By his friendly aid we got some food—yams, and fish cooked in native fashion, *i.e.* in heated holes in the ground, for which the friendly Kanakas would take no payment, although they looked murderous enough to be cannibals. It does not do to go by looks always.

Well, after a long ramble, the Scotchman and I laid our weary bodies down in the shade of a big rock, and had a grand sleep, waking up again a little before sunset. We hastened down to the beach off the town, where all my watchmates were sitting in a row, like lost sheep, waiting to be taken on board again. They had had enough of liberty; indeed, such liberty as that was hardly worth having. It seems hardly credible, but we were actually glad to get on board again, it was so miserable ashore. The natives were most unsociable at the port, and we could not make ourselves understood, so there was not much fun to be had. Even those who were inclined to drink had too little for a spree, which I was not sorry for, since doubtless a very unpleasant reception would have awaited them had they come on board drunk.

Next day the starboard watch went on liberty, while we who had received our share were told off to spend the day wooding and watering. In this most pleasant of occupations (when the weather is fine) I passed a much more satisfactory time than when wandering about with no objective, an empty pocket, and a hungry belly. No foremast hand has ever enjoyed his opportunities of making the acquaintance of his various visiting places more than I have; but the circumstances attendant upon one's leave must be a little favourable, or I would much rather stay aboard and fish. Our task was over for the day, a goodly store of wood and casks of water having been shipped. We were sitting down to supper, when, in answer to a hail from the beach, we were ordered to fetch the liberty men. When we got to them, there was a pretty how-d'ye-do. All of them were more or less drunk, some exceedingly quarrelsome. Now, Mistah Jones was steering our boat, looking as little like a man to take sauce from a drunken sailor as you could imagine. Most of the transformed crowd ya-hooing on the beach had felt the weight of his shoulder-of-mutton fist, yet so utterly had prudence forsaken them that, before we came near them, they were abusing him through all the varied gamut of filthy language they possessed. My democratic sentiments are deeply seated, but I do believe in authority, and respect for it being rigidly enforced, so this uncalled-for scene upset me, making me feel anxious that the gibbering fools might get a lesson. They got one.

Goliath stood like a tower, his eyes alone betraying the fierce anger boiling within. When we touched the beach, his voice was mild and gentle as a child's, his movements calm and deliberate. As soon as we had beached the boat he stepped ashore, and in two strides was in the middle of the snarling group. Further parley ceased at once. Snatching the loudest of them by the breast of his shirt with his right hand, another one by the collar with his left, he flung himself backwards towards the boat, knocking the interveners right and left. But a protruding fragment of rock caught his heel, bringing him with his captives to the ground in a writhing mass. The rest, maddened beyond restraint of fear, flung themselves upon the prostrate man, the glimmer of more than one knife-blade appearing. Two of us from the boat—one with the tiller, the other brandishing a paddle—rushed to the rescue; but before we arrived the giant had heaved off his assailants, and, with no other weapons than his bare hands, was doing terrific execution among them. Not knowing, I suppose, whether we were friendly to him or not, he shouted to us to keep away, nor dare to interfere. There was no need. Disregarding such trifles as a few superficial cuts—not feeling them perhaps—he so unmercifully mauled that crowd that they howled again for mercy. The battle was brief and bloody. Before hostilities had lasted five minutes, six of the aggressors were stretched insensible; the rest, comprising as many more, were pleading for mercy, completely sober. Such prowess on the part of one man against twelve seems hardly credible; but it must be remembered that Goliath fought, with all the moral force of the ship's officers behind him, against a disorganized crowd without backbone, who would never have dared to face him but for the temporary mania induced by the stuff they had drunk. It was a conflict between a lion and a troop of jackals, whereof the issue was never in doubt as long as lethal weapons were wanting.

Standing erect among the cowering creatures, the great negro looked every inch a mediæval hero. In a stern voice he bade his subjugated enemies to get into the boat, assisting those to do so who were too badly hurt to rise. Then we shoved off for the ship—a sorrowful gang indeed.

As I bent to my oar, I felt very sorry for what had happened. Here were half the crew guilty of an act of violence upon an officer, which, according to the severe code under which we lived, merited punishment as painful as could be inflicted, and lasting for the rest of the voyage. Whatever form that punishment might take, those of us who were innocent would be almost equal sufferers with the others, because discrimination in the treatment between watch and watch is always difficult, and in our case it was certain that it would not be attempted. Except as regarded physical violence, we might all expect to share alike. Undoubtedly things looked very unpleasant. My gloomy cogitations were abruptly terminated by the order to " unrow "—we were alongside. Somehow or other all hands managed to scramble on board, and assist in hoisting the boat up.

As soon as she was secured we slunk away forward, but we had hardly got below before a tremendous summons from Goliath brought us all aft again at the double quick. Most of the fracas had been witnessed from the ship, so that but a minute or two was needed to explain how or why it begun. Directly that explanation had been supplied by Mistah Jones, the order was issued for the culprits to appear.

I have before noticed how little love was lost between the skipper and his officers, Goliath having even once gone so far as to give me a very emphatic opinion of his about the "old man" of a most unflattering nature. And had such a state of things existed on board an English ship, the crew would simply have taken charge, for they would have seen the junior officers flouted, snubbed, and jeered at; and, of course, what they saw the captain do, they would not be slow to improve on. Many a promising young officer's career has been blighted in this way by the feminine spite of a foolish man unable to see that if the captain shows no respect to his officers, neither will the crew, nor obedience either.

But in an American ship, so long as an officer remains an officer, he must be treated as such by every man, under pain of prompt punishment. Yankee skippers have far too much *nous* to allow their hands to grow saucy in consequence of division among the after-guard. So now a sort of court-martial was held upon the unfortunates who had dared to attack Goliath, at which that sable hero might have been the apple of Captain Slocum's eye, so solicitous was he of Mistah Jones' honour and the reparation to be made.

This sort of thing was right in his line. Naturally cruel, he seemed to thoroughly enjoy himself in the prospect of making human beings twist and writhe in pain. Nor would he be baulked of a jot of his pleasure.

Goliath approached him, and muttered a few words, meant, I felt sure, to appease him by letting him know how much they had suffered at his strong hands; but he turned upon the negro with a savage curse, bidding him be silent. Then every one of the culprits was stripped, and secured to the lash-rail by the wrists; scourges were made of cotton fish-line, knotted at intervals, and secured to a stout handle; the harpooners were told off as executioners, and the flogging began. Perhaps it was necessary for the maintenance of discipline—certainly it was trivial compared with the practice, till recently, in our own army and navy; but I am glad to say that, compelled to witness it, I felt quite sick—physically sick—trembling so in every limb that my legs would not support me. It was not fear, for I had nothing to fear had I been ever such a coward. Whatever it was, I am not sorry either to have felt it or to own it, even while I fully admit that for some forms of wickedness nothing but the lash seems adequate punishment.

Some of the victims fainted, not being in the best condition at the outset for undergoing so severe a trial; but all were treated alike, buckets of salt water being flung over them. This drastic reviver, while adding to their pain, brought them all into a state of sufficient activity to get forward when they were released. Smarting and degraded, all their temporary bravado effectually banished, they were indeed pitiable objects, their deplorable state all the harder to bear from its contrast to our recent pleasure when we entertained the visiting crews.

Having completed our quantum of wood, water, and fresh provisions for the officers, we got under way again for the fishing grounds. I did not see how we could hope for a successful season, knowing the utterly despondent state of the crew, which even affected the officers, who, not so callous or cruel as the skipper, seemed to be getting rather tired of the constant drive and kick, now the normal condition of affairs. But the skipper's vigilance was great. Whether he noted any sign of slackness or indifference on the part of his coadjutors or not, of course I cannot say, but he certainly seemed to put more vigour into his attentions than had been his wont, and so kept everybody up to the mark.

Hitherto we had always had our fishing to ourselves; we were now to see something of the ways of other men employed in the same manner. For though the general idea or plan of campaign against the whales is the same in all American whalers, every ship has some individual peculiarity of tactics, which, needless to say, are always far superior to those of any other ship. When we commenced our cruise on this new ground, there were seven whalers in sight, all quite as keen on the chase as ourselves, so that I anticipated considerable sport of the liveliest kind should we "raise" whales with such a fleet close at hand.

But for a whole week we saw nothing but a grampus or so, a few loitering finbacks, and an occasional lean humpback bull certainly not worth chasing. On the seventh afternoon, however, I was in the main crow's-nest with the chief, when I noticed a ship to windward of us alter her course, keeping away three or four points on an angle that would presently bring her across our bows a good way ahead. I was getting pretty well versed in the tricks of the trade now, so I kept mum, but strained my eyes in the direction for which the other ship was steering. The chief was looking astern at some finbacks, the look-out men forward were both staring to leeward, thus for a minute or so I had a small arc of the horizon to myself. The time was short, but it sufficed, and for the first time that voyage I had the privilege of "raising" a sperm whale. My voice quivered with excitement as I uttered the war-whoop, "Ah blo-o-o-o-w!" Round spun the mate on his heel, while the hands clustered like bees roused from their hive. "Where away—where?" gasped the mate. And I pointed to a spot about half a point on the lee bow, at the same time calling his attention to the fact that the stranger to windward was keeping away. In answer to the skipper's hurried queries from below, Mr. Count gave him the general outline of affairs, to which he replied by crowding every stitch of canvas on the vessel that was available.

The spout I had seen was a good ten miles off, and, for the present, seemed to belong to a "lone" whale, as it was the only one visible. There was a good breeze blowing, as much, in fact, as we could carry all sail to, the old barky making a tremendous commotion as she blundered along under the unusual press of canvas. In the excitement of the race all our woes were forgotten; we only thought of the possibility of the ship getting there first. We drew gradually nearer to the stranger, who, like us, was carrying all the sail he had got, but, being able to go a point or two free, was outsailing us.

It was anybody's race as yet, though, when we heard the skipper's hail, "'Way down from aloft!" as he came up to take our place. The whale had sounded, apparently heading to leeward, so that the weather-gage held by our rival was not much advantage to him now. We ran on for another two miles, then shortened sail, and stood by to lower away the moment he should reappear. Meanwhile another ship was working up from to leeward, having evidently noted our movements, or else, like the albatross, "smelt whale," no great distance to windward of him. Waiting for that whale to rise was one of the most exciting experiences we had gone through as yet, with two other ships so near. Everybody's nerves seemed strung up to concert pitch, and it was quite a relief when from half a dozen throats at once burst the cry, "There she white-waters! Ah blo-o-o-o-w!" Not a mile away, dead to leeward of us, quietly beating the water with the flat of his flukes, as if there was no such thing in the watery world as a whale-ship. Splash! almost simultaneously went the four boats. Out we shot from the ship, all on our mettle; for was not the skipper's eye upon us from his lofty eerie, as well as the crew of the other ship, now not more than a mile away? We seemed a terrible time getting the sails up, but the officers dared not risk our willingness to pull while they could be independent of us.

By the time we were fairly off, the other ship's boats were coming like the wind, so that eight boats were now converging upon the unconscious monster. We fairly flew over the short, choppy sea, getting drenched with the flying spray, but looking out far more keenly at the other boats than at the whale. Up we came to him, Mr. Count's boat to the left, the other mate's boat to the right. Almost at the same moment the irons flew from the hands of the rival harpooners; but while ours was buried to the hitches in the whale's side, the other man's just ploughed up the skin on the animal's back, as it passed over him and pierced our boat close behind the harpooner's leg. Not seeing what had happened to his iron, or knowing that we were fast, the other harpooner promptly hurled his second iron, which struck solidly. It was a very pretty tangle, but our position was rather bad. The whale between us was tearing the bowels of the deep up in his rage and fear ; we were struggling frantically to get our sail down ; and at any moment that wretched iron through our upper strake might tear a plank out of us. Our chief, foaming at the mouth with rage and excitement, was screeching inarticulate blasphemy at the other mate, who, not knowing what was the matter, was yelling back all his copious vocabulary of abuse. I felt very glad the whale was between us, or there would surely have been murder done. At last, out drops the iron, leaving a jagged hole you could put your arm through. Wasn't Mr. Count mad ? I really thought he would split with rage, for it was impossible for us to go on with that hole in our bilge. The second mate came alongside and took our line as the whale was just commencing to sound, thus setting us free. We made at once for the other ship's "fast" boat, and the compliments that had gone before were just casual conversation to what filled the air with dislocated language now. Presently both the champions cooled down a bit from want of breath, and we got our case stated. It was received with a yell of derision from the other side as a splendid effort of lying on our part ; because the first ship fast claims the whale, and such a prize as this one we were quarrelling about was not to be tamely yielded.

However, as reason asserted her sway over Mr. Count, he quieted down, knowing full well that the state of the line belonging to his rival would reveal the truth when the whale rose again. Therefore we returned to the ship, leaving our three boats busy waiting the whale's pleasure to rise again. When the skipper heard what had happened, he had his own boat manned, proceeding himself to the battle-field in expectation of complications presently. By the time he arrived upon the scene there were two more boats lying by, which had come up from the third ship, mentioned as working up from to leeward. "Pretty fine ground this's got ter be!" growled the old man. "Caint strike whale 'thout bein' crowded eout uv yer own propputty by a gang ov bunco steerers like this. Shall hev ter quit it, en keep a pawnshop."

And still the whale kept going steadily down, down, down. Already he was on the second boat's lines, and taking them out faster than ever. Had we been alone, this persistence on his part, though annoying, would not have mattered much; but, with so many others in company, the possibilities of complication, should we need to slip our end, were numerous. The ship kept near, and Mr. Count, seeing how matters were going, had hastily patched his boat, returning at once with another tub of line. He was but just in time to bend on, when to our great delight we saw the end slip from our rival's boat. This in no wise terminated his lien on the whale, supposing he could prove that he struck first, but it got him out of the way for the time.

Meanwhile we were running line faster than ever. There was an enormous length attached to the animal now—some twelve thousand feet—the weight of which was very great, to say nothing of the many "drogues" or "stopwaters" attached to it at intervals. Judge, then, of my surprise when a shout of "Blo-o-o-w!" called my attention to the whale himself just breaking water about half a mile away. It was an awkward predicamont;

for if we let go our end, the others would be on the whale immediately; if we held on, we should certainly be dragged below in a twinkling; and our disengaged boats could do nothing, for they had no line. But the difficulty soon settled itself. Out ran our end, leaving us bare of line as pleasure skiffs. The new-comer, who had been prowling near, keeping a close watch upon us, saw our boat jump up when released from the weight. Off he flew like an arrow to the labouring leviathan, now a "free fish," except for such claims as the two first comers had upon it, which claims are legally assessed, where no dispute arises. In its disabled condition, dragging so enormous a weight of line, it was but a few minutes before the fresh boat was fast, while we looked on helplessly, boiling with impotent rage. All that we could now hope for was the salvage of some of our line, a mile and a half of which, inextricably mixed up with about the same length of our rival's, was towing astern of the fast-expiring cachalot.

So great had been the strain upon that hardly-used animal that he did not go into his usual "flurry," but calmly expired without the faintest struggle. In the mean time two of our boats had been sent on board again to work the ship, while the skipper proceeded to try his luck in the recovery of his gear. On arriving at the dead whale, however, we found that he had rolled over and over beneath the water so many times that the line was fairly frapped round him, and the present possessors were in no mood to allow us the privilege of unrolling it.

During the conversation we had drawn very near the carcass, so near, in fact, that one hand was holding the boat alongside the whale's "small" by a bight of the line. I suppose the skipper's eagle eye must have caught sight of the trailing part of the line streaming beneath, for suddenly he plunged overboard, reappearing almost immediately with the line in his hand. He scrambled into the boat with it, cutting it from the whale at once, and starting his boat's crew hauling in.

Then there was a hubbub again. The captain of the *Narragansett*, our first rival, protested vigorously against our monopoly of the line; but in grim silence our skipper kept on, taking no notice of him, while we steadily hauled. Unless he of the *Narragansett* choose to fight for what he considered his rights, there was no help for him. And there was something in our old man's appearance eminently calculated to discourage aggression of any kind.

At last, disgusted apparently with the hopeless turn affairs had taken, the *Narragansett's* boats drew off, and returned on board their ship. Two of our boats had by this time accumulated a mountainous coil of line each, with which we returned to our own vessel, leaving the skipper to visit the present holder of the whale, the skipper of the *John Hampden.*

What arrangements they made, or how they settled the *Narragansett's* claim between them, I never knew, but I dare say there was a costly law-suit about it in New Bedford years after.

This was not very encouraging for a start, nor did the next week see us do any better. Several times we saw other ships with whales alongside, but we got no show at all. Now, I had hoped a great deal from our cruise on these grounds, because I had heard whispers of a visit to the icy Sea of Okhotsk, and the prospect was to me a horrible one. I never did take any stock in

Arctic work. But if we made a good season on the Japan grounds, we should not go north, but gradually work down the Pacific again, on the other side, cruising as we went.

Day after day went by without any fresh capture or even sight of fish, until I began to believe that the stories I had heard of the wonderful fecundity of the Coast of Japan waters were fables without foundation, in fact. Had I known what sort of fishing our next bout would be, I should not have been so eager to sight whales again. If this be not a platitude of the worst kind, I don't know the meaning of the word; but, after all, platitudes have their uses, especially when you want to state a fact baldly.

CHAPTER XV.

WHICH COMES UNCOMFORTABLY NEAR BEING THE LAST.

All unversed as I am in the finer shades of literary craftsmanship, there is great uncertainty in my mind whether it is good or bad "art" to anticipate your next chapter by foreshadowing its contents; but whether good or bad art, the remembrance of my miseries on the eventful occasion I wish to describe was so strong upon me as I wrote the last few lines of the previous chapter that I just had to let those few words leak out.

Through all the vicissitudes of this strange voyage I had hitherto felt pretty safe, and as the last thing a man anticipates (if his digestion is all right) is the possibility of coming to grief himself, while fully prepared to see everybody else go under, so I had got to think that whoever got killed I was not to be—a very pleasing sentiment, and one that carries a man far, enabling him to face dangers with a light heart which otherwise would make a nerveless animal of him.

In this optimistic mood, then, I gaily flung myself into my place in the mate's boat one morning, as we were departing in chase of a magnificent cachalot that had been raised just after breakfast. There were no other vessels in sight—much to our satisfaction—the wind was light, with a cloudless sky, and the whale was dead to leeward of us. We sped along at a good rate towards our prospective victim, who was, in his leisurely enjoyment of life, calmly lolling on the surface, occasionally lifting his enormous tail out of water and letting it fall flat upon the surface with a boom audible for miles.

We were, as usual, first boat; but, much to the mate's annoyance, when we were a short half-mile from the whale, our main-sheet parted. It became immediately necessary to roll the sail up, lest its flapping should alarm the watchful monster, and this delayed us sufficiently to allow the other boats to shoot ahead of us. Thus the second mate got fast some seconds before we arrived on the scene, seeing which we furled sail, unshipped the mast, and went in on him with the oars only. At first the proceedings were quite of the usual character, our chief wielding his lance in most brilliant fashion, while not being fast to the animal allowed us much greater freedom in our evolutions; but that fatal habit of the mate's—of allowing his boat to take care of herself so long as he was getting in some good home-thrusts—once more asserted itself. Although the whale was exceedingly vigorous, churning the sea into yeasty foam over an enormous area, there we wallowed close to him, right in the middle of the turmoil, actually courting disaster.

He had just settled down for a moment, when, glancing over the gunwale, I saw his tail, like a vast shadow, sweeping away from us towards the second mate, who was laying off the other side of him. Before I had time to think, the mighty mass of gristle leapt into the sunshine, curved back from us like a huge bow. Then with a roar it came at us, released from its tension of Heaven knows how many tons. Full on the broadside it struck us, sending every soul but me flying out of the wreckage as if fired from catapults. I did not go because my foot was jammed somehow in the well of the boat, but the wrench nearly pulled my thigh-bone out of its socket. I had hardly released my foot, when, towering above me, came the colossal head of the great creature, as he ploughed through the bundle of *débris* that had just been a boat. There was an appalling roar of water in my ears, and darkness that might be felt all around. Yet, in the midst of it all, one thought predominated as clearly as if I had been turning it over in my mind in the quiet of my bunk aboard—"What if he should swallow me?" Nor to this day can I understand how I escaped the portals of his gullet, which of course gaped wide as a church door. But the agony of holding my breath soon overpowered every other feeling and thought, till just as something was going to snap inside my head I rose to the surface. I was surrounded by a welter of bloody froth, which made it impossible for me to see; but oh, the air was sweet!

I struck out blindly, instinctively, although I could feel so strong an eddy that voluntary progress was out of the question. My hand touched and clung to a rope, which immediately towed me in some direction—I neither knew nor cared whither. Soon the motion ceased, and, with a seaman's instinct, I began to haul myself along by the rope I grasped, although no definite idea was in my mind as to where it was attached. Presently I came butt up against something solid, the feel of which gathered all my scattered wits into a compact knub of dread. It was the whale! "Any port in a storm," I murmured, beginning to haul away again on my friendly line. By dint of hard work I pulled myself right up the sloping, slippery bank of blubber, until I reached the iron, which, as luck would have it, was planted in that side of the carcass now uppermost. Carcass I said—well, certainly I had no idea of there being any life remaining within the vast mass beneath me; yet I had hardly time to take a couple of turns round myself with the rope (or whale-line, as I had proved it to be), when I felt the great animal quiver all over; and begin to forge ahead. I was now composed enough to remember that help could not be far away, and that my rescue, providing that I could keep above water, was but a question of a few minutes. But I was hardly prepared for the whale's next move. Being very near his end, the boat, or boats, had drawn off a bit, I supposed, for I could see nothing of them. Then I remembered the flurry. Almost at the same moment it began; and there was I, who with fearful admiration had so often watched the titanic convulsions of a dying cachalot, actually involved in them. The turns were off my body, but I was able to twist a couple of turns round my arms, which, in case of his sounding, I could readily let go.

Then all was lost in roar and rush, as of the heart of some mighty cataract, during which I was sometimes above, sometimes beneath, the water, but always clinging, with every ounce of energy still left, to the line. Now, one thought was uppermost—"What if he should breach?" I had seen them do so when in flurry, leaping full twenty feet in the air. Then I prayed.

Quickly as all the preceding changes had passed came perfect peace. There I lay, still alive, but so weak that, although I could feel the turns slipping off my arms, and knew that I should slide off the slope of the whale's side into the sea if they did, I could make no effort to secure myself. Everything then passed away from me, just as if I had gone to sleep.

I do not at all understand how I kept my position, nor how long, but I awoke to the blessed sound of voices, and saw the second mate's boat alongside. Very gently and tenderly they lifted me into the boat, although I could hardly help screaming with agony when they touched me, so bruised and broken up did I feel. My arms must have been nearly torn from their sockets, for the strands of the whale-line had cut deep into their flesh with the strain upon it, while my thigh was swollen enormously from the blow I received at the onset. Mr. Cruce was the most surprised man I think I ever saw. For full ten minutes he stared at me with wide-open eyes. When at last he spoke, it was with difficulty, as if wanting words to express his astonishment. At last he blurted out, "Whar you bin all de time, ennyhaow? 'Cawse ef you bin hangin' on to dat ar wale ev' sence you boat smash, w'y de debbil you hain't all ter bits, hey?" I smiled feebly, but was too weak to talk, and presently went off again into a dead faint.

When I recovered, I was snug in my bunk aboard, but aching in every joint, and as sore as if I had been pounded with a club until I was bruised all over. During the day Mr. Count was kind enough to pay me a visit. With his usual luck, he had escaped without the slightest injury; neither was any other member of the boat's crew the worse for the ducking but myself. He told me that the whale was one of the largest he had ever seen, and as fat as butter. The boat was an entire loss, so completely smashed to pieces that nothing of her or her gear had been recovered. After spending about a quarter of an hour with me, he left me considerably cheered up, promising to look after me in the way of food, and also to send me some books. He told me that I need not worry myself about my inability to be at work, because the old man was not unfavourably disposed towards me, which piece of news gave me a great deal of comfort.

When my poor, weary shipmates came below from their heavy toil of cutting in, they were almost inclined to be envious of my comfort—small blame to them—though I would gladly have taken my place among them again, could I have got rid of my hurts. But I was condemned to lie there for nearly three weeks before I was able to get about once more. In my sleep I would undergo the horrible anticipation of sliding down that awful, cavernous mouth over again, often waking with a shriek, and drenched with sweat.

While I lay there, three whales were caught, all small cows, and I was informed that the skipper was getting quite disgusted with the luck. At last I managed to get on deck, quite a different-looking man to when I went below, and feeling about ten years older. I found the same sullen quiet reigning that I had noticed several times before when we were unfortunate. I fancied that the skipper looked more morose and savage than ever, though of me, to my great relief, he took not the slightest notice.

The third day after my return to duty we sighted whales again. We lowered three boats as promptly as usual; but when within about half a mile of the "pod" some slight noise in one of the boats gallied them, and away they went in the wind's eye, it blowing a stiffish breeze at the time. It was from the first evidently a hopeless task to chase them, but we persevered until recalled to the ship, dead beat with fatigue. I was not sorry, for my recent adventure seemed to have made quite a coward of me, so much so that an unpleasant gnawing at the pit of my stomach as we neared them almost made me sick. I earnestly hoped that so inconvenient a feeling would speedily leave me, or I should be but a poor creature in a boat.

In passing, I would like to refer to the wonderful way in which these whales realize at a great distance, if the slightest sound be made, the presence of danger. I do not use the word "hear," because so abnormally small are their organs of hearing, the external opening being quite difficult to find, that I do not believe they *can* hear at all well. But I firmly believe they possess another sense by means of which they are able to detect any unusual vibration of the waves of either air or sea at a far greater distance than it would be possible for them to hear. Whatever this power may be which they possess, all whalemen are well acquainted with their exercise of it, and always take most elaborate precautions to render their approach to a whale noiseless.

Our extraordinary want of success at last so annoyed the skipper that he determined to quit the ground and go north. The near approach of the open season in those regions probably hastened his decision, but I learned from Goliath that he had always been known as a most fortunate man among the "bowheads," as the great *Mysticetæ* of that part of the Arctic seas are called by the Americans. Not that there is any difference, as far as I have been able to ascertain, between them and the "right" whale of the Greenland seas, but from some caprice of nomenclature for which there is no accounting.

So in leisurely fashion we worked north, keeping, of course, a bright look-out all the way for straggling cachalots, but not seeing any. From scraps of information that in some mysterious fashion leaked out, we learned that we were bound to the Okhotsk Sea, it being no part of the skipper's intentions to go prowling around Behrings Sea, where he believed the whales to be few and far between.

It may be imagined that we of the crew were not at all pleased with this intelligence, our life being, we considered, sufficiently miserable without the addition of extreme cold; for we did not realize that in the Arctic regions during summer the cold is by no means unbearable, and our imagination pictured a horrible waste of perpetual ice and snow, in the midst of which we should be compelled to freeze while dodging whales through the crevices of the floes. But whether our pictures of the prospects that awaited us were caricatures or no made not the slightest difference. "Growl you may, but go you must" is an old sea-jingle of the truest ring; but, while our going was inevitable, growling was a luxury none of us dare indulge in.

We had by no means a bad passage to the Kuriles, which form a natural barrier enclosing the immense area of the Okhotsk Sea from the vast stretch of the Pacific. Around this great chain of islands the navigation is exceedingly difficult, and dangerous as well, from the ever-varying currents as from the frequent fogs and sudden storms. But these impediments to swift and safe navigation are made light of by the whalemen, who, as I feel never weary of remarking, are the finest navigators in the world where speed is not the first consideration.

The most peculiar features of these inhospitable shores to a seaman are the vast fields of seaweed surrounding them all, which certainly helps to keep the sea down during gales, but renders navigation most difficult on account of its concealment of hidden dangers. These islands are aptly named, the word "Kurile" being Kamschatkan for smoke; and whether it be regarded as given in consequence of the numerous volcanoes which pour their fumes into the air, or the all-prevailing fog fostered by the Kuro Siwo, or Japanese counterpart of the Gulf stream, the designation is equally appropriate.

We entered the Okhotsk Sea by the Nadeshda Channel, so-named after Admiral Krusenstern's ship, which was the first civilized vessel that passed through its turbulent waters. It separates the islands Rashau and Mataua by about twenty miles, yet so conflicting and violent are the currents which eddy and swirl in all parts of it, that without a steady, strong fair wind it is most dangerous to a sailing vessel. Thenceforward the navigation was free from difficulty, or at least none that we could recognize as such, so we gave all our attention to the business which brought us there.

Scarcely any change was needed in our equipment, except the substitution of longer harpoons for those we had been using, and the putting away of the bomb-guns. These changes were made because the blubber of the bowhead is so thick that ordinary harpoons will not penetrate beyond it to the muscle, which, unless they do, renders them liable to draw, upon a heavy strain. As for the bombs, Yankees hold the mysticetæ in such supreme contempt that none of them would dream of wasting so expensive a weapon as a bomb upon them. I was given to understand by my constant crony, Mistah Jones, that there was no more trouble in killing a bowhead than in slaughtering a sheep; and that while it was quite true that accidents *did* occur, they were entirely due to the carelessness or clumsiness of the whalemen, and not in any way traceable to a desire on the victim's part to do any one harm.

The sea was little encumbered with ice, it being now late in June, so that our progress was not at all impeded by the few soft, brashy floes that we encountered, none of them hard enough to do a ship's hull any damage. In most places the sea was sufficiently shallow to permit of our anchoring. For this purpose we used a large kedge, with stout hawser for cable, never furling all the sails in case of a strong breeze suddenly springing up, which would cause us to drag. This anchoring was very comfortable. Besides allowing us to get much more rest than when on other cruising-grounds, we were able to catch enormous quantities of fish, mostly salmon, of which there were no less than fourteen varieties. So plentiful were these splendid fish that we got quite critical in our appreciation of them, very soon finding that one kind, known as the "nerker," was far better flavoured than any of the others. But as the daintiest food palls the quickest, it was not long before we got tired of salmon, and wished most heartily for beef.

Much fun has been made of the discontent of sailors with food which is considered a luxury ashore, and wonder expressed that if, as we assert, the ordinary dietary of the seaman be so bad, he should be so ready to rebel when fed with delicacies. But in justice to the sailor, it ought to be remembered that the daintiest food may be rendered disgusting by bad cookery, such as is the rule on board merchant ships. "God sends meat, but the devil sends cooks" is a proverb which originated on board ship, and no one who has ever served any time in a ship's forecastle would deny that it is abundantly justified. Besides which, even good food well cooked of one kind only, served many times in succession, becomes very trying, only the plainest foods, such as bread, rice, potatoes, etc., retaining their command of the appetite continually.

I remember once, when upon the Coromandel coast in a big Greenock ship, we found fowls very cheap. At Bimliapatam the captain bought two or three hundred, which, as we had no coops, were turned loose on deck. We had also at the same time prowling about the decks three goats, twenty pigs, and two big dogs.

Consequently the state of the ship was filthy, nor could all our efforts keep her clean. This farmyard condition of things was permitted to continue for about a week, when the officers got so tired of it, and the captain so annoyed at the frequent loss of fowls by their flying overboard, that the edict went forth to feed the foremast hands on poultry till further orders. Great was our delight at the news. Fowl for dinner represented to our imagination almost the apex of high living, only indulged in by such pampered children of fortune as the officers of ships or well-to-do people ashore.

When dinner-time arrived, we boys made haste to the galley with watering mouths, joyfully anticipating that rare delight of the sailor—a good "feed." The cook uncovered his coppers, plunged his tormentors therein, and produced such a succession of ugly corpses of fowls as I had never seen before. To each man a whole one was allotted, and we bore the steaming hecatomb into the forecastle. The boisterous merriment became hushed at our approach, and faces grew lengthy when the unwholesome aspect of the "treat" was revealed. Each man secured his bird, and commenced operations. But oh, the disappointment, *and* the bad words! What little flesh there was upon the framework of those unhappy fowls was like leather itself, and utterly flavourless. It could not well have been otherwise. The feathers had been simply scalded off, the heads chopped off, and bodies split open to facilitate drawing (I am sure I wonder the cook took the trouble to do that much), and thus prepared they were cast into a cauldron of boiling salt water. There, with the water fiercely bubbling, they were kept for an hour and a half, then pitchforked out into the mess kid and set before us. We simply could not eat them; no one but a Noumean Kanaka could, for his teeth are equal to husking a cocoa-nut, or chopping off a piece of sugar-cane as thick as your wrist.

After much heated discussion, it was unanimously resolved to protest at once against the substitution of such a fraud as this poultry for our legitimate rations of "salt horse." So, bearing the *disjecta membra* of our meal, the whole crowd marched aft, and requested an interview with the skipper. He came out of the cabin at once, saying, "Well, boys, what's the matter?" The spokesman, a bald-headed Yankee, who had been bo'sun's mate of an American man-of-war, stepped forward and said, offering his kid, "Jest have a look at that, sir." The skipper looked, saying, inquiringly, "Well?"

"D'yew think, sir," said Nat, "*thet's* proper grub for men?" "Proper grub! Why, you old sinner, you don't mean to say you're goin' to growl about havin' chicken for dinner?" "Well, sir, it depends muchly upon the chicken. All I know is, that I've et some dam queer tack in my time, but sence I ben fishin' I never had no such bundles of sticks parcelled with leather served out to me. I *hev* et boot—leastways gnawed it when I was cast away in a open boat for three weeks—but it wa'n't bad boot, as boots go. Now, if yew say that these things is boots, en thet it's necessary we should eat 'em, or starve, w'y, we'll think about it. But if yew call 'em chickens, 'n say you're doin' us a kindness by stoppin' our 'lowance of meat wile we're wrastlin' with em, then we say we don't feel obliged to yew, 'n 'll thank yew kindly to keep such lugsuries for yerself, 'n give us wot we signed for." A murmur of assent confirmed this burst of eloquence, which we all considered a very fine effort indeed. A moment's silence ensued; then the skipper burst out, "I've often heard of such things, but hang me if I ever believed 'em till now! You ungrateful beggars! I'll see you get your whack, and no more, from this out. When you get any little extras aboard this ship agen, you'll be thankful for 'em; now I tell you." "All right, sir," said Nat; "so long as we don't hev to chaw any more of yer biled Bimly crows, I dessay we shall worry along as usual." And, as the Parliamentary reports say, the proceedings then terminated.

Now, suppose the skipper had told that story to some of his shore friends, how very funny the sailors' conduct would have been made to appear.

On another occasion long after, when I was mate of a barque loading mahogany in Tonala, Mexico, the skipper thought he would practise economy by buying a turtle instead of beef. A large turtle was obtained for twenty-five cents, and handed over to the cook to be dealt with, particular instructions being given him as to the apportionment of the meat.

At eight bells there was a gathering of the men in front of the poop, and a summons for the captain. When he appeared, the usual stereotyped invitation to "have a look at *that*, if you please, sir," was uttered. The skipper was, I think, prepared for a protest, for he began to bluster immediately. "Look here!" he bawled, "I ain't goin' to 'ave any of your dam nonsense. You *want* somethin' *to* growl about, you do." "Well, Cap'n George," said one of the men, "you shorely don't think we k'n eat shells, do yer?" Just then I caught sight of the kid's contents, and could hardly restrain my indignation. For in a dirty heap, the sight of which might have pleased an Esquimaux, but was certainly enough to disgust any civilized man, lay the calipee, or undershell of the turtle, hacked into irregular blocks. It had been simply boiled, and flung into the kid, an unclean, disgusting heap of shell, with pieces of dirty flesh attached in ragged lumps. But the skipper, red-faced and angry, answered, "W'y, yer so-and-so ijits, that's wot the Lord Mayor of London gives about a guinea a hounce for w'en 'e feeds lords n' dooks. Only the haristocracy at 'ome get a charnce to stick their teeth in such grub as that. An' 'ere are you lot a-growlin' at 'avin' it for a change!" "That's all right, cap'n," said the man; "bein' brort up ter such lugsuries, of corse *you* kin appreshyate it. So if yer keep it fer yer own eatin', an' giv us wot we signed for, we shall be werry much obliged." "Now, I ain't a-goin' to 'ave none o' *your* cheek, so you'd better git forrard. You can betcher life you won't get no more fresh messes this voy'ge." So, with grumbling and ill-will on both sides, the conference came to an end. But I thought, and still think, that the mess set before those men, who had been working hard since six a.m., was unfit for the food of a good dog.

Out of my own experience I might give many other instances of the kind, but I hope these will suffice to show that Jack's growling is often justified, when both sides of the story are heard.

CHAPTER XVI.

"BOWHEAD" FISHING.

DAY and night being now only distinguishable by the aid of the clock, a constant look-out aloft was kept all through the twenty-four hours, watch and watch, but whales were apparently very scarce. We did a good deal of "pelagic" sealing; that is, catching seals swimming. But the total number obtained was not great, for these creatures are only gregarious when at their rocky haunts during the breeding season, or among the ice just before that season begins. Our sealing, therefore, was only a way of passing the time in the absence of nobler game, to be abandoned at once with whales in sight.

It was on the ninth or tenth morning after our arrival on the grounds that a bowhead was raised, and two boats sent after him. It was my first sight of the great *Mysticetus*, and I must confess to being much impressed by his gigantic bulk. From the difference in shape, he looked much larger than the largest sperm whale we had yet seen, although we had come across some of the very biggest specimens of cachalot.

The contrast between the two animals is most marked, so much so, in fact, that one would hardly credit them with belonging to the same order. Popular ideas of the whale are almost invariably taken from the *Mysticetus*, so that the average individual generally defines a whale as a big fish which spouts water out of the top of his head, and cannot swallow a herring. Indeed, so lately as last year a popular M.P., writing to one of the religious papers, allowed himself to say that "science will not hear of a whale with a gullet capable of admitting anything larger than a man's fist"—a piece of crass ignorance, which is also perpetrated in the appendix to a very widely-distributed edition of the Authorized Version of the Bible. This opinion, strangely enough, is almost universally held, although I trust that the admirable models now being shown in our splendid Natural History Museum at South Kensington will do much to remove it. Not so many people, perhaps, believe that a whale is a fish, instead of a mammal, but few indeed are the individuals who do not still think that a cetacean possesses a sort of natural fountain on the top of its head, whence, for some recondite reason, it ejects at regular intervals streams of water into the air.

But a whale can no more force water through its spiracle or blow-hole than you or I through our nostrils. It inhales, when at the surface, atmospheric air, and exhales breath like ours, which, coming warm into a cooler medium, becomes visible, as does our breath on a frosty morning.

Now, the *Mysticetus* carries his nostrils on the summit of his head, or crown, the orifice being closed by a beautifully-arranged valve when the animal is beneath the water. Consequently, upon coming to the surface to breathe, he sends up a jet of visible breath into the air some ten or twelve feet. The cachalot, on the other hand, has the orifice at the point of his square snout, the internal channel running in a slightly diagonal direction downwards, and back through the skull to the lungs. So when *he* spouts, the breath is projected forward diagonally, and, from some peculiarity which I do not pretend to explain, expends itself in a short, bushy tuft of vapour, very distinct from the tall vertical spout of the bowhead or right whale.

There was little or no wind when we sighted the individual I am now speaking of, so we did not attempt to set sail, but pulled straight for him "head and head." Strange as it may appear, the *Mysticetus*' best point of view is right behind, or "in his wake," as we say; it is therefore part of the code to approach him from right ahead, in which direction he cannot see at all. Some time before we reached him he became aware of our presence, showing by his uneasy actions that he had his doubts about his personal security. But before he had made up his mind what to do we were upon him, with our harpoons buried in his back. The difference in his behaviour to what we had so long been accustomed to was amazing. He did certainly give a lumbering splash or two with his immense flukes, but no one could possibly have been endangered by them. The water was so shallow that when he sounded it was but for a very few minutes; there was no escape for him that way. As soon as he returned to the surface he set off at his best gait, but that was so slow that we easily hauled up close alongside of him, holding the boats in that position without the slightest attempt to guard ourselves from reprisals on his part, while the officers searched his vitals with the lances as if they were probing a haystack.

Really, the whole affair was so tame that it was

impossible to get up any fighting enthusiasm over it; the poor, unwieldy creature died meekly and quietly as an overgrown seal. In less than an hour from the time of leaving the ship we were ready to bring our prize alongside.

Upon coming up to the whale, sail was shortened, and as soon as the fluke-chain was passed we anchored. It was, I heard, our skipper's boast that he could "skin a bowhead in forty minutes;" and although we were certainly longer than that, the celerity with which what seemed a gigantic task was accomplished was marvellous. Of course, it was all plain-sailing, very unlike the complicated and herculean task inevitable at the commencement of cutting-in a sperm whale.

Except for the head work, removing the blubber was effected in precisely the same way as in the case of the cachalot. There was a marked difference between the quantity of lard enveloping this whale and those we had hitherto dealt with. It was nearly double the thickness, besides being much richer in oil, which fairly dripped from it as we hoisted in the blanket-pieces. The upper jaw was removed for its long plates of whalebone or baleen—that valuable substance which alone makes it worth while nowadays to go after the *Mysticetus*, the price obtained for the oil being so low as to make it not worth while to fit out ships to go in search of it alone. "Trying-out" the blubber, with its accompaniments, is carried on precisely as with the sperm whale. The resultant oil, when recent, is of a clear white, unlike the golden-tinted fluid obtained from the cachalot. As it grows stale it developes a nauseous smell, which sperm does not, although the odour of the oil is otto of roses compared with the horrible mass of putridity landed from the tanks of a Greenland whaler at the termination of a cruise. For in those vessels, the fishing-time at their disposal being so brief, they do not wait to boil down the blubber, but, chopping it into small pieces, pass it below as it is into tanks, to be rendered down by the oil-mills ashore on the ship's return.

This first bowhead yielded us eighteen tuns of oil and a ton of baleen, which made the catch about equal in value to that of a seven-tun cachalot. But the amount of labour and care necessary in order to thoroughly dry and cleanse the baleen was enormous; in fact, for months after we began the bowhead fishery there was almost always something being done with the wretched stuff—drying, scraping, etc.—which, as it was kept below, also necessitated hoisting it up on deck and getting it down again.

After this beginning, it was again a considerable time before we sighted any more; but when we did, there were quite a number of them—enough to employ all the boats with one each. I was out of the fun this time, being almost incapable of moving by reason of several boils on my legs—the result, I suppose, of a long abstinence from fresh vegetables, or anything to supply their place.

As it happened, however, I lost no excitement by remaining on board; for while all the boats were away a large bowhead rose near the ship, evidently being harassed in some way by enemies, which I could not at first see. He seemed quite unconscious of his proximity to the ship, though, and at last came so near that the whole performance was as visible as if it had been got up for my benefit. Three "killers" were attacking him at once, like wolves worrying a bull.

except that his motions were far less lively than those of any bull would have been.

The "killer," or *Orca gladiator*, is a true whale, but, like the cachalot, has teeth. He differs from that great cetacean, though, in a most important particular; *i.e.* by having a complete set in both upper and lower jaws, like any other carnivore. For a carnivore indeed is he, the very wolf of the ocean, and enjoying, by reason of his extraordinary agility as well as comparative worthlessness commercially, complete immunity from attack by man. By some authorities he is thought to be identical with the grampus, but whalers all consider the animals quite distinct. Not having had very long acquaintance with them both, I cannot speak emphatically upon this difference of opinion; so far as personal observation goes, I agree with the whalers in believing that there is much variation both of habits and shape between them.

But to return to the fight. The first inkling I got of what was really going on was the leaping of a killer high into the air by the side of the whale, and descending upon the victim's broad, smooth back with a resounding crash. I saw that the killer was provided with a pair of huge fins—one on his back, the other on his belly—which at first sight looked as if they were also weapons of offence. A little observation convinced me that they were fins only. Again and again the aggressor leaped into the air, falling each time on the whale's back, as if to beat him into submission.

The sea around foamed and boiled like a cauldron, so that it was only occasional glimpses I was able to catch of the two killers, until presently the worried whale lifted his head clear out of the surrounding smother, revealing the two furies hanging—one on either side—

to his lips, as if endeavouring to drag his mouth open — which I afterwards saw was their principal object, as whenever during the tumult I caught sight of them, they were still in the same position. At last the tremendous and incessant blows, dealt by the most active member of the trio, seemed actually to have exhausted the immense vitality of the great bowhead, for he lay supine upon the surface. Then the three joined their forces, and succeeded in dragging open his cavernous mouth, into which they freely entered, devouring his tongue. This, then, had been their sole object, for as soon as they had finished their barbarous feast they departed, leaving him helpless and dying to fall an easy prey to our returning boats.

Thus, although the four whales captured by the boats had been but small, the day's take, augmented by so great a find, was a large one, and it was a long time before we got clear of the work it entailed.

From that time forward we saw no whales for six weeks, and, from the reports we received from two whalers we "gammed," it appeared that we might consider ourselves most fortunate in our catch, since they, who had been longer on the ground than ourselves, had only one whale apiece.

In consequence of this information, Captain Slocum decided to go south again, and resume the sperm whaling in the North Pacific, near the line—at least so the rumour ran; but as we never heard anything definitely, we could not feel at all certain of our next destination.

Ever since the fracas at the Bonins between Goliath and his watch, the relations between Captain Slocum and the big negro had been very strained. Even before the outbreak, as I have remarked upon one occasion, it was noticeable that little love was lost between them. Why this was so, without anything definite to guide one's reasoning, was difficult to understand, for a better seaman or a smarter whaleman than Mistah Jones did not live—of that every one was quite sure. Still, there was no gainsaying the fact that, churlish and morose as our skipper's normal temper always was, he was never so much so as in his behaviour towards his able fourth mate, who, being a man of fine, sensitive temper, chafed under his unmerited treatment so much as to lose flesh, becoming daily more silent, nervous, and depressed. Still, there had never been an open rupture, nor did it appear as if there would be, so great was the power Captain Slocum possessed over the will of everybody on board.

One night, however, as we were nearing the Kuriles again, on our way south, leaving the Sea of Okhotsk, I was sitting on the fore side of the try-works alone, meditating upon what I would do when once I got clear of this miserable business. Futile and foolish, no doubt, my speculations were, but only in this way could I forget for awhile my surroundings, since the inestimable comfort of reading was denied me. I had been sitting thus absorbed in thought for nearly an hour, when Goliath came and seated himself by my side. We had always been great friends, although, owing to the strict discipline maintained on board, it was not often we got a chance for a "wee bit crack," as the Scotch say. Besides, I was not in his watch, and even now he should rightly have been below. He sat for a minute or two silent; then, as if compelled to speak, he began in low, fierce whispers to tell me of his miserable state of mind. At last, after recapitulating many slights and insults he had received silently from the captain, of which I had previously known nothing, he became strangely calm. In tones quite unlike his usual voice, he said that he was not an American-born negro, but a pure African, who had been enslaved in his infancy, with his mother, somewhere in the "Hinterland" of Guinea. While still a child, his mother escaped with him into Liberia, where he had remained till her death. She was, according to him, an Obeah woman of great power, venerated exceedingly by her own people for her prophetic abilities. Before her death, she had told him that he would die suddenly, violently, in a struggle with a white man in a far-off country, but that the white man would die too by his hand. She had also told him that he would be a great traveller and hunter upon the sea. As he went on, his speech became almost unintelligible, being mingled with fragments of a language I had never heard before; moreover, he spoke as a man who is only half awake. A strange terror got hold of me, for I began to think he was going mad, and perhaps about to run a-mok, as the Malays do when driven frantic by the infliction of real or fancied wrongs.

But he gradually returned to his old self, to my great relief, and I ventured somewhat timidly to remind him of the esteem in which he was held by all hands; even the skipper, I ventured to say, respected him, although, from some detestable form of ill-humour, he had chosen to be so sneering and insulting towards him. He shook his head sadly, and said, "My dear boy, youse de only man aboard dis ship—wite man, dat is—dat don't hate an' despise me becawse ob my colour, wich *I* cain't he'p; an' de God you beliebe in bless you fer dat. As fer me, w'at I done tole you's true, 'n befo' bery little w'ile you see it *come* true. 'N w'en *dat* happens w'at's gwine ter happen, I'se real glad to tink it gwine ter be better fer you—gwine ter be better fer eberybody 'bord de *Cach'lot;* but I doan keer nuffin 'bout anybody else. So long." He held out his great black hand, and shook mine heartily, while a big tear rolled down his face and fell on the deck. And with that he left me a prey to a very whirlpool of conflicting thoughts and fears.

The night was a long and weary one—longer and drearier perhaps because of the absence of the darkness, which always made it harder to sleep. An incessant day soon becomes, to those accustomed to the relief of the night, a burden grievous to be borne; and although use can reconcile us to most things, and does make even the persistent light bearable, in times of mental distress or great physical weariness one feels irresistibly moved to cry earnestly, "Come, gentle night."

When I came on deck at eight bells, it was a stark calm. The watch, under Mistah Jones' direction, were busy scrubbing decks with the usual thoroughness, while the captain, bare-footed, with trouser-legs and shirt-sleeves rolled up, his hands on his hips and a portentous frown on his brow, was closely looking on. As it was my spell at the crow's-nest, I made at once for the main-rigging, and had got halfway to the top, when some unusual sounds below arrested me.

All hands were gathered in the waist, a not unusual thing at the changing of the watch. In the midst of them, as I looked down, two men came together in a fierce struggle. They were Goliath and the skipper. Captain Slocum's right hand went naturally to his hip pocket, where he always carried a revolver; but before he could draw it, the long, black arms of his adversary wrapped around him, making him helpless as a babe. Then, with a rush that sent every one flying out of his way, Goliath hurled himself at the bulwarks, which were low, the top of the rail about thirty-three inches from the deck. The two bodies struck the rail with a heavy thud, instantly toppling overboard. That broke the spell that bound everybody, so that there was an instantaneous rush to the side. Only a hardly noticeable ripple remained on the surface of the placid sea.

But, from my lofty perch, the whole of the ghastly struggle had been visible to the least detail. The two men had struck the water locked in closest embrace, which relaxed not even when far below the surface. When the sea is perfectly smooth, objects are visible from aloft at several feet depth, though apparently diminished in size. The last thing I saw was Captain Slocum's white face, with its starting black eyes looking their last upon the huge, indefinite hull of the ship whose occupants he had ruled so long and rigidly.

The whole tragedy occupied such a brief moment of time that it was almost impossible to realize that it was actual. Reason, however, soon regained her position among the officers, who ordered the closest watch to be kept from aloft, in case of the rising of either or both of the men. A couple of boats were swung, ready to drop on the instant. But, as if to crown the tragedy with completeness, a heavy squall, which had risen unnoticed, suddenly burst upon the ship with great fury, the lashing hail and rain utterly obscuring vision even for a few yards. So unexpected was the onset of this squall that, for the only time that voyage, we lost some canvas through not being able to get it in quick enough. The topgallant halyards were let go; but while the sails were being clewed up, the fierce wind following the rain caught them from their confining gear, rending them into a thousand shreds. For an hour the squall raged—a tempest in brief—then swept away to the south-east on its furious journey, leaving peace again. Needless perhaps to say, that after such a squall it was hopeless to look for our missing ones. The sudden storm had certainly driven us several miles away from the spot where they disappeared, and, although we carefully made what haste was possible back along the line we were supposed to have come, not a vestige of hope was in any one's mind that we should ever see them again.

Nor did we. Whether that madness, which I had feared was coming upon Goliath during our previous night's conversation, suddenly overpowered him and impelled him to commit the horrible deed, what more had passed between him and the skipper to even faintly justify so awful a retaliation—these things were now matters of purest speculation. As if they had never been, the two men were blotted out—gone before God in full-blown heat of murder and revengeful fury.

On the same evening Mr. Count mustered all hands on the quarter-deck, and addressed us thus: "Men, Captain Slocum is dead, and, as a consequence, I command the ship. Behave yourself like men, not presuming upon kindness or imagining that I am a weak, vacillating old man with whom you can do as you like, and you will find in me a skipper who will do his duty by you as far as lies in his power, nor expect more from you than you ought to render. If, however, you *do* try any tricks, remember that I am an old hand, equal to most of the games that men get up to. I do want—if you will help me—to make this a comfortable as well as a successful ship. I hope with all my heart we shall succeed."

In answer to this manly and affecting little speech, which confirmed my previous estimate of Captain Count's character, were he but free to follow the bent of his natural, kindly inclinations, and which I have endeavoured to translate out of his usual dialect, a hearty cheer was raised by all hands, the first ebullition of general good feeling manifested throughout the voyage. Hearts rose joyfully at the prospect of comfort to be gained by thoughtfulness on the part of the commander; nor from that time forward did any sign of weariness of the ship or voyage show itself among us, either on deck or below.

The news soon spread among us that, in consequence of the various losses of boats and gear, the captain deemed it necessary to make for Honolulu, where fresh supplies could readily be obtained. We had heard many glowing accounts from visitors, when "gamming," of the delights of this well-known port of call for whalers, and under our new commander we had little doubt that we should be allowed considerable liberty during our stay. So we were quite impatient to get along, fretting considerably at the persistent fogs which prevented our making much progress while in the vicinity of the Kuriles. But we saw no more bowheads, for which none of us forward were at all sorry. We had got very tired of the stink of their blubber, and the never-ending worry connected with the preservation of the baleen; besides, we had not yet accumulated any fund of enthusiasm about getting a full ship, except as a reason for shortening the voyage, and we quite understood that what black oil we had got would be landed at Hawaii, so that our visit to the Okhotsk Sea, with its resultant store of oil, had not really brought our return home any nearer, as we at first hoped it would.

A great surprise was in store for me. I knew that Captain Count was favourably inclined towards me, for he had himself told me so, but nothing was further from my thoughts than promotion. However, one Sunday afternoon, when we were all peacefully enjoying the unusual rest (we had no Sundays in Captain Slocum's time), the captain sent for me. He informed me that, after mature consideration, he had chosen me to fill the vacancy made by the death of Mistah Jones. Mr. Cruce was now mate; the waspish little third had become second; Louis Silva, the captain's favourite harpooner, was third; and I was to be fourth. Not feeling at all sure of how the other harpooners would take my stepping over their heads, I respectfully demurred to the compliment offered me, stating my reasons. But the captain said he had fully made up his mind, after consultation with the other officers, and that I need have no apprehension on the score of the harpooners' jealousy; that they had been spoken to on the subject, and they were all agreed that the captain's choice was the best, especially as none of them knew anything of navigation, or could write their own names.

In consequence of there being none of the crew fit to take a harpooner's place, I was now really harpooner of the captain's boat, which he would continue to work, when necessary, until we were able to ship a harpooner, which he hoped to do at Hawaii.

The news of my promotion was received in grim silence by the Portuguese forward, but the white men all seemed pleased. This was highly gratifying to me, for I had tried my best to be helpful to all, as far as my limited abilities would let me; nor do I think I had an enemy in the ship. Behold me, then, a full-blown "mister," with a definite substantial increase in my prospects of pay of nearly one-third, in addition to many other advantages, which, under the new captain, promised exceedingly well.

More than half the voyage lay behind us, looking like the fast-settling bank of storm-clouds hovering above the tempest-tossed sea so lately passed, while ahead the bright horizon was full of promise of fine weather for the remainder of the journey.

CHAPTER XVII.

VISIT TO HONOLULU.

RIGHT glad were we all when, after much fumbling and box-hauling about, we once more felt the long, familiar roll of the Pacific swell, and saw the dim fastnesses of the smoky islands fading into the lowering gloom astern. Most deep-water sailors are familiar, by report if not by actual contact, with the beauties of the Pacific islands, and I had often longed to visit them to see for myself whether the half that had been told me was true. Of course, to a great number of seafaring men, the loveliness of those regions counts for nothing, their desirability being founded upon the frequent opportunities of unlimited indulgence in debauchery. To such men, a "missionary" island is a howling wilderness, and the missionaries themselves the subjects of the vilest abuse as well as the most boundless lying.

No one who has travelled with his eyes open would assert that all missionaries were wise, prudent, or even godly men; while it is a great deal to be regretted that so much is made of hardships which in a large proportion of cases do not exist, the men who are supposed to be enduring them being immensely better off and more comfortable than they would ever have been at home. Undoubtedly the pioneers of missionary enterprise had, almost without exception, to face dangers and miseries past telling, but that is the portion of pioneers in general. In these days, however, the missionary's lot in Polynesia is not often a hard one, and in many cases it is infinitely to be preferred to a life among the very poor of our great cities.

But when all has been said that can be said against the missionaries, the solid bastion of fact remains that, in consequence of their labours, the whole vile character of the populations of the Pacific has been changed, and where wickedness runs riot to-day, it is due largely to the hindrances placed in the way of the noble efforts of the missionaries by the unmitigated scoundrels who vilify them. The task of spreading Christianity would not, after all, be so difficult were it not for the efforts of those apostles of the devil to keep the islands as they would like them to be—places where lust runs riot day and night, murder may be done with impunity, slavery flourishes, and all evil may be indulged in free from law, order, or restraint.

It speaks volumes for the inherent might of the Gospel that, in spite of the object-lessons continually provided for the natives by white men of the negation of all good, that it has stricken its roots so deeply into the soil of the Pacific islands. Just as the best proof of the reality of the Gospel here in England is that it survives the incessant assaults upon it from within by its professors, by those who are paid, and highly paid, to propagate it, by the side of whose deadly doings the efforts of so-called infidels are but as the battery of a summer breeze; so in Polynesia, were not the principles of Christianity vital with an immortal and divine life, missionary efforts might long ago have ceased in utter despair at the fruitlessness of the field.

We were enjoying a most uneventful passage, free from any serious changes either of wind or weather, which quiet time was utilized to the utmost in making many much-needed additions to running gear, repairing rigging, etc. Any work involving the use of new material had been put off from time to time during the previous part of the voyage till the ship aloft was really in a dangerous condition. This was due entirely to the peculiar parsimony of our late skipper, who could scarcely bring himself to broach a coil of rope, except for whaling purposes. The same false economy had prevailed with regard to paint and varnish, so that the vessel, while spotlessly clean, presented a worn-out, weather-beaten appearance. Now, while the condition of life on board was totally different to what it had been, as regards comfort and peace, discipline and order were maintained at the same high level as always, though by a different method—in fact, I believe that a great deal more work was actually done, certainly much more that was useful and productive; for Captain Count hated, as much as any foremast hand among us, the constant, remorseless grind of iron-work polishing, paint-work scrubbing, and holystoning, all of which, though necessary in a certain degree, when kept up continually for the sole purpose of making work—a sort of elaborated tread-mill, in fact—becomes the refinement of cruelty to underfed, unpaid, and hopeless men.

So, while the *Cachalot* could have fearlessly challenged comparison with any ship afloat for cleanliness and neatness of appearance, the hands no longer felt that they were continually being "worked up" or "hazed" for the sole, diabolical satisfaction of keeping them "at it." Of course, the incidence of the work was divided, since so many of the crew were quite unable to do any sailorizing, as we term work in sails and rigging. Upon them, then, fell all the common labour, which can be done by any unskilled man or woman afloat or ashore.

Of this work a sailor's duties are largely made up, but when good people ashore wonder "whatever sailors do with their time," it would be useful for them to remember that a ship is a huge and complicated machine, needing constant repairs, which can only be efficiently performed by skilled workmen. An "A.B." or able seaman's duties are legally supposed to be defined by the three expressions, "hand, reef, and steer." If he can do those three things, which mean furling or making fast sails, reefing them, and steering the ship, his wages cannot be reduced for incompetency. Yet these things are the A B C of seamanship only. A good *seaman* is able to make all the various knots, splices, and other arrangements in hempen or wire rope, without which a ship cannot be rigged; he can make a sail, send up or down yards and masts, and do many other things, the sum total of which need several years of steady application to learn, although a good seaman is ever learning.

Such seamen are fast becoming extinct. They are almost totally unnecessary in steamships, except when the engines break down in a gale of wind, and the crowd of navvies forming the crew stand looking at one another when called upon to set sail or do any other job aloft. *Then* the want of seamen is rather severely felt. But even in sailing ships—the great, overgrown tanks of two thousand tons and upwards—mechanical genius has utilized iron to such an extent in their rigging that sailor-work has become very largely a matter of blacksmithing. I make no complaint of this, not believing that the "old was better;" but, since the strongest fabric of man's invention comes to grief sometimes in conflict with the irresistible sea, some provision should be made for having a sufficiency of seamen who could exercise their skill in refitting a dismasted ship or temporarily replacing broken blacksmith work by old-fashioned rope and wood.

But, as the sailing ship is doomed inevitably to disappear before steam, perhaps it does not matter much. The economic march of the world's progress will never be stayed by sentimental considerations, nor will all the romance and poetry in the world save the seaman from extinction, if his place can be more profitably filled by the engineer. From all appearances, it soon will be, for even now marine superintendents of big lines are sometimes engineers, and in their hands lie the duty of engaging the officers. It would really seem as if the ship of the near future would be governed by the chief engineer, under whose direction a pilot or sailing-master would do the necessary navigation, without power to interfere in any matter of the ship's economy. Changes as great have taken place in other professions; seafaring cannot hope to be the sole exception.

So, edging comfortably along, we gradually neared the Sandwich Islands without having seen a single spout worth watching since the tragedy. At last the lofty summits of the island mountains hove in sight, and presently we came to an anchor in that paradise of whalers, missionaries, and amateur statesmen—Honolulu. As it is as well known to most reading people as our own ports—better, perhaps—I shall not attempt to describe it, or pit myself against the able writers who have made it so familiar. Yet to me it was a new world. All things were so strange, so delightful, especially the lovable, lazy, fascinating Kanakas, who could be so limply happy over a dish of poë, or a green cocoa-nut, or even a lounge in the sun, that it seemed an outrage to expect them to work. In their sports they could be energetic enough. I do not know of any more delightful sight than to watch them bathing in the tremendous surf, simply intoxicated with the joy of living, as unconscious of danger as if swinging in a hammock while riding triumphantly upon the foaming summit of an incoming breaker twenty feet high, or plunging with a cataract over the dizzy edge of its cliff, swallowed up in the hissing vortex below, only to reappear with a scream of riotous laughter in the quiet eddy beyond.

As far as I could judge, they were the happiest of people, literally taking no thought for the morrow, and content with the barest necessaries of life, so long as they were free and the sun shone brightly. We had many opportunities of cultivating their acquaintance, for the captain allowed us much liberty, quite one-half of the crew and officers being ashore most of the time. Of course, the majority spent all their spare time in the purlieus of the town, which, like all such places anywhere, were foul and filthy enough; but that was their own faults. I have often wondered much to see men, who on board ship were the pink of cleanliness and neatness, fastidious to a fault in all they did, come ashore and huddle in the most horrible of kennels, among the very dregs and greaves of the 'long-shore district. It certainly wants a great deal of explanation; but I suppose the most potent reason is, that sailors, as a class, never learn to enjoy themselves rationally. They are also morbidly suspicious of being taken in hand by anybody who would show them anything worth seeing, preferring to be led by the human sharks that infest all seaports into ways of strange nastiness, and so expensive withal that one night of such wallowing often costs them more than a month's sane recreation and good food would. All honour to the devoted men and women who labour in our seaports for the moral and material benefit of the sailor, passing their lives amidst sights and sounds shocking and sickening to the last degree, reviled, unthanked, unpaid. Few are the missionaries abroad whose lot is so hard as theirs.

We spent ten happy days in Honolulu, marred only by one or two drunken rows among the chaps forward, which, however, resulted in their getting a severe dressing-down in the forecastle, where good order was now kept. There had been no need for interference on the part of the officers, which I was glad to see, remembering what would have happened under such circumstances not long ago. Being short-handed, the captain engaged a number of friendly islanders for a limited period, on the understanding that they were to be discharged at their native place, Vau Vau. There were ten of them, fine, stalwart fellows, able-bodied, and willing as possible. They were cleanly in their habits, and devout members of the Wesleyan body, so that their behaviour was quite a reproach to some of our half-civilized crew. Berths were found for them in the forecastle, and they took their places among us quite naturally, being fairly well used to a whale-ship.

CHAPTER XVIII.

ON THE "LINE" GROUNDS.

We weighed at last, one morning, with a beautiful breeze, and, bidding a long farewell to the lovely isles and their amiable inhabitants, stood to sea, bound for the "line" or equatorial grounds on our legitimate business of sperm whaling. It was now a long while since we had been in contact with a cachalot, the last one having been killed by us on the Coast of Japan some six months before. But we all looked forward to the coming campaign with considerable joy, for we were now a happy family, interested in the work, and, best of all, even if the time was still distant, we were, in a sense, homeward bound. At any rate, we all chose so to think, from the circumstance that we were now working to the southward, towards Cape Horn, the rounding of which dreaded point would mark the final stage of our globe-encircling voyage.

We had, during our stay at Honolulu, obtained a couple of grand boats in addition to our stock, and were now in a position to man and lower five at once, if occasion should arise, still leaving sufficient crew on board to work the vessel. The captain had also engaged an elderly seaman of his acquaintance—out of pure philanthropy, as we all thought, since he was in a state of semi-starvation ashore—to act as a kind of sailing-master, so as to relieve the captain of ship duty at whaling time, allowing him still to head his boat. This was not altogether welcome news to me, for, much as I liked the old man and admired his pluck, I could not help dreading his utter recklessness when on a whale, which had so often led to a smash-up that might have been easily avoided. Moreover, I reasoned that if he had been foolhardy before, he was likely to be much more so now, having no superior to look black or use language when a disaster occurred. For now I was his harpooner, bound to take as many risks as he chose to incur, and anxious also to earn a reputation among the more seasoned whalemen for smartness sufficient to justify my promotion.

The Kanakas shipped at Honolulu were distributed among the boats, two to each, being already trained whalemen, and a fine lot of fellows they were. My two—Samuela and Polly—were not very big men, but sturdy, nimble as cats, as much at home in the water as on deck, and simply bubbling over with fun and good-humour. From my earliest sea-going, I have always had a strong liking for natives of tropical countries, finding them affectionate and amenable to kindness. Why, I think, white men do not get on with darkies well, as a rule, is, that they seldom make an appeal to the *man* in them. It is very degrading to find one's self looked down upon as a sort of animal without reason or feelings; and if you degrade a man, you deprive him of any incentive to make himself useful, except the brute one you may feel bound to apply yourself. My experience has been limited to Africans (of sorts), Kanakas, natives of Hindostan,

Malagasy, and Chinese; but with all these I have found a little *camaraderie* answer excellently. True, they are lazy; but what inducement have they to work? The complicated needs of our civilized existence compel *us* to work, or be run over by the unresting machine; but I take leave to doubt whether any of us with a primitive environment would not be as lazy as any Kanaka that ever dozed under a banana tree through daylight hours. Why, then, make an exalted virtue of the necessity which drives us, and objurgate the poor black man because he prefers present ease to a doubtful prospective retirement on a competency? Australian blackfellows and Malays are said to be impervious to kind treatment by a great number of witnesses, the former appearing incapable of gratitude, and the latter unable to resist the frequent temptation to kill somebody. Not knowing anything personally of either of these races, I can say nothing for or against them.

All the coloured individuals that I have had to do with have amply repaid any little kindness shown them with fidelity and affection, but especially has this been the case with Kanakas. The soft and melodious language spoken by them is easy to acquire, and is so pleasant to speak that it is well worth learning, to say nothing of the convenience to yourself, although the Kanaka speedily picks up the mutilated jargon which does duty for English on board ship.

What I specially longed for now was a harpooner, or even two, so that I might have my boat to myself, the captain taking his own boat with a settled harpooner. Samuela, the biggest of my two Kanakas, very earnestly informed me that he was no end of a "number one" whale slaughterer; but I judged it best to see how things went before asking to have him promoted. My chance, and his, came very promptly; so nicely arranged, too, that I could not have wished for anything better. The skipper had got a fine, healthy boil on one knee-cap, and another on his wrist, so that he was, as you may say, *hors de combat*. While he was impatiently waiting to get about once more, sperm whales were raised. Although nearly frantic with annoyance, he was compelled to leave the direction of things to Mr. Cruce, who was quite puffed up with the importance of his opportunity.

Such a nice little school of cow-whales, a lovely breeze, clear sky, warm weather—I felt as gay as a lark at the prospect. As we were reaching to windward, with all boats ready for lowering, the skipper called me aft and said, "Naow, Mr. Bullen, I cain't lower, because of this condemned leg 'n arm of mine; but how'r yew goin' ter manage 'thout a harpooneer?" I suggested that if he would allow me to try Samuela, who was suffering for a chance to distinguish himself, we would "come out on top." "All right," he said; "but let the other boats get fast first, 'n doan be in too much of a hurry to tie yerself up till ye see what's doin'. If everythin's goin' bizness-fashion', 'n yew git a chance, sail right in; yew got ter begin some time. But ef thet Kanaka looks skeered goin' on, take the iron frum him ter onct." I promised, and the interview ended.

When I told Samuela of his chance, he was beside himself with joy. As to his being scared, the idea was manifestly absurd. He was as pleased with the prospect as it was possible for a man to be, and hardly able to contain himself for impatience to be off. I almost envied him his exuberant delight, for a sense of responsibility began to weigh upon me with somewhat depressing effect.

We gained a good weather-gage, rounded to, and lowered four boats. Getting away in good style, we had barely got the sails up, when something gallied the school. We saw or heard nothing to account for it, but undoubtedly the "fish" were off at top speed dead to windward, so that our sails were of no use. We had them in with as little delay as possible, and lay to our oars for all we were worth, being fresh and strong, as well as anxious to get amongst them. But I fancy all our efforts would have availed us little had it not been for the experience of Mr. Cruce, whose eager eye detected the fact that the fish were running on a great curve, and shaped our course to cut them off along a chord of the arc.

Two and a half hours of energetic work was required of us before we got on terms with the fleeing monsters; but at last, to our great joy, they broke water from sounding right among us. It was a considerable surprise, but we were all ready, and before they had spouted twice, three boats were fast, only myself keeping out, in accordance with my instructions. Samuela was almost distraught with rage and grief at the condition of things. I quite pitied him, although I was anything but pleased myself. However, when I ranged up alongside the mate's fish, to render what assistance was needed, he shouted to me, "We's all right; go'n git fas', if yew kin." That was enough, and away we flew after a retreating spout to leeward. Before we got there, though, there was an upheaval in the water just ahead, and up came a back like a keelless ship bottom up. Out came the head belonging to it, and a spout like an explosion burst forth, denoting the presence of an enormous bull-cachalot. Close by his side was a cow of about one-third his size, the favoured sultana of his harem, I suppose. Prudence whispered, "Go for the cow;" Ambition hissed, "All or none—the bull, the bull." Fortunately emergencies of this kind leave one but a second or two to decide, as a rule; in this case, as it happened, I was spared even that mental conflict, for as we ran up between the two vast creatures, Samuela, never even looking at the cow, hurled his harpoon, with all the energy that he had been bursting with so long, at the mighty bull. I watched its flight—saw it enter the black mass and disappear to the shaft, and almost immediately came the second iron, within a foot of the first, burying itself in the same solid fashion.

"Starn—starn all!" I shouted; and we backed slowly away, considerably hampered by the persistent attentions of the cow, who hung round us closely. The temptation to lance her was certainly great, but I remembered the fate that had overtaken the skipper on the first occasion we struck whales, and did not meddle with her ladyship. Our prey was not apparently disposed to kick up much fuss at first, so, anxious to settle matters, I changed ends with Samuela, and pulled in on the whale. A good, steady lance-thrust—the first I had ever delivered—was obtained, sending a thrill of triumph through my whole body. The recipient, thoroughly roused by this, started off at a great lick, accompanied, somewhat to my surprise, by the cow. Thenceforward for another hour, in spite of all our efforts, we could not get within striking distance, mainly because of the close attention of the cow, which stuck to her lord like a calf to its mother. I was getting so impatient of this hindrance, that it was all I could do to restrain myself from lancing the cow, though I felt convinced that, if I did, I should spoil a good job. Suddenly I caught sight of the ship right ahead. We were still flying along, so that in a short time we were comparatively close to her. My heart beat high, and I burned to distinguish myself under the friendly and appreciative eye of the skipper.

None of the other boats were in sight, from our level at least, so that I had a reasonable hope of being able to finish my game, with all the glory thereunto attaching, unshared by any other of my fellow-officers. As we ran quite closely past the ship, calling on the crew to haul up for all they were worth, we managed actually to squeeze past the cow, and I got in a really deadly blow. The point of the lance entered just between the fin and the eye, but higher up, missing the broad plate of the shoulder-blade, and sinking its whole four feet over the hitches right down into the animal's vitals. Then, for the first time, he threw up his flukes, thrashing them from side to side almost round to his head, and raising such a turmoil that we were half full of water in a moment. But Samuela was so quick at the steer-oar, so lithe and forceful, and withal appeared so to anticipate every move of mine, that there seemed hardly any danger.

After a few moments of this tremendous exertion, our victim settled down, leaving the water deeply stained with his gushing blood. With him disappeared his constant companion, the faithful cow, who had never left his side a minute since we first got fast. Down, down they went, until my line began to look very low, and I was compelled to make signals to the ship for more. We had hardly elevated the oars, when down dropped the last boat with four men in her, arriving by my side in a few minutes with two fresh tubs of tow-line. We took them on board, and the boat returned again.

By the time the slack came we had about four hundred and fifty fathoms out—a goodly heap to pile up loose in our stern-sheets. I felt sure, however, that we should have but little more trouble with our fish; in fact, I was half afraid that he would die before getting to the surface, in which case he might sink and be lost. We hauled steadily away, the line not coming in very easily, until I judged there was only about another hundred fathoms out. Our amazement may be imagined, when suddenly we were compelled to slack away again, the sudden weight on the line suggesting that the fish was again sounding. If ever a young hand was perplexed, it was I. Never before had I heard of such unseemly behaviour, nor was my anxiety lessened when I saw, a short distance away, the huge body of my prize at the surface spouting blood. At the same time, I was paying out line at a good rate, as if I had a fast fish on which was sounding briskly.

The skipper had been watching me very closely from his seat on the taffrail, and had kept the ship within easy distance. Now, suspecting something out of the common, he sent the boat again to my assistance, in charge of the cooper. When that worthy arrived, he said, "Th' ol' man reckens yew've got snarled erp 'ith thet ar' loose keow, 'n y'r irons hev draw'd from th' other. I'm gwine ter wait on him, 'n get him 'longside 'soon's he's out'er his flurry. Ole man sez yew'd best wait on what's fast t' yer an' nev' mine th' other." Away he went, reaching my prize just as the last feeble spout exhaled, leaving the dregs of that great flood of life trickling lazily down from the widely-expanded spiracle. To drive a harpoon into the carcass, and run the line on board, was the simplest of jobs, for, as the captain had foreseen, my irons were drawn clean. I had no leisure to take any notice of them now, though, for whatever was on my line was coming up hand-over-fist.

With a bound it reached the surface—the identical cow so long attendant upon the dead whale. Having been so long below for such a small whale, she was quite exhausted, and before she had recovered we had got alongside of her and lanced her, so thoroughly that she died without a struggle. The ship was so close that we had her alongside in a wonderfully short time, and with scarcely any trouble.

When I reached the deck, the skipper called me, and said several things that made feel about six inches taller. He was, as may be thought, exceedingly pleased, saying that only once in his long career had he seen a similar case; for I forgot to mention that the line was entangled around the cow's down-hanging jaw, as if she had actually tried to bite in two the rope that held her consort, and only succeeded in sharing his fate. I would not like to say that whales do not try to thus sever a line, but, their teeth being several inches apart, conical, and fitting into sockets in the upper jaw instead of meeting the opposed surfaces of other teeth, the accomplishment of such a feat must, I think, be impossible.

The ship being now as good as anchored by the vast mass of flesh hanging to her, there was a tremendous task awaiting us to get the other fish alongside. Of course they were all to windward; they nearly always are, unless the ship is persistently "turned to windward" while the fishing is going on. Whalers believe that they always work up into the wind while fast, and, when dead, it is certain that they drift at a pretty good rate right in the "wind's eye." This is accounted for by the play of the body, which naturally lies head to wind; and the wash of the flukes, which, acting somewhat like the "sculling" of an oar at the stern of a boat, propel the carcass in the direction it is pointing. Consequently we had an awful amount of towing to do before we got the three cows alongside. Many a time we blessed ourselves that they were no bigger, for of all the clumsy things to tow with boats, a sperm whale is about the worst. Owing to the great square mass of the head, they can hardly be towed head-on at all, the practice being to cut off the tips of the flukes, and tow them tail first. But even then it is slavery. To dip your oar about three times in the same hole from whence you withdrew it, to tug at it with all your might, apparently making as much progress as though you were fast to a dock-wall, and to continue this fun for four or five hours at a stretch, is to wonder indeed whether you have not mistaken your vocation.

However, "it's dogged as does it," so by dint of sheer sticking to the oar, we eventually succeeded in getting all our prizes alongside before eight bells that evening, securing them around us by hawsers to the cows, but giving the big bull the post of honour alongside on the best fluke-chain.

We were a busy company for a fortnight thence, until the last of the oil was run below—two hundred and fifty barrels, or twenty-five tuns, of the valuable fluid having rewarded our exertions. During these operations we had drifted night and day, apparently without anybody taking the slightest account of the direction we were taking; when, therefore, on the day after clearing up the last traces of our fishing, the cry of "Land ho!" came ringing down from the crow's-nest, no one was surprised, although the part of the Pacific in which we were cruising has but few patches of *terra firma* scattered about over its immense area when compared with the crowded archipelagoes lying farther south and east.

We could not see the reported land from the deck for two hours after it was first seen from aloft, although the odd spectacle of a scattered group of cocoa-nut trees apparently growing out of the sea was for some time presented to us before the island itself came into view. It was Christmas Island, where the indefatigable Captain Cook landed on December 24, 1777, for the purpose of making accurate observations of an eclipse of the sun. He it was who gave to this lonely atoll the name it has ever since borne, with characteristic modesty giving his own great name to a tiny patch of coral which almost blocks the entrance to the central lagoon. Here we lay "off and on" for a couple of days, while foraging parties went ashore, returning at intervals with abundance of turtle and sea-fowls' eggs. But any detailed account of their proceedings must be ruthlessly curtailed, owing to the scanty limits of space remaining.

CHAPTER XIX.

EDGING SOUTHWARD.

The line whaling grounds embrace an exceedingly extensive area, over the whole of which sperm whales may be found, generally of medium size. No means of estimating the probable plenty or scarcity of them in any given part of the grounds exist, so that falling in with them is purely a matter of coincidence. To me it seems a conclusive proof of the enormous numbers of sperm whales frequenting certain large breadths of ocean, that they should be so often fallen in with, remembering what a little spot is represented by a day's cruise, and that the signs which denote almost infallibly the vicinity of right whales are entirely absent in the case of the cachalot. In the narrow waters of the Greenland seas, with quite a small number of vessels seeking, it is hardly possible for a whale of any size to escape being seen; but in the open ocean a goodly fleet may cruise over a space of a hundred thousand square miles without meeting any of the whales that may yet be there in large numbers. So that when one hears talk of the extinction of the cachalot, it is well to bear in mind that such a thing would take a long series of years to effect, even were the whaling business waxing instead of waning. While, however, South Sea whaling is conducted on such old-world methods as still obtain; while steam, with all the power it gives of rapidly dealing with a catch, is not made use of, the art and mystery of the whale-fisher must continually decrease. No such valuable lubricant has ever been found as sperm oil; but the cost of its production, added to the precarious nature of the supply, so handicaps it in the competition with substitutes that it has been practically eliminated from the English markets, except in such greatly adulterated forms as to render it a lie to speak of the mixture as sperm oil at all.

Except to a few whose minds to them are kingdoms, and others who can hardly be said to have any minds at all, the long monotony of unsuccessful seeking for whales is very wearying. The ceaseless motion of the vessel rocking at the centre of a circular space of blue, with a perfectly symmetrical dome of azure enclosing her above, unflecked by a single cloud, becomes at last almost unbearable from its changeless sameness of environment. Were it not for the trivial round and common task of everyday ship duty, some of the crew must become idiotic, or, in sheer rage at the want of interest in their lives, commit mutiny.

Such a weary time was ours for full four weeks after sighting Christmas Island. The fine haul we had obtained just previous to that day seemed to have exhausted our luck for the time being, for never a spout did we see. And it was with no ordinary delight that we hailed the advent of an immense school of black-fish, the first we had run across for a long time. Determined to have a big catch, if possible, we lowered all five boats, as it was a beautifully calm day, and the ship might almost safely have been left to look after herself. After what we had recently been accustomed to, the game seemed trifling to get up much excitement over; but still, for a good day's sport, commend me to a few lively black-fish,

In less than ten minutes we were in the thick of the crowd, with harpoons flying right and left. Such a scene of wild confusion and uproarious merriment ensued as I never saw before in my life. The skipper, true to his traditions, got fast to four, all running different ways at once, and making the calm sea boil again with their frantic gyrations. Each of the other boats got hold of three; but, the mate getting too near me, our fish got so inextricably tangled up that it was hopeless to try and distinguish between each other's prizes. However, when we got the lances to work among them, the hubbub calmed down greatly, and the big bodies one by one ceased their gambols, floating supine.

So far, all had been gay; but the unlucky second mate must needs go and do a thing that spoiled a day's fun entirely. The line runs through a deep groove in the boat's stem, over a brass roller so fitted that when the line is running out it remains fixed, but when hauling in it revolves freely, assisting the work a great deal. The second mate had three fish fast, like the rest of us—the first one on the end of the main line, the other two on "short warps," or pieces of whale-line some eight or ten fathoms long fastened to harpoons, with the other ends running on the main line by means of bowlines round it. By some mistake or other he had allowed the two lines to be hauled together through the groove in his boat's stem, and before the error was noticed two fish spurted off in opposite directions, ripping the boat in two halves lengthways, like a Dutchman splitting a salt herring.

Away went the fish with the whole of the line, nobody being able to get at it to cut; and, but for the presence of mind shown by the crew in striking out and away from the tangle, a most ghastly misfortune, involving the loss of several lives, must have occurred. As it was, the loss was considerable, almost outweighing the gain on the day's fishing, besides the inconvenience of having a boat useless on whaling grounds.

The accident was the fruit of gross carelessness, and should never have occurred; but then, strange to say, disasters to whale-boats are nearly always due to want of care, the percentage of unavoidable casualties being very small as compared with those like the one just related. When the highly dangerous nature of the work is remembered, this statement may seem somewhat overdrawn; but it has been so frequently corroborated by others, whose experience far outweighs my own, that I do not hesitate to make it with the fullest confidence in its truth.

Happily no lives were lost on this occasion, for it would have indeed been grievous to have seen our shipmates sacrificed to the *manes* of a mere black-fish, after successfully encountering so many mighty whales. The episode gave us a great deal of unnecessary work getting the two halves of the boat saved, in addition to securing our fish, so that by the time we got the twelve remaining carcasses hove on deck we were all quite fagged out. But under the new *régime* we were sure of a good rest, so that did not trouble us; it rather made the lounge on deck in the balmy evening air and the well-filled pipe of peace doubly sweet.

Our next day's work completed the skinning of the

haul we had made, the last of the carcasses going overboard with a thunderous splash at four in the afternoon. The assemblage of sharks round the ship on this occasion was incredible for its number and the great size of the creatures. Certainly no mariners see so many or such huge sharks as whalemen; but, in spite of all our previous experience, this day touched high-water mark. Many of these fish were of a size undreamed of by the ordinary seafarer, some of them full thirty feet in length, more like whales than sharks. Most of them were striped diagonally with bands of yellow, contrasting curiously with the dingy grey of their normal colour. From this marking is derived their popular name—"tiger sharks," not, as might be supposed, from their ferocity. That attribute cannot properly be applied to the *squalus* at all, which is one of the most timid fish afloat, and whose ill name, as far as regards blood-thirstiness, is quite undeserved. Rapacious the shark certainly is; but what sea-fish is not? He is not at all particular as to his diet; but what sea-fish is? With such a great bulk of body, such enormous vitality and vigour to support, he must needs be ever eating; and since he is not constructed on swift enough lines to enable him to prey upon living fish, like most of his neighbours, he is perforce compelled to play the humble but useful part of a sea-scavenger.

He eats man, as he eats anything else eatable, because in the water man is easily caught, and not from natural depravity or an acquired taste begetting a decided preference for human flesh. All natives of shores infested by sharks despise him and his alleged man-eating propensities, knowing that a very feeble splashing will suffice to frighten him away even if ever so hungry.

Demerara River literally swarms with sharks, yet I have often seen a negro, clad only in a beaming smile, slip into its muddy waters, and, after a few sharp blows with his open hand upon the surface, calmly swim down to the bottom, clear a ship's anchor, or do whatever job was required, coming up again as leisurely as if in a swimming-bath. A similar disregard of the dangerous attributes awarded by popular consent to the shark may be witnessed everywhere among the people who know him best. The cruelties perpetrated upon sharks by seamen generally are the result of ignorance and superstition combined, the most infernal forces known to humanity. What would be said at home of such an act, if it could be witnessed among us, as the disembowelling of a tiger, say, and then letting him run in that horrible condition somewhere remote from the possibility of retaliating upon his torturers? Yet that is hardly comparable with a similar atrocity performed upon a shark, because he will live hours to the tiger's minutes in such a condition.

I once caught a shark nine feet long, which we hauled on board and killed by cutting off its head and tail. It died very speedily—for a shark—all muscular motion ceasing in less than fifteen minutes. It was my intention to prepare that useless and unornamental article so dear to sailors—a walking-stick made of a shark's backbone. But when I came to cut out the vertebra, I noticed a large scar, extending from one side to the other, right across the centre of the back. Beneath it the backbone was thickened to treble its normal size, and perfectly rigid; in fact, it had become a mass of solid bone. At some time or other this shark had been harpooned so severely that, in wrenching himself free, he must have nearly torn his body in two halves, severing the spinal column completely. Yet such a wound as that had been healed by natural process, the bone knit together again with many times the strength it had before—minus, of course, its flexibility—and I can testify from the experience of securing him that he could not possibly have been more vigorous than he was.

A favourite practice used to be—I trust it is so no longer—to catch a shark, and, after driving a sharpened stake down through his upper jaw and out underneath the lower one, so that its upper portion pointed diagonally forward, to let him go again. The consequence of this cruelty would be that the fish was unable to open his mouth, or go in any direction without immediately coming to the surface. How long he might linger in such torture, one can only guess; but unless his fellows, finding him thus helpless, came along and kindly devoured him, no doubt he would exist in extreme agony for a very long time.

Two more small cows were all that rewarded our search during the next fortnight, and we began to feel serious doubts as to the success of our season upon the line grounds, after all. Still, on the whole, our voyage up to the present had not been what might fairly be called unsuccessful, for we were not yet two years away from New Bedford, while we had considerably more than two thousand barrels of oil on board—more, in fact, than two-thirds of a full cargo. But if a whale were caught every other day for six months, and then a month elapsed without any being seen, grumbling would be loud and frequent, all the previous success being forgotten in the present stagnation. Perhaps it is not so different in other professions nearer home?

Christmas Day drew near, beloved of Englishmen all the world over, though thought little of by Americans. The two previous ones spent on board the *Cachalot* have been passed over without mention, absolutely no notice being taken of the season by any one on board, to all appearance. In English ships some attempt is always made to give the day somewhat of a festive character, and to maintain the national tradition of good-cheer and goodwill in whatever part of the world you may happen to be. For some reason or other, perhaps because of the great increase in comfort we had all experienced lately, I felt the approach of the great Christian anniversary very strongly; although, had I been in London, I should probably have spent it in lonely gloom, having no relatives or friends whom I might visit. But what of that? Christmas is Christmas; and, if we have no home, we think of the place where our home should be; and whether, as cynics sneer, Dickens invented the English Christmas or not, its observance has taken deep root among us. May its shadow never be less!

On Christmas morning I mounted to the crow's-nest at daybreak, and stood looking with never-failing awe at the daily marvel of the sunrise. Often and often have I felt choking for words to express the tumult of thoughts aroused by this sublime spectacle. Hanging there in cloudland, the tiny microcosm at one's feet forgotten, the grandeur of the celestial outlook is overwhelming. Many and many a time I have bowed my head and wept in pure reverence at the majesty manifested around me while the glory of the dawn increased and brightened, till with one exultant bound the sun appeared.

For some time I stood gazing straight ahead of me

with eyes that saw not, filled with wonder and admiration. I must have been looking directly at the same spot for quite a quarter of an hour, when suddenly, as if I had but just opened my eyes, I saw the well-known bushy spout of a sperm whale. I raised the usual yell, which rang through the stillness discordantly, startling all hands out of their lethargy like bees out of a hive. After the usual preliminaries, we were all afloat with sails set, gliding slowly over the sleeping sea towards the unconscious objects of our attention. The captain did not lower this time, as there only appeared to be three fish, none of them seeming large. Though at any distance it is extremely difficult to assess the size of whales, the spout being very misleading. Sometimes a full-sized whale will show a small spout, while a twenty-barrel cow will exhale a volume of vapour extensive enough for two or three at once.

Now although, according to etiquette, I kept my position in the rear of my superior officers, I had fully determined in my own mind, being puffed up with previous success, to play second fiddle to no one, if I could help it, this time. Samuela was decidedly of the same opinion; indeed, I believe he would have been delighted to tackle a whole school single-handed, while my crew were all willing and eager for the fight. We had a long, tedious journey before we came up with them, the wind being so light that even with the occasional assistance of the paddles our progress was wretchedly slow. When at last we did get into their water, and the mate's harpooner stood up to dart, his foot slipped, and down he came with a clatter enough to scare a cachalot twenty miles away. It gallied our friends effectually, sending them flying in different directions at the top of their speed. But being some distance astern of the other boats, one of the fish, in his headlong retreat, rose for a final blow some six or seven fathoms away, passing us in the opposite direction. His appearance was only momentary, yet in that moment Samuela hurled his harpoon into the air, where it described a beautiful parabola, coming down upon the disappearing monster's back just as the sea was closing over it. Oh, it was a splendid dart, worthy of the finest harpooner that ever lived! There was no time for congratulations, however, for we spun round as on a pivot, and away we went in the wake of that fellow at a great rate. I cast one look astern to see whether the others had struck, but could see nothing of them; we seemed to have sprung out of their ken in an instant.

The speed of our friend was marvellous, but I comforted myself with the knowledge that these animals usually run in circles—sometimes, it is true, of enormous diameter, but seldom getting far away from their starting-point. But as the time went on, and we seemed to fly over the waves at undiminished speed, I began to think this whale might be the exception necessary to prove the rule, so I got out the compass and watched his course. Due east, not a degree to north or south of it, straight as a bee to its hive. The ship was now far out of sight astern, but I knew that keen eyes had been watching our movements from the masthead, and that every effort possible would be made to keep the run of us. The speed of our whale was not only great, but unflagging. He was more like a machine than an animal capable of tiring; and though we did our level best, at the faintest symptom of slackening, to get up closer and lance him, it was for some time impossible. After, at a rough estimate, running in a direct easterly course for over two hours, he suddenly sounded, without having given us the ghost of a chance to "land him one where he lived." Judging from his previous exertions, though, it was hardly possible he would be able to stay down long, or get very deep, as the strain upon these vast creatures at any depth is astonishingly exhausting. After a longer stay below than usual, when they have gone extra deep, they often arrive at the surface manifestly "done up" for a time. Then, if the whaleman be active and daring, a few well-directed strokes may be got in which will promptly settle the business out of hand.

Now, when my whale sounded he was to all appearance as frightened a beast as one could wish—one who had run himself out endeavouring to get away from his enemies, and as a last resource had dived into the quietness below in the vain hope to get away. So I regarded him, making up my mind to wait on him with diligence upon his arrival, and not allow him to get breath before I had settled him. But when he did return, there was a mighty difference in him. He seemed as if he had been getting some tips on the subject from some school below where whales are trained to hunt men; for his first move was to come straight for me with a furious rush, carrying the war into the enemy's country with a vengeance. It must be remembered that I was but young, and a comparatively new hand at this sort of thing; so when I confess that I felt more than a little scared at this sudden change in the tactics of my opponent, I hope I shall be excused. Remembering, however, that all our lives depended on keeping cool, I told myself that even if I was frightened I must not go all to pieces, but compel myself to think and act calmly, since I was responsible for others. If the animal had not been in so blind a fury, I am afraid my task would have been much harder; but he was mad, and his savage rushes were, though disquieting, unsystematic and clumsy. It was essential, however, that he should not be allowed to persist too long in his evil courses; for a whale learns with amazing rapidity, developing such cunning in an hour or two that all a man's smartness may be unable to cope with his newly-acquired experience. Happily, Samuela was perfectly unmoved. Like a machine, he obeyed every gesture, every look even, swinging the boat "off" or "on" the whale with such sweeping strokes of his mighty oar that she revolved as if on a pivot, and encouraging the other chaps with his cheerful cries and odd grimaces, so that the danger was hardly felt. During a momentary lull in the storm, I took the opportunity to load my bomb-gun, much as I disliked handling the thing, keeping my eye all the time on the water around where I expected to see mine enemy popping up murderously at any minute. Just as I had expected, when he rose, it was very close, and on his back, with his jaw in the first biting position, looking ugly as a vision of death. Finding us a little out of reach, he rolled right over towards us, presenting as he did so the great rotundity of his belly. We were not twenty feet away, and I snatched up the gun, levelled it, and fired the bomb point-blank into his bowels. Then all was blank. I do not even remember the next moment. A rush of roaring waters, a fighting with fearful, desperate energy for air and life, all in a hurried, flurried phantasmagoria about which there was nothing clear except the primitive desire for life, life, life! Nor do I know how long this struggle lasted, except that, in the nature of things, it could not have been very long.

When I returned to a consciousness of external things, I was for some time perfectly still, looking at the sky, totally unable to realize what had happened or where I was. Presently the smiling, pleasant face of Samuela bent over me. Meeting my gratified look of recognition, he set up a perfect yell of delight. "So glad, so glad you blonga life! No go Davy Jonesy dis time, hay?" I put my hand out to help myself to a sitting posture, and touched blubber. That startled me so that I sprung up as if shot. Then I took in the situation at a glance. There were all my poor fellows with me, stranded upon the top of our late antagonist, but no sign of the boat to be seen. Bewildered at the state of affairs, I looked appealingly from one to the other for an explanation. I got it from Abner, who said, laconically, "When yew fired thet ole gun, I guess it mus' have bin loaded fer bear, fer ye jest tumbled clar head over heels backwards outen the boat. Et that very same moment I suspicion the bomb busted in his belly, fer he went clean rampageous loony. He rolled right over an' over to'rds us, n' befo' we c'd rightly see wat wuz comin', we cu'dnt see anythin' 'tall; we wuz all grabbin' at nothin', some'rs underneath the whale. When I come to the top, I lit eout fer the fust thing I c'd see to lay holt of, which wuz old squarhead himself, deader 'n pork. I guess thet ar bomb o' yourn kinder upset his commissary department. Anyway, I climed up onto him, 'n bime-by the rest ov us histed themselves alongside ov me. Sam Weller here; he cum last, towin' you 'long with him. I don'no whar he foun' ye, but ye was very near a goner, 'n's full o' pickle as ye c'd hold." I turned a grateful eye upon my dusky harpooner, who had saved my life, but was now apparently blissfully unconscious of having done anything meritorious.

Behold us, then, a half-drowned row of scarecrows perched, like some new species of dilapidated birds, upon the side of our late foe. The sun was not so furiously hot as usual, for masses of rain-laden *nimbi* were filling the sky, so that we were comparatively free from the awful roasting we might have expected; nor was our position as precarious for a while as would be thought. True, we had only one harpoon, with its still fast line, to hold on by; but the side of the whale was somehow hollowed, so that, in spite of the incessant movement imparted to the carcass by the swell, we sat fairly safe, with our feet in the said hollow. We discussed the situation in all its bearings, unable to extract more than the faintest gleam of hope from any aspect of the case. The only reasonable chance we had was, that the skipper had almost certainly taken our bearings, and would, we were sure, be anxiously seeking us on the course thus indicated. Meanwhile, we were ravenously hungry and thirsty. Samuela and Polly set to work with their sheath-knives, and soon excavated a space in the blubber to enable them to reach the meat. Then they cut off some good-sized junks, and divided it up. It was not half bad; and as we chewed on the tough black fibre, I could hardly help smiling as I thought how queer a Christmas dinner we were having. But eating soon heightened our thirst, and our real sufferings then began. We could eat very little once the want of drink made itself felt. Hardly two hours had elapsed, though, before one of the big-bellied clouds which had been keeping the sun off us most considerately emptied out upon us a perfect torrent of rain. It filled the cavity in the whale's side in a twinkling; and though the water was greasy, stained with blood, and vilely flavoured, it was as welcome a drink as I have ever tasted. Thus fed, and with our thirst slaked, we were able to take a more hopeful view of things, while the prospect of our being found seemed much more probable than it had done before the rain fell.

Still, we had to endure our pillory for a long while yet. The sharks and birds began to worry us, especially the former, who in their eagerness to get a portion of the blubber fought, writhed, and tore at the carcass with tireless energy. Once, one of the smaller ones actually came sliding up right into our hollow; but Samuela and Polly promptly dispatched him with a cut throat, sending him back to encourage the others. The present relieved us of most of their attentions for a short time at least, as they eagerly divided the remains of their late comrade among them.

To while away the time we spun yarns—without much point, I am afraid; and sung songs, albeit we did not feel much like singing—till after a while our poor attempts at gaiety fizzled out like a damp match, leaving us silent and depressed. The sun, which had been hidden for some time, now came out again, his slanting beams revealing to us ominously the flight of time and the near approach of night. Should darkness overtake us in our present position, we all felt that saving us would need the performance of a miracle; for in addition to the chances of the accumulated gases within the carcass bursting it asunder, the unceasing assault of the sharks made it highly doubtful whether they would not in a few hours more have devoured it piecemeal. Already they had scooped out some deep furrows in the solid

ON HIS BACK, WITH HIS JAW IN THE FIRST BITING POSITION.

blubber, making it easier to get hold and tear off more, and their numbers were increasing so fast that the surrounding sea was fairly alive with them. Lower and lower sank the sun, deeper and darker grew the gloom upon our faces, till suddenly Samuela leaped to his feet in our midst, and emitted a yell so ear-piercing as to nearly deafen us. He saw the ship! Before two minutes had passed we all saw her—God bless her!—coming down upon us like some angelic messenger. There were no fears among us that we should be overlooked. We knew full well how anxiously and keenly many pairs of eyes had been peering over the sea in search of us, and we felt perfectly sure they had sighted us long ago. On she came, gilded by the evening glow, till she seemed glorified, moving in a halo of celestial light, all her homeliness and clumsy build forgotten in what she then represented to us.

Never before or since has a ship looked like that to me, nor can I ever forget the thankfulness, the delight, the reverence, with which I once more saw her approaching. Straight down upon us she bore, rounding to within a cable's length, and dropping a boat simultaneously with her windward sweep. They had no whale—well for us they had not. In five minutes we were on board, while our late resting-place was being hauled alongside with great glee.

The captain shook hands with me cordially, pooh-poohing the loss of the boat as an unavoidable incident of the trade, but expressing his heart-felt delight at getting us all back safe. The whale we had killed was ample compensation for the loss of several boats, though such was the vigour with which the sharks were going for him, that it was deemed advisable to cut in at once, working all night. We who had been rescued, however, were summarily ordered below by the skipper, and forbidden, on pain of his severe displeasure, to reappear until the following morning. This great privilege we gladly availed ourselves of, awaking at daylight quite well and fit, not a bit the worse for our queer experience of the previous day.

The whale proved a great acquisition, for although not nearly so large as many we had caught, he was so amazingly rich in blubber that he actually yielded twelve and a half tuns of oil, in spite of the heavy toll taken of him by the hungry multitudes of sharks. In addition to the oil, we were fortunate enough to secure a lump of ambergris, dislodged perhaps by the explosion of my bomb in the animal's bowels. It was nearly black, wax-like to the touch, and weighed seven pounds and a half. At the current price, it would be worth about £200, so that, taken altogether, the whale very nearly approached in value the largest one we had yet caught. I had almost omitted to state that incorporated with the substance of the ambergris were several of the horny cuttle-fish beaks, which, incapable of being digested, had become in some manner part of this peculiar product.

CHAPTER XX.

"HUMPBACKING" AT VAU VAU.

ANOTHER three weeks' cruising brought us to the end of the season on the line, which had certainly not answered all our expectations, although we had perceptibly increased the old barky's draught during our stay. Whether from love of change or belief in the possibilities of a good haul, I can hardly say, but Captain Count decided to make the best of his way south, to the middle group of the "Friendly" Archipelago, known as Vau Vau, the other portions being called Hapai and Tongataboo respectively, for a season's "humpbacking." From all I could gather, we were likely to have a good time there, so I looked forward to the visit with a great deal of pleasurable anticipation.

We were bound to make a call at Vau Vau, in any case, to discharge our Kanakas shipped at Honolulu, although I fervently hoped to be able to keep my brave harpooner Samuela. So when I heard of our destination, I sounded him cautiously as to his wishes in the matter, finding that, while he was both pleased with and proud of his position on board, he was longing greatly for his own orange grove and the embraces of a certain tender "fafinè" that he averred was there awaiting him. With such excellent reasons for his leaving us, I could but forbear to persuade him, sympathizing with him too deeply to wish him away from such joys as he described to me.

So we bade farewell to the line grounds, and commenced another stretch to the south, another milestone, as it were, on the long road home. Prosaic and uneventful to the last degree was our passage, the only incident worth recording being our "gamming" of the *Passamaquoddy*, of Martha's Vineyard, South Sea whaler; eighteen months out, with one thousand barrels of sperm oil on board. We felt quite veterans alongside of her crew, and our yarns laid over theirs to such an extent that they were quite disgusted at their lack of experience. Some of them had known our late skipper, but none of them had a good word for him, the old maxim, "Speak nothing but good of the dead," being most flagrantly set at nought. One of her crew was a Whitechapelian, who had been roving about the world for a good many years.

Amongst other experiences, he had, after "jumping the bounty" two or three times, found himself a sergeant in the Federal Army before Gettysburg. During that most bloody battle, he informed me that a "Reb" drew a bead on him at about a dozen yards distance, and fired. He said he felt just as if somebody had punched him in the chest, and knocked him flat on his back on top of a sharp stone—no pain at all, nor any further recollection of what had happened, until he found himself at the base, in hospital. When the surgeons came to examine him for the bullet, they found that it had struck the broad brass plate of his cross-belt fairly in the middle, penetrating it and shattering his breast bone. But after torturing him vilely with the probe, they were about to give up the search in despair, when he told them he felt a pain in his back. Examining the spot indicated by him, they found a bullet just beneath the skin, which a touch with the knife allowed to tumble out. Further examination revealed the strange fact that the bullet, after striking his breast-bone, had glanced aside and travelled round his body just beneath the skin, without doing him any further harm. In proof of his story, he showed me the two scars and the perforated buckle-plate.

At another time, being in charge of a picket of Germans, he and his command were captured by a party of Confederates, who haled him before their colonel, a southern gentleman of the old school. In the course of his interrogation by the southern officer, he was asked where he hailed from. He replied, "London, England." "Then," said the colonel, "how is it you find yourself fighting for these accursed Yankees?" The cockney faltered out some feeble excuse or another, which his captor cut short by saying, "I've a great respect for the English, and consequently I'll let you go this time. But if ever I catch you again, you're gone up. As for those d——d Dutchmen, they'll be strung up inside of five minutes." And they were.

So with yarn, song, and dance, the evening passed pleasantly away; while the two old hookers jogged amicably along side by side, like two market-horses whose drivers are having a friendly crack. Along about midnight we exchanged crews again, and parted with many expressions of good-will—we to the southward, she to the eastward, for some particular preserve believed in by her commander.

In process of time we made the land of Vau Vau, a picturesque, densely wooded, and in many places precipitous, group of islands, the approach being singularly free from dangers in the shape of partly hidden reefs. Long and intricate were the passages we threaded, until we finally came to anchor in a lovely little bay perfectly sheltered from all winds. We moored, within a mile of a dazzling white beach, in twelve fathoms. A few native houses embowered in orange and cocoa-nut trees showed here and there, while the two horns of the bay were steep-to, and covered with verdure almost down to the water's edge. The anchor was hardly down before a perfect fleet of canoes flocked around us, all carrying the familiar balancing outrigger, without which those narrow dugouts cannot possibly keep upright. Their occupants swarmed on board, laughing and playing like so many children, and with all sorts of winning gestures and tones besought our friendship. "You my flem?" was the one question which all asked; but what its import might be we could not guess for some time. By-and-by it appeared that when once you had agreed to accept a native for your "flem," or friend, he from henceforward felt in duty bound to attend to all your wants which it lay within his power to supply. This important preliminary settled, fruit and provisions of various kinds appeared as if by magic. Huge baskets of luscious oranges, massive bunches of gold and green bananas, clusters of green cocoa-nuts, conch-shells full of chillies, fowls loudly protesting against their hard fate, gourds full of eggs, and a few vociferous swine—all came tumbling on board in richest profusion, and, strangest thing of all, not a copper was asked in return. I might have as truly said nothing was asked, since money must have been useless here. Many women came alongside, but none climbed on board. Surprised at this, I asked Samuela the reason, as soon as I could disengage him for a few moments from the caresses of his friends. He informed me that the ladies' reluctance to favour us with their society was owing to their being in native dress, which it is punishable to appear in among white men, the punishment consisting of a rather heavy fine. Even the men and boys, I noticed, before they ventured to climb on board, stayed a while to put on trousers, or what did duty for those useful articles of dress. At any rate, they were all clothed, not merely enwrapped with a fold or two of "tapa," the native bark-cloth, but made awkward and ugly by dilapidated shirts and pants.

She was a busy ship for the rest of that day. The anchor down, sails furled and decks swept, the rest of the time was our own, and high jinks were the result. The islanders were amiability personified, merry as children, nor did I see or hear one quarrelsome individual among them. While we were greedily devouring the delicious fruit, which was piled on deck in mountainous quantities, they encouraged us, telling us that the trees ashore were breaking down under their loads, and what a pity it was that there were so few to eat such bountiful supplies.

We were, it appeared, the first whale-ship that had anchored there that year, and, in that particular bay where we lay, no vessel had moored for over two years. An occasional schooner from Sydney called at the "town" about ten miles away, where the viceroy's house was, and at the present time of speaking one of Godeffroi's Hamburg ships was at anchor there, taking in an accumulation of copra from her agent's store. But the natives all spoke of her with a shrug—"No like Tashman. Tashman no good." Why, I could not ascertain.

Our Kanakas had promised to remain with us till our departure for the south, so, hard as it seemed to them, they were not allowed to go ashore, in case they might not come back, and leave us short-handed. But as their relatives and friends could visit them whenever they felt inclined, the restriction did not hurt them much. The next day, being Sunday, all hands were allowed liberty to go ashore by turns (except the Kanakas), with strict injunctions to molest no one, but to behave as if in a big town guarded by policemen. As no money could be spent, none was given, and, best of all, it was impossible to procure any intoxicating liquor.

Our party got ashore about 9.30, but not a soul was visible either on the beach or in the sun-lit paths which led through the forest inland. Here and there a house, with doors wide open, stood in its little cleared space, silent and deserted. It was like a country without inhabitants. Presently, however, a burst of melody arrested us, and borne upon the scented breeze came—oh, so sweetly!—the well-remembered notes of "Hollingside." Hurriedly getting behind a tree, I let myself go, and had a perfectly lovely, soul-refreshing cry. Reads funny, doesn't it? Sign of weakness perhaps. But when childish memories come back upon one torrent-like in the swell of a hymn or the scent of the hawthorn, it seems to me that the flood-gates open without you having anything to do with it. When I was a little chap in the Lock Chapel choir, before the evil days came, that tune was my favourite; and when I heard it suddenly come welling up out of the depths of the forest, my heart just stood still for a moment, and then the tears came. Queer idea, perhaps, to some people; but I do not know when I enjoyed myself so much as I did just then, except when a boy of sixteen home from a voyage, and strolling along the Knightsbridge Road, I "happened" into the Albert Hall. I did not in the least know what was coming; the notices on the bills did not mean anything to me; but I paid my shilling, and went up into the gallery. I had hardly edged myself into a corner by the refreshment-stall, when a great breaker of sound caught me, hurled me out of time, thought, and sense in one intolerable ecstasy—"For unto us a Child is born; unto us a Son is given"—again and again—billows and billows of glory. I gasped for breath, shook like one in an ague fit; the tears ran down in a continuous stream; while people stared amazed at me, thinking, I suppose, that I was another drunken sailor. Well, I *was* drunk, helplessly intoxicated, but not with drink, with something Divine, untellable, which, coming upon me unprepared, simply swept me away with it into a heaven of delight, to which only tears could testify.

But I am in the bush, whimpering over the tones of "Hollingside." As soon as I had pulled myself together a bit, we went on again in the direction of the sound. Presently we came to a large clearing, in the middle of which stood a neat wooden, pandanus-thatched church. There were no doors or windows to it, just a roof supported upon posts, but a wide verandah ran all round, upon the edge of which we seated ourselves; for the place was full—full to suffocation, every soul within miles, I should think, being there. No white man was present, but the service, which was a sort of prayer-meeting, went with a swing and go that was wonderful to see. There was no perfunctory worship here; no one languidly enduring it because it was "the right sort of thing to show up at, you know;" but all were in earnest, terribly in earnest. When they sang, it behoved us to get away to a little distance, for the vigour of the voices, unless mellowed by distance, made the music decidedly harsh. Every one was dressed in European clothing—the women in neat calico gowns; but the men, nearly all of them, in woollen shirts, pilot-coats, and trousers to match, and sea-boots! Whew! it nearly stifled me to look at them. The temperature was about ninety degrees in the shade, with hardly a breath of air stirring, yet those poor people, from some mistaken notion of propriety, were sweating in torrents under that Arctic rig. However they could worship, I do not know! At last the meeting broke up. The men rushed out, tore off their coats, trousers, and shirts, and flung themselves panting upon the grass, mother-naked, except for a chaplet of cocoa-nut leaves, formed by threading them on a vine-tendril, and hanging round the waist.

Squatting by the side of my "flem," whom I had recognized, I asked him why ever he outraged all reason by putting on such clothes in this boiling weather. He looked at me pityingly for a moment before he replied, "You go chapella Belitani? No put bes' close on top?" "Yes," I said; "but in hot weather put on thin clothes; cold weather, put on thick ones." "S'pose no got more?" he said, meaning, I presumed, more than the one suit. "Well," I said, "more 'better stop 'way than look like big fool, boil all away, same like duff in pot. You savvy duff?" He smiled a wide comprehensive smile, but looked very solemn again, saying directly, "You no go chapella; you no mishnally. No mishnally [missionary=godly]; vely bad. Me no close; no go chapella; vely bad. Evelly tangata, evelly fafiné, got close all same papâlang [every man and woman has clothes like a white man]; go chapella all day Sunday." That this was no figure of speech I proved fully that day, for I declare that the recess between any of the services never lasted more than an hour. Meanwhile the worshippers did not return to their homes, for in many cases they had journeyed twenty or thirty miles, but lay about in the verdure, refreshing themselves with fruit, principally the delightful green cocoa-nuts, which furnish meat and drink both—cool and refreshing in the extreme, as well as nourishing.

We were all heartily welcome to whatever was going, but there was a general air of restraint, a fear of breaking the Sabbath, which prevented us from trespassing too much upon the hospitality of these devout children of the sun. So we contented ourselves with strolling through the beautiful glades and woods, lying down, whenever we felt weary, under the shade of some spreading orange tree loaded with golden fruit, and eating our fill, or rather eating until the smarting of our lips warned us to desist. Here was a land where, apparently, all people were honest, for we saw a great many houses whose owners were absent, not one of which was closed, although many had a goodly store of such things as a native might be supposed to covet. At last, not being able to rid ourselves of the feeling that we were doing something wrong, the solemn silence and Sundayfied air of the whole region seeming to forbid any levity even in the most innocent manner, we returned on board again, wonderfully impressed with what we had seen, but wondering what would have happened if some of the ruffianly crowds composing the crews of many ships had been let loose upon this fair island.

In the evening we lowered a stage over the bows to the water's edge, and had a swimming-match, the water being perfectly delightful, after the great heat of the day, in its delicious freshness; and so to bunk, well pleased indeed with our first Sunday in Vau Vau.

I have no doubt whatever that some of the gentry

who swear at large about the evils of missionaries would have been loud in their disgust at the entire absence of drink and debauchery, and the prevalence of what they would doubtless characterize as adjective hypocrisy on the part of the natives; but no decent man could help rejoicing at the peace, the security, and friendliness manifested on every hand, nor help awarding unstinted praise to whoever had been the means of bringing about so desirable a state of things. I felt that their Sabbatarianism was carried to excess; that they would have been better, not worse, for a little less church, and a little more innocent fun; but ten thousand times better thus than such scenes of lust let loose and abandoned animalism as we witnessed at Honolulu. What pleased me mightily was the absence of the white man with his air of superiority and sleek overlordship. All the worship, all the management of affairs, was entirely in the hands of the natives themselves, and excellently well did they manage everything.

I shall never forget once going ashore in a somewhat similar place, but very far distant, one Sunday morning, to visit the mission station. It was a Church mission, and a very handsome building the church was. By the side of it stood the parsonage, a beautiful bungalow, nestling in a perfect paradise of tropical flowers. The somewhat intricate service was conducted, and the sermon preached, entirely by natives—very creditably too. After service I strolled into the parsonage to see the reverend gentleman in charge, whom I found supporting his burden in a long chair, with a tall glass of brandy and soda within easy reach, a fine cigar between his lips, and a late volume of Ouida's in his hand. All very pleasant and harmless, no doubt, but hardly reconcilable with the ideal held up in missionary magazines. Yet I have no doubt whatever that this gentleman would have been heartily commended by the very men who can hardly find words harsh enough to express their opinion of missionaries of the stamp of Paton, Williams, Moffat, and Mackenzie.

Well, it is highly probable—nay, almost certain, that I shall be accused of drawing an idyllic picture of native life from first impressions, which, if I had only had sufficient subsequent experience among the people, I should have entirely altered. All I can say is, that although I did not live among them ashore, we had a number of them on board; we lay in the island harbour five months, during which I was ashore nearly every day, and from habit I observed them very closely; yet I cannot conscientiously alter one syllable of what I have written concerning them. Bad men and women there were, of course, to be found—as where not?—but the badness, in whatever form, was not allowed to flaunt itself, and was so sternly discountenanced by public (entirely native) opinion, that it required a good deal of interested seeking to find.

But after all this chatter about my amiable friends, I find myself in danger of forgetting the purpose of our visit. We lost no time in preparation, since whaling of whatever sort is conducted in these ships on precisely similar lines, but on Monday morning, at daybreak, after a hurried breakfast, lowered all boats and commenced the compaign. We were provided with boxes—one for each boat—containing a light luncheon, but no ordered meal, because it was not considered advisable to in any way hamper the boat's freedom to chase. Still, in consideration of its being promptly dumped overboard on attacking a whale, a goodly quantity of fruit was permitted in the boats.

In the calm beauty of the pearly dawn, with a gentle hush over all nature, the lofty, tree-clad hills reflected with startling fidelity in the glassy, many-coloured waters, the only sound audible the occasional cra-a-ake of the advance-guard of a flight of fruit-bats (*pèca*) homeward from their nocturnal depredations, we shipped our oars and started, pulling to a certain position whence we could see over an immense area. Immediately upon rounding the horn of our sheltered bay, the fresh breeze of the south-east trades met us right on end with a vigour that made a ten-mile steady pull against it somewhat of a breather. Arriving at the station indicated by the chief, we set sail, and, separating as far as possible without losing sight of each other, settled down for the day's steady cruise. Anything more delightful than that excursion to those who love seashore scenery combined with boat-sailing would be difficult to name. Every variety of landscape, every shape of strait, bay, or estuary, reefs awash, reefs over which we could sail, ablaze with loveliness inexpressible; a steady, gentle, caressing breeze, and overhead one unvarying canopy of deepest blue. Sometimes, when skirting the base of some tremendous cliffs, great caution was necessary, for at one moment there would obtain a calm, death-like in its stillness; the next, down through a cañon cleaving the mountain to the water's edge would come rushing, with a shrill howl, a blast fierce enough to almost lift us out of the water. Away we would scud with flying sheets dead before it, in a smother of spray, but would hardly get full way on her before it was gone, leaving us in the same hush as before, only a dark patch on the water far to leeward marking its swift rush. These little diversions gave us no uneasiness, for it was an unknown thing to make a sheet fast in one of our boats, so that a puff of wind never caught us unprepared.

On that first day we seemed to explore such a variety of stretches of water that one would hardly have expected there could be any more discoveries to make in that direction. Nevertheless, each day's cruise subsequently revealed to us some new nook or other, some quiet haven or pretty passage between islands that, until closely approached, looked like one. When, at sunset, we returned to the ship, not having seen anything like a spout, I felt like one who had been in a dream, the day's cruise having surpassed all my previous experience. Yet it was but the precursor of many such. Oftentimes I think of those halcyon days, with a sigh of regret that they can never more be renewed to me; but I rejoice to think that nothing can rob me of the memory of them.

Much to the discomfort of the skipper, it was four days before a solitary spout was seen, and then it was so nearly dark that before the fish could be reached it was impossible to distinguish her whereabouts. A careful bearing was taken of the spot, in the hope that she might be lingering in the vicinity next morning, and we hastened on board.

Before it was fairly light we lowered, and paddled as swiftly as possible to the bay where we had last seen the spout overnight. When near the spot we rested on our paddles a while, all hands looking out with intense eagerness for the first sign of the whale's appearance. There was a strange feeling among us of unlawfulness and stealth, as of ambushed pirates waiting to attack some unwary merchantman, or highwaymen waylaying a fat alderman on a country road. We spoke in whispers, for the morning was so still that a voice raised but ordinarily would have reverberated among the rocks which almost overhung us, multiplied indefinitely. A turtle rose ghost-like to the surface at my side, lifting his queer head, and, surveying us with stony gaze, vanished as silently as he came.

What a sigh! One looked at the other inquiringly, but the repetition of that long expiration satisfied us all that it was the placid breathing of the party we sought somewhere close at hand. The light grew rapidly better, and we strained our eyes in every direction to discover the whereabouts of our friend, but for some minutes without result. There was a ripple just audible, and away glided the mate's boat right for the near shore. Following him with our eyes, we almost immediately beheld a pale, shadowy column of white, shimmering against the dark mass of the cliff not a quarter of a mile away. Dipping our paddles with the utmost care, we made after the chief, almost holding our breath. His harpooner rose, darted once, twice, then gave a yell of triumph that rang re-echoing all around in a thousand eerie vibrations, startling the drowsy *pèca* in myriads from where they hung in inverted clusters on the trees above. But, for all the notice taken by the whale, she might never have been touched. Close nestled to her side was a youngling of not more, certainly, than five days old, which sent up its baby-spout every now and then about two feet into the air. One long, wing-like fin embraced its small body, holding it close to the massive breast of the tender mother, whose only care seemed to be to protect her young, utterly regardless of her own pain and danger. If sentiment were ever permitted to interfere with such operations as ours, it might well have done so now; for while the calf continually sought to escape from the enfolding fin, making all sorts of puny struggles in the attempt, the

A TEN-MILE STEADY PULL TO WINDWARD.

mother scarcely moved from her position, although streaming with blood from a score of wounds. Once, indeed, as a deep-searching thrust entered her very vitals, she raised her massy flukes high in air with an apparently involuntary movement of agony; but even in that dire throe she remembered the possible danger to her young one, and laid the tremendous weapon as softly down upon the water as if it were a feather fan.

So in the most perfect quiet, with scarcely a writhe, nor any sign of flurry, she died, holding the calf to her side until her last vital spark had fled, and left it to a swift despatch with a single lance-thrust. No slaughter of a lamb ever looked more like murder. Nor, when the vast bulk and strength of the animal was considered, could a mightier example have been given of the force and quality of maternal love.

The whole business was completed in half an hour from the first sight of her, and by the mate's hand alone, none of the other boats needing to use their gear. As soon as she was dead, a hole was bored through the lips, into which a tow-line was secured, the two long fins were lashed close into the sides of the animal by an encircling line, the tips of the flukes were cut off, and away we started for the ship. We had an eight-mile tow in the blazing sun, which we accomplished in a little over eight hours, arriving at the vessel just before two p.m. News of our coming had preceded us, and the whole native population appeared to be afloat to make us welcome. The air rang again with their shouts of rejoicing, for our catch represented to them a gorgeous feast, such as they had not indulged in for many a day. The flesh of the humpbacked whale is not at all bad, being but little inferior to that of the porpoise; so that, as these people do not despise even the coarse rank flesh of the cachalot, their enthusiasm was natural. Their offers of help were rather embarrassing to us, as we could find little room for any of them in the boats, and the canoes only got in our way. Unable to assist us, they vented their superfluous energies on the whale in the most astounding aquatic antics imaginable—diving under it; climbing on to it; pushing and rolling each other headlong over its broad back; shrieking all the while with the frantic, uncontrollable laughter of happy children freed from all restraint. Men, women, and children all mixed in this wild, watery spree; and as to any of them getting drowned, the idea was utterly absurd.

When we got it alongside, and prepared to cut in, all the chaps were able to have a rest, there were so many eager volunteers to man the windlass, not only willing, but, under the able direction of their compatriots belonging to our crew, quite equal to the work of heaving in blubber. All their habitual indolence was cast aside. Toiling like Trojans, they made the old windlass rattle again as they spun the brakes up and down, every blanket-piece being hailed with a fresh volley of eldritch shrieks, enough to alarm a deaf and dumb asylum.

With such ample aid, it was, as may be supposed, a brief task to skin our prize, although the strange arrangement of the belly blubber caused us to lift some disappointing lengths. This whale has the blubber underneath the body lying in longitudinal corrugations, which, when hauled off the carcass at right angles to their direction, stretch out flat to four or five times their normal area. Thus, when the cutting-blocks had reached their highest limit, and the piece was severed from the body, the folds flew together again, leaving dangling aloft but a miserable square of some four or five feet, instead of a fine "blanket" of blubber twenty by five. Along the edges of these *rugæ*, as also upon the rim of the lower jaw, abundance of limpets and barnacles had attached themselves, some of the former large as a horse's hoof, and causing prodigious annoyance to the toiling carpenter, whose duty it was to keep the spades ground. It was no unusual thing for a spade to be handed in with two or three gaps in its edge half an inch deep, where they had accidentally come across one of those big pieces of flinty shell, undistinguishable from the grey substance of the belly blubber.

But, in spite of these drawbacks, in less than ninety minutes the last cut was reached, the vertebra severed, and away went the great mass of meat, in tow of countless canoes, to an adjacent point, where, in eager anticipation, fires were already blazing for the coming cookery. An enormous number of natives had gathered from far and near, late arrivals continually dropping in from all points of the compass with breathless haste. No danger of going short need have troubled them, for, large as were their numbers, the supply was evidently fully equal to all demands. All night long the feast proceeded, and, even when morning dawned, busy figures were still discernible coming and go̊ing between the reduced carcass and the fires, as if determined to make an end of it before their operations ceased.

CHAPTER XXI.

PROGRESS OF THE "HUMPBACK" SEASON.

It will probably be inferred from the foregoing paragraph that we were little troubled with visits from the natives next day; but it would be doing them an injustice if I omitted to state that our various "flems" put in an appearance as usual with their daily offerings of fruit, vegetables, etc. They all presented a somewhat jaded and haggard look, as of men who had dined not wisely but too well, nor did the odour of stale whale-meat that clung to them add to their attractions. Repentance for excesses or gluttony did not seem to trouble them, for they evidently considered it would have been a sin not to take with both hands the gifts the gods had so bountifully provided. Still, they did not stay long, feeling, no doubt, sore need of a prolonged rest after their late arduous exertions; so, after affectionate farewells, they left us again to our greasy task of trying-out.

The cow proved exceedingly fat, making us, though by no means a large specimen, fully fifty barrels of oil. The whalebone (baleen) was so short as to be not worth the trouble of curing, so, with the exception of such pieces as were useful to the "scrimshoners" for ornamenting their nicknacks, it was not preserved. On the evening of the third day the work was so far finished that we were able to go ashore for clothes washing, which necessary process was accompanied with a good deal of fun and hilarity. In the morning cruising was resumed again.

For a couple of days we met with no success, although we had a very aggravating chase after some smart bulls we fell in with, to our mutual astonishment, just as we rounded a point of the outermost island. They were lazily sunning themselves close under the lee of the cliffs, which at that point were steep-to, having a depth of about twenty fathoms close alongside. A fresh breeze was blowing, so we came round the point at a great pace, being almost among them before they had time to escape. They went away gaily along the land, not attempting to get seaward, we straining every nerve to get alongside of them. Whether they were tantalizing us or not, I cannot say, but certainly it looked like it. In spite of their well-known speed, we were several times so close in their wake that the harpooners loosed the tacks of the jibs to get a clear shot; but as they did so the nimble monsters shot ahead a length or two, leaving us just out of reach. It was a fine chase while it lasted, though annoying; yet one could hardly help feeling amused at the way they wallowed along—just like a school of exaggerated porpoises. At last, after nearly two hours of the fun, they seemed to have had enough of it, and with one accord headed seaward at a greatly accelerated pace, as who should say, "Well, s' long, boys; company's very pleasant and all that, but we've got important business over at Fiji, and can't stay fooling around here any longer." In a quarter of an hour they were out of sight, leaving us disgusted and outclassed pursuers sneaking back again to shelter, feeling very small. Not that we could have had much hope of success under the circumstances, knowing the peculiar habits of the hump back and the almost impossibility of competing with him in the open sea; but they had lured us on to forget all these things in the ardour of the chase, and then exposed our folly.

Then ensued a week or two of uneventful cruising, broken only by the capture of a couple of cows—one just after the fruitless chase mentioned above, and one several days later. These events, though interesting enough to us, were marked by no such deviation from the ordinary course as to make them worthy of special attention; nor do I think that the cold-blooded killing of a cow-whale, who dies patiently endeavouring to protect her young, is a subject that lends itself to eulogium.

However, just when the delightful days were beginning to pall upon us, a real adventure befell us, which, had we been attending strictly to business, we should not have encountered. For a week previous we had been cruising constantly without ever seeing a spout, except those belonging to whales out at sea, whither we knew it was folly to follow them. We tried all sorts of games to while away the time, which certainly did hang heavy, the most popular of which was for the whole crew of the boat to strip, and, getting overboard, be towed along at the ends of short warps, while I sailed her. It was quite mythological—a sort of rude reproduction of Neptune and his attendant Tritons. At last, one afternoon as we were listlessly lolling (half asleep, except the look-out man) across the thwarts, we suddenly came upon a gorge between two cliffs that we must have passed before several times unnoticed. At a certain angle it opened, disclosing a wide sheet of water, extending a long distance ahead. I put the helm up, and we ran through the passage, finding it about a boat's length in width and several fathoms deep, though overhead the cliffs nearly came together in places. Within, the scene was very beautiful, but not more so than many similar ones we had previously witnessed. Still, as the place was new to us, our languor was temporarily dispelled, and we paddled along, taking in every feature of the shores with keen eyes that let nothing escape. After we had gone on in this placid manner for maybe an hour, we suddenly came to a stupendous cliff—that is, for those parts—rising almost sheer from the water for about a thousand feet. Of itself it would not have arrested our attention, but at its base was a semicircular opening, like the mouth of a small tunnel. This looked alluring, so I headed the boat for it, passing through a deep channel between two reefs which led straight to the opening. There was ample room for us to enter, as we had lowered the mast; but just as we were passing through, a heave of the unnoticed swell lifted us unpleasantly near the crown of this natural arch. Beneath us, at a great depth, the bottom could be dimly discerned, the water being of the richest blue conceivable, which the sun, striking down through, resolved into some most marvellous colour-schemes in the path of its rays. A delicious sense of coolness, after the fierce heat outside, saluted us as we entered a vast hall, whose roof rose to a minimum height of forty feet, but in places could not be seen at all. A sort of diffused light, weak, but sufficient to reveal the general contour of the place, existed, let in, I supposed, through some unseen crevices in the roof or walls. At first, of course, to our eyes fresh from the fierce glare outside, the place seemed wrapped in impenetrable gloom, and we dared not stir lest we should run into some hidden danger. Before many minutes, however, the gloom lightened as our pupils enlarged, so that, although the light was faint, we could find our way about with ease. We spoke in low tones, for the echoes were so numerous and resonant that even a whisper gave back from those massy walls in a series of recurring hisses, as if a colony of snakes had been disturbed.

We paddled on into the interior of this vast cave, finding everywhere the walls rising sheer from the silent, dark waters, not a ledge or a crevice where one might gain foothold. Indeed, in some places there was a considerable overhang from above, as if a great dome whose top was invisible sprang from some level below the water. We pushed ahead until the tiny semicircle of light through which we had entered was only faintly visible; and then, finding there was nothing to be seen except what we were already witnessing, unless we cared to go on into the thick darkness, which extended apparently into the bowels of the mountain, we turned and started to go back. Do what we would, we could not venture to break the solemn hush that surrounded us as if we were shut within the dome of some vast cathedral in the twilight. So we paddled noiselessly along for the exit, till suddenly an awful, inexplicable roar set all our hearts thumping fit to break our bosoms. Really, the sensation was most painful, especially as we had not the faintest idea whence the noise came or what had produced it. Again it filled that immense cave with its thunderous reverberations; but this time all the sting was taken out of it, as we caught sight of its author. A goodly bull-humpback had found his way in after us, and the sound of his spout, exaggerated a thousand times in the confinement of that mighty cavern, had frightened us all so that we nearly lost our breath. So far, so good; but, unlike the old nigger, though we were "doin' blame well," we did not "let blame well alone." The next spout that intruder gave, he was right alongside of us. This was too much for the semi-savage instincts of my gallant harpooner, and before I had time to shout a caution he had plunged his weapon deep into old Blowhard's broad back.

I should like to describe what followed, but, in the first place, I hardly know; and, in the next, even had I been cool and collected, my recollections would sound like the ravings of a fevered dream. For of all the hideous uproars conceivable, that was, I should think, about the worst. The big mammal seemed to have gone frantic with the pain of his wound, the surprise of the attack, and the hampering confinement in which he found himself. His tremendous struggles caused such a commotion that our position could only be compared to that of men shooting Niagara in a cylinder at night. How we kept afloat, I do not know. Some one had the gumption to cut the line, so that by the radiation of the disturbance we presently found ourselves close to the wall, and trying to hold the boat in to it with our finger tips. Would he never be quiet? we thought, as the thrashing, banging, and splashing still went on with unfailing vigour. At last, in, I suppose, one supreme effort to escape, he leaped clear of the water like a salmon. There was a perceptible hush, during which we shrank together like unfledged chickens on a frosty night; then, in a never-to-be-forgotten crash that ought to have brought down the massy roof, that mountainous carcass fell. The consequent violent upheaval of the water should have smashed the boat against the rocky walls, but that final catastrophe was mercifully spared us. I suppose the rebound was sufficient to keep us a safe distance off.

A perfect silence succeeded, during which we sat

speechless, awaiting a resumption of the clamour. At last Abner broke the heavy silence by saying, "I doan' see the do'way any mo' at all, sir." He was right. The tide had risen, and that half-moon of light had disappeared, so that we were now prisoners for many hours, it not being at all probable that we should be able to find our way out during the night ebb. Well, we were not exactly children, to be afraid of the dark, although there is considerable difference between the velvety darkness of a dungeon and the clear, fresh night of the open air. Still, as long as that beggar of a whale would only keep quiet or leave the premises, we should be fairly comfortable. We waited and waited until an hour had passed, and then came to the conclusion that our friend was either dead or gone out, as he gave no sign of his presence.

That being settled, we anchored the boat, and lit pipes, preparatory to passing as comfortable a night as might be under the circumstances, the only thing troubling me being the anxiety of the skipper on our behalf. Presently the blackness beneath was lit up by a wide band of phosphoric light, shed in the wake of no ordinary-sized fish, probably an immense shark. Another and another followed in rapid succession, until the depths beneath were all ablaze with brilliant foot-wide ribands of green glare, dazzling to the eye and bewildering to the brain. Occasionally, a gentle splash or ripple alongside, or a smart tap on the bottom of the boat, warned us how thick the concourse was that had gathered below. Until that weariness which no terror is proof against set in, sleep was impossible, nor could we keep our anxious gaze from that glowing inferno beneath, where one would have thought all the population of Tartarus were holding high revel. Mercifully, at last we sank into a fitful slumber, though fully aware of the great danger of our position. One upward rush of any of those ravening monsters, happening to strike the frail shell of our boat, and a few fleeting seconds would have sufficed for our obliteration as if we had never been.

But the terrible night passed away, and once more we saw the tender, irridescent light stream into that abode of dread. As the day strengthened, we were able to see what was going on below, and a grim vision it presented. The water was literally alive with sharks of enormous size, tearing with never-ceasing energy at the huge carcass of the whale lying on the bottom, who had met his fate in a singular but not unheard-of way. At that last titanic effort of his he had rushed downward with such terrific force that, striking his head on the bottom, he had broken his neck. I felt very grieved that we had lost the chance of securing him; but it was perfectly certain that before we could get help to raise him, all that would be left on his skeleton would be quite valueless to us. So with such patience as we could command we waited near the entrance until the receding ebb made it possible for us to emerge once more into the blessed light of day. I was horrified at the haggard, careworn appearance of my crew, who had all, excepting the two Kanakas, aged perceptibly during that night of torment. But we lost no time in getting back to the ship, where I fully expected a severe wigging for the scrape my luckless curiosity had led me into. The captain, however, was very kind, expressing his pleasure at seeing us all safe back again, although he warned me solemnly against similar investigations in future. A hearty meal and a good rest did wonders in removing the severe effects of our adventure, so that by next morning we were all fit and ready for the day's work again.

It certainly seemed as if I was in for a regular series of troubles. After cruising till nearly two p.m., we fell in with the mate's boat, and were sailing quietly along side by side, when we suddenly rounded a point and ran almost on top of a bull-humpback that was basking in the beautiful sunshine. The mate's harpooner, a wonderfully smart fellow, was not so startled as to lose his chance, getting an iron well home before the animal realized what had befallen him. We had a lovely fight, lasting over an hour, in which all the marvellous agility with which this whale is gifted was exerted to the full in order to make his escape. But with the bottom not twenty fathoms away, we were sure of him. With all his supple smartness, he had none of the dogged savagery of the cachalot about him, nor did we feel any occasion to beware of his rushes, rather courting them, so as to finish the game as quickly as possible.

He was no sooner dead than we hurried to secure him, and had actually succeeded in passing the tow-line through his lips, when, in the trifling interval that passed while we were taking the line aft to begin towing, he started to sink. Of course it was, "Let go all!" If you can only get the slightest way on a whale of this kind, you are almost certain to be able to keep him afloat, but once he begins to sink you cannot stop him. Down he went, till full twenty fathoms beneath us he lay comfortably on the reef, while we looked ruefully at one another. We had no gear with us fit to raise him, and we were ten miles from the ship; evening was at hand, so our prospects of doing anything that night were faint.

However, the mate decided to start off for home at once, leaving us there, but promising to send back a boat as speedily as possible with provisions and gear for the morning. There was a stiff breeze blowing, and he was soon out of sight; but we were very uncomfortable. The boat, of course, rode like a duck, but we were fully exposed to the open sea; and the mighty swell of the Pacific, rolling in over those comparatively shallow grounds, sometimes looked dangerously like breaking. Still, it was better than the cave, and there was a good prospect of supper. Long before we expected her, back came the boat, bringing bountiful provision of yams, cold pork and fruit—a regular banquet to men who were fasting since daylight. A square meal, a comforting pipe, and the night's vigil, which had looked so formidable, no longer troubled us, although, to tell the truth, we were heartily glad when the dawn began to tint the east with pale emerald and gold. We set to work at once, getting the huge carcass to the surface without as much labour as I had anticipated. Of course all hands came to the rescue.

But, alas for the fruit of our labours! Those hungry monsters had collected in thousands, and, to judge from what we were able to see of the body, they had reduced its value alarmingly. However, we commenced towing, and were getting along fairly well, when a long spur of reef to leeward of us, over which the sea was breaking frightfully, seemed to be stretching farther out to intercept us before we could get into smooth water. The fact soon faced us that we were in the remorseless grip of a current that set right over that reef, and against its steady stream all our efforts were the merest triviality. Still, we hung on, struggling desperately to keep what we had earned, until so close to the roaring, foaming line of broken water, that one wave breaking farther out than the rest very nearly swamped us all. One blow of an axe, one twirl of the steer-oars, and with all the force we could muster, we were pulling away from the very jaws of death, leaving our whale to the hungry crowds, who would make short work of him. Downcast indeed, at our bad luck, we returned on board, disappointing the skipper very much with our report. Like the true gentleman he was though, recognizing that we had done our best, he did not add to the trouble by cursing us all for a set of useless trash, as his predecessor would have done; on the contrary, a few minutes after the receipt of the bad news his face was as bright as ever, his laugh as hearty as if there was no such thing as a misfortune in the world.

And now I must come to what has been on my mind so long—a tragedy that, in spite of all that had gone before, and of what came after, is the most indelible of all the memories which cling round me of that eventful time. Abner Cushing, the Vermonter, had declared at different times that he should never see his native Green Mountain again. Since the change in our commander, however, he had been another man—always silent and reserved, but brighter, happier, and with a manner so improved as to make it hard to recognize him for the same awkward, ungainly slab of a fellow that had bungled everything he put his hand to. Taking stock of him quietly during our day-long leisurely cruises in the boat, I often wondered whether his mind still kept its gloomy forebodings, and brooded over his tragical life-history. I never dared to speak to him on the subject, for fear of arousing what I hoped was growing too faint for remembrance. But at times I saw him in the moonlit evenings sitting on the rail alone, steadfastly gazing down into the star-besprent waters beneath him, as if coveting their unruffled peace.

Two-thirds of our stay in the islands had passed way, when, for a wonder, the captain took it into his head to go up to the chief village one morning. So he retained me on board, while the other three boats left for the day's cruise as usual. One of the mate's crew was sick, and to replace him he took Abner out of my boat. Away they went; and shortly after breakfast-time I lowered, received the captain on board, and we started for the capital. Upon our arrival there we interviewed the chief, a stout, pleasant-looking man of about fifty, who was evidently held in great respect by the natives, and had a chat with the white Wesleyan missionary in charge of the station. About two p.m., after the captain's business was over, we were returning under sail, when we suddenly caught sight of two of our boats heading in towards one of the islands. We helped her with the paddles to get up to them, seeing as we neared them the two long fins of a whale close ahead of one of them. As we gazed breathlessly at the exciting scene, we saw the boat rush in between the two flippers, the harpooner at the same time darting an iron straight down. There was a whirl in the waters, and quick as thought the vast flukes of the whale rose in the air, recurving with a sidelong sweep as of some gigantic scythe. The blow shore off the bow of the attacking boat as if it had been an egg-shell.

At the same moment the mate stooped, picked up the tow-line from its turn round the loggerhead, and threw it forward from him. He must have unconsciously given a twist to his hand, for the line fell in a kink round Abner's neck just as the whale went down with a rush. Struggling, clutching at the fatal noose, the hapless man went flying out through the incoming sea, and in one second was lost to sight for ever. Too late, the harpooner cut the line which attached the wreck to the retreating animal, leaving the boat free, but gunwale under. We instantly hauled alongside of the wreck and transferred her crew, all dazed and horror-stricken at the awful death of their late comrade.

I saw the tears trickle down the rugged, mahogany-coloured face of the captain, and honoured him for it, but there was little time to waste in vain regrets. It was necessary to save the boat, if possible, as we were getting short of boat-repairing material; certainly we should not have been able to build a new one. So, drawing the two sound boats together, one on either side of the wreck, we placed the heavy steering oars across them from side to side. We then lifted the battered fore part upon the first oar, and with a big effort actually succeeded in lifting the whole of the boat out of water upon this primitive pontoon. Then taking the jib, we "frapped" it round the opening where the bows had been, lashing it securely in that position. Several hands were told off to jump into her stern on the word, and all being ready we launched her again. The weight of the chaps in her stern-sheets cocked her bows right out of water, and in that position we towed her back to the ship, arriving safely before dusk.

That evening we held a burial service, at which hundreds of natives attended with a solemnity of demeanour and expressions of sorrow that would not have been out of place at the most elaborate funeral in England or America. It was a memorable scene. The big cressets were lighted, shedding their wild glare over the dark sea, and outlining the spars against the moonless sky with startling effect. When we had finished the beautiful service, the natives, as if swayed by an irresistible impulse, broke into the splendid tune St. Ann's; and I afterwards learned that the words they sang were Dr. Watts' unsurpassable rendering of Moses'

THE VAST FLUKES OF THE WHALE . . . SHORE OFF THE BOW OF THE ATTACKING BOAT.

pean of praise, "O God, our help in ages past." No elaborate ceremonial in towering cathedral could begin to compare with the massive simplicity of poor Abner's funeral honours, the stately hills for many miles re-iterating the sweet sounds, and carrying them to the farthest confines of the group.

Next day was Sunday, and, in pursuance of a promise given some time before, I went ashore to my "flem's" to dinner, he being confined to the house with a hurt leg. It was not by any means a festive gathering, for he was more than commonly taciturn; his daughter Irene, a buxom lassie of fourteen, who waited on us, appeared to be dumb; and his wife was "in the straw." These trifling drawbacks, however, in nowise detracted from the hospitality offered. The dining-room was a large apartment furnished with leaves, the uprights of cocoa-nut tree, the walls and roof of pandanus leaf. Beneath the heaps of leaves, fresh and sweet-scented, was the earth. The inner apartment, or chamber of state, had a flooring of highly-polished planks, and contained, I presume, the household gods; but as it was in possession of my host's secluded spouse, I did not enter.

A couch upon a pile of leaves was hastily arranged, upon which I was bidden to seat myself, while a freshly-cut cocoa-nut of enormous size was handed to me, the soft top sliced off so that I might drink its deliciously cool contents. These nuts must grow elsewhere, but I have never before or since seen any so large. When green—that is, before the meat has hardened into indigestible matter—they contain from three pints to two quarts of liquid, at once nourishing, refreshing, and palatable. The natives appeared to drink nothing else, and I never saw a drop of fresh water ashore during our stay.

Taking a huge knife from some hiding-place, Irene handed it to her father, who at once commenced to dig in the ground by his side, while I looked on wondering and amused. Presently he fished up a bundle of leaves bound with a vine-tendril, which he laid carefully aside. More digging brought to light a fine yam about three pounds in weight, which, after carefully wiping the knife on some leaves, he proceeded to peel. It was immediately evident that the yam was perfectly cooked, for it steamed as he removed the skin, revealing the inside as white as milk. Some large, round leaves were laid in front of me, and the yam placed upon them. Then mine host turned his attention to the bundle first unearthed, which concealed a chicken, so perfectly done that, although the bones drew out of the meat as if it had been jelly, it was full of juice and flavour; and except for a slight foreign twang, referrible, doubtless, to the leaves in which it had been enwrapped, I do not think it could have been possible to cook anything in a better way, or one more calculated to retain all the natural juices of the meat. The fowl was laid beside the yam, another nut broached; then, handing me the big knife, my "flem" bade me welcome, informing me that I saw my dinner. As nothing would induce him to join me, the idea being contrary to his notions of respect due to a guest, I was fain to fall to, and an excellent meal I made. For dessert, a basketful of such oranges freshly plucked as cannot be tasted under any other conditions, and crimson bananas, which upon being peeled looked liked curved truncheons of golden jelly, after tasting which I refused to touch anything else.

A corn-cob cigarette closed the banquet. After expressing my thanks, I noticed that the pain of his leg was giving my friend considerable uneasiness, which he was stolidly enduring upon my account rather than appear discourteously anxious to get rid of me. So with the excuse that I must needs be going, having another appointment, I left the good fellow and strolled around to the chapel, where I sat enjoying the sight of those simple-minded Kanakas at their devotions till it was time to return on board. Before closing this chapter, I would like, for the benefit of such of my readers who have not heard yet of Kanaka cookery, to say that it is simplicity itself. A hole is scooped in the earth, in which a fire is made (of wood), and kept burning until a fair-sized heap of glowing charcoal remains. Pebbles are then thrown in until the charcoal is covered. Whatever is to be cooked is enveloped in leaves, placed upon the pebbles, and more leaves heaped upon it. The earth is then thrown back into the cavity, and well stamped down. A long time is, of course, needed for the viands to get cooked through; but so subtle is the mode that overdoing anything is almost an impossibility. A couple of days may pass from the time of "putting down" the joint, yet when it is dug up it will be smoking hot, retaining all its juices, tender as jelly, but, withal, as full of flavour as it is possible for cooked meat to be. No matter how large the joint is, or how tough the meat, this gentle suasion will render it succulent and tasty; and no form of civilized cookery can in the least compare with it.

CHAPTER XXII.

FAREWELL TO VAU VAU.

Taking it all round, our visit to the Friendly Islands had not been particularly fortunate up till the time of which I spoke at the conclusion of the last chapter. Two-thirds of the period during which the season was supposed to last had expired, but our catch had not amounted to more than two hundred and fifty barrels of oil. Whales had been undoubtedly scarce, for our ill-success on tackling bulls was not at all in consequence of our clumsiness, these agile animals being always a handful, but due to the lack of cows, which drove us to take whatever we could get, which, as has been noted, was sometimes a severe drubbing. Energy and watchfulness had been manifested in a marked degree by everybody, and when the news circulated that our stay was drawing to a close, there was, if anything, an increase of zeal in the hope that we might yet make a favourable season.

But none of these valuable qualities exhibited by us could make up for the lack of "fish" which was lamentably evident. It was not easy to understand why, because these islands were noted as a breeding-place for the humpbacked whale. Yet for years they had not been fished, so that a plausible explanation of the paucity of their numbers as a consequence of much harassing could not be reasonably offered. Still, after centuries of whale-fishing, little is known of the real habits of whales. Where there is abundance of "feed," in the case of *Mysticeta* it may be reasonably inferred that whales may be found in proportionately greater numbers. With regard to the wider-spread classes of the great marine mammalia, beyond the fact, ascertained from continued observation, that certain parts of the ocean are more favoured by them than others, there is absolutely no data to go upon as to why at times they seem to desert their usual haunts and scatter themselves far and wide.

The case of the cachalot is still more difficult. All the *Balaenæ* seem to be compelled, by laws which we can only guess at, to frequent the vicinity of land possessing shallows at their breeding times, so that they may with more or less certainty be looked for in such places at the seasons which have been accurately fixed. They may be driven to seek other haunts, as was undoubtedly the case at Vau Vau in a great measure, by some causes unknown, but to land they must come at those times. The sperm whale, however, needs no shelter at such periods, or, at any rate, does not avail herself of any. They may often be seen in the vicinity of land where the water is deep close to, but seldom with calves. Schools of cows with recently-born young gambolling about them are met with at immense distances from land, showing no disposition to seek shelter either. For my part, I firmly believe that the cachalot is so terrible a foe, that the great sharks who hover round a gravid cow of the *Balaenæ*, driving her in terror to some shallow spot where she may hope to protect her young, never dare to approach a sperm cow on kidnapping errands, or any other if they can help it, until their unerring guides inform them that life is extinct. When a sperm whale is in health, nothing that inhabits the sea has any chance with him; neither does he scruple to carry the war into the enemy's country, since all is fish that comes to his net, and a shark fifteen feet in length has been found in the stomach of a cachalot.

The only exception he seems to make is in the case of man. Instances have several—nay, many times occurred where men have been slain by the jaws of a cachalot crushing the boat in which they were; but their death was of course incidental to the destruction of the boat. Never, as far as I have been able to ascertain, has a cachalot attacked a man swimming or clinging to a piece of wreckage, although such opportunities occur innumerably. I have in another place told the story of how I once saw a combat between a bull-cachalot and so powerful a combination of enemies that even one knowing the fighting qualities of the sperm whale would have hesitated to back him to win, but the yarn will bear repetition.

Two "killers" and a sword-fish, all of the largest size. Description of these warriors is superfluous, since they are so well known to museums and natural histories; but unless one has witnessed the charge of a *Xiphias*, he cannot realize what a fearful foe it is. Still, as a practice, these creatures leave the cachalot respectfully alone, knowing instinctively that he is not their game. Upon this memorable occasion, however, I guess the two *Orcas* were starving, and they had organized a sort of forlorn hope with the *Xiphias* as an auxiliary who might be relied upon to ensure success if it could be done. Anyhow, the syndicate led off with their main force first; for while the two killers hung on the cachalot's flanks, diverting his attention, the sword-fish, a giant some sixteen feet long, launched himself at the most vulnerable part of the whale, for all the world like a Whitehead torpedo. The wary eye of the whale saw the long, dark mass coming, and, like a practised pugilist, coolly swerved, taking for the nonce no notice of those worrying wolves astern. The shock came; but instead of the sword penetrating three, or maybe four feet just where the neck (if a whale has any neck) encloses the huge heart, it met the mighty, impenetrable mass of the head, solid as a block of thirty tons of india-rubber.

So the blow glanced, revealing a white streak running diagonally across the eye, while the great *Xiphias* rolled helplessly over the top of that black bastion. With a motion so rapid that the eye could scarcely follow it, the whale turned, settling withal, and, catching the momentarily motionless aggressor in the lethal sweep of those awful shears, crunched him in two halves, which writhing sections he swallowed *seriatim*. And the allied forces aft—what of them? Well, they had been rash—they fully realized that fact, and would have fled, but one certainly found that he had lingered on the scene too long. The thoroughly-roused leviathan, with a reversal of his huge bulk that made the sea boil like a pot, brandished his tail aloft and brought it down upon the doomed "killer," making him at once the "killed." He was crushed like a shrimp under one's heel.

The survivor fled—never faster—for an avalanche of living, furious flesh was behind him, and coming with enormous leaps half out of the sea every time. Thus they disappeared, but I have no doubts as to the issue. Of one thing I am certain—that, if any of the trio survived, they never afterwards attempted to rush a cachalot.

Strange to say, the sperm whale does not appear to be a fond mother. At the advent of danger she often deserts her offspring, and in such cases it is hardly conceivable that she ever finds it again. It is true that she is not gifted with such long "arms" as the *Balaenæ*, wherewith to cuddle her young one to her capacious bosom while making tracks from her enemies; nor is she much "on the fight," not being so liberally furnished with jaw as the fierce and much larger bull—for this is the only species of whale in which there exists a great disproportion between the sexes in point of size. Such difference as may obtain between the *Mysticeta* is slightly in favour of the female. I never heard of a cow-cachalot yielding more than fifty barrels of oil; but I have both heard of, and seen, bulls carrying one hundred and fifty. One individual taken by us down south was seventy feet long, and furnished us with more than the latter amount; but I shall come to him by-and-by. Just one more point before leaving this (to me) fascinating subject for the present.

To any one studying the peculiar configuration of a cachalot's mouth, it would appear a difficult problem how the calf could suck. Certainly it puzzled me more than a little. But, when on the "line" grounds we got among a number of cows one calm day, I saw a little fellow about fifteen feet long, apparently only a few days old, in the very act. The mother lay on one side, with the breast nearly at the water's edge; while the calf, lying parallel to its parent, with its head in the same direction, held the teat sideways in the angle of its jaw, with its snout protruding from the surface. Although we caught several cow-humpbacks with newly-born calves, I never had an opportunity of seeing *them* suck.

Gradually our pleasant days at Vau Vau drew to a close. So quiet and idyllic had the life been, so full of simple joys, that most of us, if not all, felt a pang at the thought of our imminent departure from the beautiful place. Profitable, in a pecuniary sense, the season had certainly failed to be, but that was the merest trifle compared with the real happiness and peace enjoyed during our stay. Even the terrible tragedy which had taken one of our fellows from us could not spoil the actual enjoyment of our visit, sad and touching as the event undoubtedly was. There was always, too, a sufficiently arduous routine of necessary duties to perform, preventing us from degenerating into mere lotus eaters in that delicious afternoon-land. Nor even to me, friendless nomad as I was, did the thought ever occur, "I will return no more."

But those lovely days spent in softly gliding over the calm, azure depths, bathed in golden sunlight, gazing dreamily down at the indescribable beauties of the living reefs, feasting daintily on abundance of never-cloying fruit, amid scenes of delight hardly to be imagined by the cramped mind of the town dweller; islands, air, and sea all shimmering in an enchanted haze, and silence scarcely broken by the tender ripple of the gently-parted waters before the boat's steady keel—though these joys have all been lost to me, and I in "populous city pent" endure the fading years, I would not barter the memory of them for more than I can say, so sweet it is to me. And, then, our relations with the natives had been so perfectly amicable, so free from anything to regret. Perhaps this simple statement will raise a cynical smile upon the lips of those who know Tahiti, the New Hebrides, and kindred spots with all their savage, bestial orgies of alternate unbridled lust and unnamable cruelty. Let it be so. For my part, I rejoice that I have no tale of weeks of drunkenness, of brutal rape, treacherous murder, and almost unthinkable torture to tell.

For of such is the paradise of the beach-comber, and the hell of the clean man. Not that I have been able to escape it altogether. When I say that I once shipped, unwittingly, as sailing-master of a little white schooner in Noumea, bound to Apia, finding when too late that she was a "blackbirder," "labour vessel," the wise call it, nothing more will be needed to convince the initiated that I have moved in the "nine circles" of Polynesia.

Some time before the day fixed for our departure, we were busy storing the gifts so liberally showered upon us by our eager friends. Hundreds of bunches of bananas, many thousands of oranges, yams, taro, chillies, fowls, and pigs were accumulated, until the ship looked like a huge market-boat. But we could not persuade any of the natives to ship with us to replace those whose contract was now expiring. Samuela and Polly were, after much difficulty, prevailed upon by me to go with us to New Zealand, much to my gratification; but still we were woefully short-handed. At last, seeing that there was no help for it, the skipper decided to run over to Futuna, or Horn Island, where he felt certain of obtaining recruits without any trouble. He did so most unwillingly, as may well be believed, for the new-comers would need much training, while our present Kanaka auxiliaries were the smartest men in the ship.

The slop-chest was largely drawn upon, to the credit of the crew, who wished in some tangible way to show their appreciation of the unremitting kindness shown them by their dusky friends. Not a whisper had been uttered by any native as to desire of remuneration for what he had given. If they expected a return, they certainly exercised great control over themselves in keeping their wishes quiet. But when they received the clothing, all utterly unsuited to their requirements as it was, their beaming faces eloquently proclaimed the reality of their joy. Heavy woollen shirts, thick cloth trousers and jackets, knitted socks; but acceptable beyond all was a pilot-suit—warm enough for the Channel in winter. Happy above all power of expression was he who secured it. With an eared cloth cap and a pair of half-boots, to complete his preposterous rig, no Bond Street exquisite could feel more calmly conscious of being a well-dressed man than he. From henceforth he would be the observed of all observers at chapel on Sunday, exciting worldly desires and aspirations among his cooler but coveting fellow-worshippers.

The ladies fared very badly, until the skipper, with a twinkling eye, announced that he had "dug up" some rolls of "cloth" (calico), which he was prepared to supply us with at reasonable rates. Being of rather pretty pattern, it went off like hot pies, and as the "fathoms" of gaudy, flimsy material were distributed to the delighted fafinès, their shrill cries of gratitude were almost deafening.

Inexorable time brought round the morning of our departure. Willing hands lifted our anchor, and hoisted the sails, so that we had nothing to do but look on. A scarcely perceptible breeze, stealing softly over the tree-tops, filled our upper canvas, sparing us the labour of towing her out of the little bay where we had lain so long, and gradually wafted us away from its lovely shores, amid the fast-flowing tears of the great crowd. With multitudinous cries of "Ofa, al-ofa, papalang" ringing in our ears ("Good-bye; good-bye, white man"), we rounded the point, and, with increasing pace, bore away through the outlying islands for the open sea. There was a strong trade blowing, making the old barky caper like a dancing-master, which long unfamiliar motion almost disagreed with some of us, after our long quiet. Under its hastening influence we made such good time that before dinner Vau Vau had faded into nothingness, mingling like the clouds with the soft haze on the horizon, from henceforth only a memory.

We were not a very cheerful crowd that night, most of us being busy with his own reflections. I must confess that I felt far greater sorrow at leaving Vau Vau than ever I did at leaving England; because by the time I was able to secure a berth, I have usually drank pretty deep of the bitter cup of the "outward bounder," than whom there is no more forlorn, miserable creature on earth. No one but the much abused boarding-master will have anything to do with him, and that worthy is generally careful to let him know that he is but a hanger-on, a dependant on sufferance for a meal, and that his presence on shore is an outrage. As for the sailors' homes, I have hardly patience to speak of them. I know the sailor is usually a big baby that wants protecting against himself, and that once within the four walls of the institution he is safe; but right there commendation must end. Why are good folks ashore systematically misled into the belief that the sailor is an object of charity, and that it is necessary to subscribe continually and liberally to provide him with food and shelter when ashore? Most of the contributors would be surprised to know that the cost of board and lodging at the "home" is precisely the same as it is outside, and much higher than a landsman of the same grade can live for in better style. With the exception of the sleeping accommodation, most men prefer the boarding-house, where, if they preserve the same commercial status which is a *sine qua non* at the "home," they are treated like gentlemen; but in what follows lies the essential difference, and the reason for this outburst of mine, smothered in silence for years. An "outward bounder" —that is, a man whose money is exhausted and who is living upon the credit of his prospective advance of pay —is unknown at the "home." No matter what the condition of things is in the shipping world; though the man may have fought with energy to get his discharge accepted among the crowd at the "chain-locker;" though he be footsore and weary with "looking for a ship," when his money is done, out into the street he must go, if haply he may find a speculative boarding-master to receive him. This act, although most unlikely in appearance, is often performed; and though the boarding-master, of course, expects to recoup himself out of the man's advance note, it is none the less as merciful as the action of the "home" authorities is merciless. Of course a man may go to the "straw house," or, as it is grandiloquently termed, the "destitute seaman's asylum," where for a season he will be fed on the refuse from the "home," and sheltered from the weather. But the ungrateful rascals do not like the "straw house," and use very bad language about it.

The galling thing about the whole affair is that the "sailors' home" figures in certain official publications as a charity, which must be partially supported by outside contributions. It may be a charitable institution, but it certainly is not so to the sailor, who pays fully for everything he receives. The charity is bestowed upon a far different class of people to merchant Jack. Let it be granted that a man is sober and provident, always getting a ship before his money is all gone, he will probably be well content at the home, although very few seamen like to be reminded ashore of their sea routine, as the manner of the home is. If the institution does not pay a handsome dividend, with its clothing shops and refreshment bars, as well as the boarding-house business on such a large scale, only one inference can be fairly drawn—there must be something radically wrong with the management.

After this burst of temper, perhaps I had better get back to the subject in hand. It was, I suppose, in the usual contrary nature of things that, while we were all in this nearly helpless condition, one evening just before sunset, along comes a sperm whale. Now, the commonest prudence would have suggested letting him severely alone, since we were not only short-handed, but several of our crew were completely crippled by large boils; but it would have been an unprecedented thing to do while there was any room left in the hold. Consequently we mustered the halt and the lame, and manned two boats—all we could do—leaving the almost useless cripples to handle the ship. Not to displace the rightful harpooner, I took an oar in one of them, headed by the captain.

At first my hopes were high that we should not succeed in reaching the victim before dark, but I was grievously disappointed in this. Just as the whale was curving himself to sound, we got fairly close, and the harpooner made a "pitch-pole" dart; that is, he hurled his weapon into the air, where it described a fine curve, and fell point downward on the animal's back just as he was disappearing. He stopped his descent immediately, and turned savagely to see what had struck him so unexpectedly. At that moment the sun went down.

After the first few minutes' "kick-up," he settled down for a steady run, but not before the mate got good and fast to him likewise. Away we went at a rare rate into the gathering gloom of the fast-coming night. Now, had it been about the time of full moon or thereabouts, we should doubtless have been able, by the flood of molten light she sends down in those latitudes, to give a good account of our enemy; but alas for us, it was not. The sky overhead was a deep blue-black, with steely sparkles of starlight scattered all over it, only serving to accentuate the darkness. After a short time our whale became totally invisible, except for the phosphoric glare of the water all around him as he steadily ploughed his way along. There was a good breeze blowing, which soon caused us all to be drenched with the spray, rendering the general effect of things cold as well as cheerless. Needless to say, we strove with all our might to get alongside of him, so that an end might be put to so unpleasant a state of affairs; but in our crippled condition it was not at all easy to do so.

We persevered, however, and at last managed to get near enough for the skipper to hurl a lance into the brightness of which the whale formed the centre. It must have touched him, for he gave a bound forward and disappeared. We suddenly came to a standstill, but in a moment were whirled round as if on a pivot, and away we went in the opposite direction. He had turned a complete somersault in the water beneath us, giving us a "grue" as we reflected what would have happened had he then chosen to come bounding to the surface. This manœuvre seemed to please him mightily, for he ran at top speed several minutes, and then repeated it. This time he was nearly successful in doing us some real harm, for it was now so dark that we could hardly see the other boat's form as she towed along parallel to us about three or four lengths away. The two boats swung round in a wide circle, rushing back at each other out of the surrounding darkness as if bent on mutual destruction. Only by the smartest manipulation was a collision avoided, which, as each boat's bows bristled with lances and harpoons, would have been a serious matter for some of us. However, the whale did not have it all his own way, for the skipper, having charged his bomb-gun, patiently laid for him, and fired. It was rather a long shot, but it reached him, as we afterwards ascertained, making an ugly wound in the small near his tail.

Its effect upon him was startling and immediate. He rushed off at so furious a rate dead to windward that for a great while we had all our work cut out to keep her free by baling. The sea had risen a little, and as we leapt from one wave to another the spray flew over us in an almost continuous cloud. Clearly our situation was a parlous one. We could not get near him; we were becoming dangerously enfeebled, and he appeared to be gaining strength instead of losing it. Besides all this, none of us could have the least idea of how the ship now bore from us, our only comfort being that, by observation of the Cross, we were not making a direct course, but travelling on the circumference of an immense circle. Whatever damage we had done to him so far was evidently quite superficial, for, accustomed as we were to tremendous displays of vigour on the part of these creatures, this specimen fairly surprised us.

The time could only be guessed at; but, judging from

our feelings, it might have been two or three nights long. Still, to all things an end, so in the midst of our dogged endurance of all this misery we felt the pace give, and took heart of grace immediately. Calling up all our reserves, we hauled up on to him, regardless of pain or weariness. The skipper and mate lost no opportunities of lancing, once they were alongside, but worked like heroes, until a final plunging of the fast-dying leviathan warned us to retreat. Up he went out of the glittering foam into the upper darkness, while we held our breath at the unique sight of a whale breaching at night. But when he fell again, the effect was marvellous. Green columns of water arose on either side of the descending mass as if from the bowels of the deep, while their ghostly glare lit up the encircling gloom with a strange, weird radiance, which, reflected in our anxious faces, made us look like an expedition from the *Flying Dutchman*. A short spell of gradually-quieting struggle succeeded as the great beast succumbed, until all was still again, except the strange, low surge made by the waves as they broke over the bank of flesh passively obstructing their free sweep.

While the final touch was being given to our task—*i.e.* the hole-boring through the tail-fin—all hands lay around in various picturesque attitudes, enjoying a refreshing smoke, care forgetting. While thus pleasantly employed, sudden death, like a bolt from the blue, leapt into our midst in a terrible form. The skipper was labouring hard at his task of cutting the hole for the tow-line, when without warning the great fin swung back as if suddenly released from tremendous tension. Happily for us, the force of the blow was broken by its direction, as it struck the water before reaching the boat's side, but the upper lobe hurled the boat-spade from the captain's hands back into our midst, where it struck the tub oarsman, splitting his head in two halves. The horror of the tragedy, the enveloping darkness, the inexplicable revivifying of the monster, which we could not have doubted to be dead, all combined to stupefy and paralyze us for the time. Not a sound was heard in our boat, though the yells of inquiry from our companion craft arose in increasing volume. It was but a brief accession of energy, only lasting two or three minutes, when the whale collapsed finally. Having recovered from our surprise, we took no further chances with so dangerous an opponent, but bored him as full of holes as a colander.

Mournful and miserable were the remaining hours of our vigil. We sat around poor Miguel's corpse with unutterable feelings, recalling all the tragical events of the voyage, until we reached the nadir of despondency. With the rosy light of morning came more cheerful feelings, heightened by the close proximity of the ship, from which it is probable we had never been more than ten miles distant during the whole night. She had sighted us with the first light, and made all sail down to us, all hands much relieved at our safety. We were so sorely exhausted that we could hardly climb on board; and how we hoisted the boats, I hardly know. The whale was secured by the efforts of the cripples we had left on board, while we wayfarers, after a good meal, were allowed four hours' sound, sweet sleep.

When we returned to our duties, the first thing that awaited us was the burial of the poor body. Very reverently were the last sad offices performed, the flag hoisted half-mast, the bell solemnly tolled. Then we gathered at the gangway while the eternal words of hope and consolation were falteringly read, and with a sudden plunge the long, straight parcel slid off the hatch into the vast tomb ever ready for the dead sailor.

Our dead out of sight, work claimed all our attention and energy, wiping out with its beneficent influence all gloomy musings over the inevitable, and replacing them with the pressing needs of life. The whale was not a large one, but peculiar to look at. Like the specimen that fought so fiercely with us in the Indian Ocean, its jaw was twisted round in a sort of hook, the part that curved being so thickly covered with long barnacles as to give the monster a most eerie look. One of the Portuguese expressed his decided opinion that we had caught Davy Jones himself, and that, in consequence, we should have no more accidents. It was impossible not to sympathize with the conceit, for of all the queer-looking monstrosities ever seen, this latest acquisition of ours would have taken high honours. Such malformations of the lower mandible of the cachalot have often been met with, and variously explained; but the most plausible opinion seems to be that they have been acquired when the animal is very young, and its bones not yet indurated, since it is impossible to believe that an adult could suffer such an accident without the broken jaw drooping instead of being turned on one side.

The yield of oil was distressingly scanty, the whale being what is technically known as a "dry skin." The blubber was so hard and tough that we could hardly cut it up for boiling, and altogether it was one of the most disappointing affairs we had yet dealt with. This poorness of blubber was, to my mind, undoubtedly due to the difficulty the animal must have had in obtaining food with his disabling defect of jaw. Whatever it was, we were heartily glad to see the last of the beast, fervently hoping we should never meet with another like him.

During the progress of these melancholy operations we had drifted a considerable distance out of our course, no attention being paid, as usual, to the direction of our drift until the greasy work was done. Once the mess was cleared away, we hauled up again for our objective—Futuna—which, as it was but a few hours' sail distant, we hoped to make the next day.

CHAPTER XXIII.

AT FUTUNA, RECRUITING.

Sure enough, in accordance with our expectations, break of day revealed the twin masses of Futuna ahead, some ten or fifteen miles away. With the fine, steady breeze blowing, by breakfast-time we were off the entrance to a pretty bight, where sail was shortened and the ship hove-to. Captain Count did not intend to anchor, for reasons of his own, he being assured that there was no need to do so. Nor was there. Although the distance from the beach was considerable, we could see numbers of canoes putting off, and soon they began to arrive. Now, some of the South Sea Islands are famous for the elegance and seaworthiness of their canoes; nearly all of them have a distinctly definite style of canoe-building; but here at Futuna was a bewildering collection of almost every type of canoe in the wide world. Dugouts, with outriggers on one side, on both sides, with none at all; canoes built like boats, like prams, like irregular egg-boxes, many looking like the first boyish attempt to knock something together that would float; and—not to unduly prolong the list by attempted classification of these unclassed craft—*coracles*. Yes; in that lonely Pacific island, among that motley crowd of floating nondescripts, were specimens of the ancient coracle of our own islands, constructed in exactly the same way;

that is, of wicker-work, covered with some waterproof substance, whether skin or tarpaulin. But the ingenious Kanaka, not content with his coracles, had gone one better, and copied them in dugouts of solid timber. The resultant vessel was a sort of cross between a butcher's tray and a wash-basin—

> "A thing beyond
> Conception: such a wretched wherry,
> Perhaps ne'er ventured on a pond,
> Or crossed a ferry."

The proud possessors of the coracles, both wicker and wood, must have been poor indeed, for they did not even own a paddle, propelling their basins through the water with their hands. It may be imagined what a pace they put on! At a little distance they were very puzzling, looking more like a water-beetle grown fat and lazy than aught else.

And so, in everything floatable, the whole male population of that part of the coast came to visit us. We were speedily the centre of a great crowd of canoes, some of which were continually capsizing and spilling their occupants, who took no more notice of such incidents than one would of a sneeze. Underneath a canoe, or on top, made but little difference to these amphibious creatures. They brought nothing with them to trade; in fact, few of their vessels were capable of carrying anything that could not swim and take care of itself. As they came on board, each crossed himself more or less devoutly, revealing the teaching of a Roman Catholic mission; and as they called to one another, it was not hard to recognize, even in their native garb, such names as Errènèo (Irenæus), Al'seo (Aloysius), and other favourite cognomens of saints.

A laughing, chattering, good-tempered crowd they

were—just like a bevy of children breaking up, and apparently destitute of the slightest sense of responsibility. They spoke a totally different dialect, or maybe language, to that of Vau Vau, for it was only an isolated word here and there that Samuela could make out. But presently, going forward through the crowd that thronged every part of the deck, I saw a man leaning nonchalantly against the rail by the fore-rigging, who struck me at once as being an American negro. The most casual observer would not have mistaken him for a Kanaka of those latitudes, though he might have passed as a Papuan. He was dressed in all the dignity of a woollen shirt, with a piece of fine "tapa" for a waistcloth, feet and legs bare. Around his neck was a necklace composed of a number of strings of blue and white beads plaited up neatly, and carrying as a pendant a George shilling. Going up to him, I looked at the coin, and said, "Belitani money?" "Oh yes," he said, "that's a shilling of old Georgey Fourf," in perfectly good English, but with an accent which quite confirmed my first idea. I at once invited him aft to see the skipper, who was very anxious to find an interpreter among the noisy crowd, besides being somewhat uneasy at having so large a number on board.

To the captain's interrogations he replied that he was "Tui Tongoa"—that is, King of Tongoa, an island a little distance away—but that he was at present under a cloud, owing to the success of a usurper, whom he would reckon with by-and-by.

In the mean time he would have no objection to engaging himself with us as a harpooner, and would get us as many men as we wanted, selecting from among the crowd on board, fellows that would, he knew, be useful to us.

A bargain was soon struck, and Tui entered upon his self-imposed task. It was immediately evident that he had a bigger contract on hand than he had imagined. The natives, who had previously held somewhat aloof from him in a kind of deferential respect, no sooner got wind of the fact that we needed some of them than they were seized with a perfect frenzy of excitement. There were, I should think, at least a hundred and fifty of them on board at the time. Of this crowd, every member wanted to be selected, pushing his candidature with voice and gesture as vigorously as he knew how. The din was frightful. Tui, centre of the frantic mob, strove vainly to make himself heard, to reduce the chaos to some sort of order, but for a great while it was a hopeless attempt. At last, extricating himself from his importunate friends, he gained the captain's side. Panting, almost breathless, with sweat streaming off him, he gasped out, "Oh, cap'n, dese yer darn niggers all gone mad! Dribe 'em oberbord; clar 'em out, 'n I'll stan' by to grab some o' der likely ones as de res' scatter." "But what about the wages?" said the skipper. "I'm not goin' ter give 'em whatever they like to ask." "You leab it ter me, cap'n. I bet you'll be satisfy. Anyhow, dishyers no time fer tradin'; de blame niggers all off dere coco-nuts. Anybody fink you'se payin' off 'stead o' shippin', an' deyse all afraid dey won't get 'nough."

Unpleasant as the job was to all of us, it had to be done; so we armed ourselves with ropes'-ends, which we flourished threateningly, avoiding where possible any actual blows. Many sprang overboard at once, finding their way ashore or to their canoes as best they could. The majority, however, had to swim, for we now noticed that, either in haste or from carelessness, they had in most cases omitted to fasten their canoes securely when coming alongside, so that many of them were now far out to sea. The distance to shore being under three miles, that mattered little, as far as their personal safety was concerned.

This summary treatment was eminently successful, quiet being rapidly restored, so that Tui was able to select a dozen men, who he declared were the best in the islands for our purpose. Although it seems somewhat premature to say so, the general conduct of the successful candidates was so good as to justify Tui fully in his eulogium. Perhaps his presence had something to do with it?

We now had all that we came for, so that we were anxious to be off. But it was a job to get rid of the visitors still remaining on board. They stowed themselves away in all manner of corners, in some cases ludicrously inadequate as hiding-places, and it was not until we were nearly five miles from the land that the last of them plunged into the sea and struck out for home. It was very queer. Ignorant of our destination, of what would be required of them; leaving a land of ease and plenty for a certainty of short commons and hard work, without preparation or farewells, I do not think I ever heard of such a strange thing before. Had their home been famine or plague-stricken, they could not have evinced greater eagerness to leave it, or to face the great unknown.

As we drew farther off the island the wind freshened, until we had a good, whole-sail breeze blustering behind us, the old ship making, with her usual generous fuss, a tremendous rate of seven knots an hour. Our course was shaped for the southward, towards the Bay of Islands, New Zealand. In that favourite haunt of the

South-seaman we were to wood and water, find letters from home (those who had one), and prepare for the stormy south.

Obviously the first thing to be done for our new shipmates was to clothe them. When they arrived on board, all, with the single exception of Tui, were furnished only with a "maro" of "tapa," scanty in its proportions, but still enough to wrap round their loins. But when they were accepted for the vacant positions on board, they cast off even the slight apology for clothing which they had worn, flinging the poor rags to their retreating and rejected compatriots. Thus they were strutting about, in native majesty unclad, which, of course, could not be endured among even so unconventional a crowd as we were. So they were mustered aft, and, to their extravagant delight, a complete rig-out was handed to each of them, accompanied by graphic instructions how to dress themselves. Very queer they looked when dressed, but queerer still not long afterwards, when some of them, galled by the unaccustomed restraint of the trousers, were seen prowling about with shirts tied round their waists by the sleeves, and pants twisted turban-wise about their heads. Tui was called, and requested to inform them that they must dress properly, after the fashion of the white man, for that any impromptu improvements upon our method of clothes-wearing could not be permitted. As they were gentle, tractable fellows, they readily obeyed, and, though they must have suffered considerably, there were no further grounds for complaint on the score of dress.

It has been already noticed that they were Roman Catholics—all except Tui, who from his superior mental elevation looked down upon their beliefs with calm contempt, although really a greater heathen than any of them had ever been. It was quite pathetic to see how earnestly they endeavoured to maintain the form of worship to which they had been accustomed, though how they managed without their priest, I could not find out. Every evening they had prayers together, accompanied by many crossings and genuflexions, and wound up by the singing of a hymn in such queer Latin that it was almost unrecognizable. After much wondering, I did manage to make out "O Salutaris Hostia!" and "Tantum Ergo," but not until their queer pronunciation of consonants had become familiar. Some of the hymns were in their own tongue, only one of which I can now remember. Phonetically, it ran thus—

> "Mah-lee-ah, Kollyeea leekee;
> Ohselloh mo mallamah.
> Alofah, keea ma toh;
> Fah na oh, Mah lah ee ah"—

which I understood to be a native rendering of "O Stella Maris!" It was sung to the well-known "Processional" in good time, and on that account, I suppose, fixed itself in my memory.

Whenever any of them were ordered aloft, they never failed to cross themselves before taking to the rigging, as if impressed with a sense of their chance of not returning again in safety. To me was given the congenial task of teaching them the duties required, and I am bound to admit that they were willing, biddable, and cheerful learners. Another amiable trait in their characters was especially noticeable: they always held everything in common. No matter how small the portion received by any one, it was scrupulously shared with the others who lacked, and this subdivision was often carried to ludicrous lengths.

As there was no reason to hurry south, we took a short cruise on the Vasquez ground, more, I think, for the purpose of training our recruits than anything else. As far as the results to our profit were concerned, we might almost as well have gone straight on, for we only took one small cow-cachalot. But the time spent thus cruising was by no means wasted. Before we left finally for New Zealand, every one of those Kanakas was as much at home in the whale-boats as he would have been in a canoe. Of course they were greatly helped by their entire familiarity with the water, which took from them all that dread of being drowned which hampers the white "greenie" so sorely; besides which, the absolute confidence they had in our prowess amongst the whales freed them from any fear on that head.

Tui proved himself to be a smart harpooner, and was chosen for the captain's boat. During our conversations, I was secretly amused to hear him allude to himself as Sam, thinking how little it accorded with his *soi-disant* Kanaka origin. He often regaled me with accounts of his royal struggles to maintain his rule, all of which narrations I received with a goodly amount of reserve, though confirmed in some particulars by the Kanakas, when I became able to converse with them. But I was hardly prepared to find, as I did many years after, upon looking up some detail in Findlay's "South Pacific Directory," this worthy alluded to as "the celebrated Sam," in a brief account of Futuna. There he was said to be king of the twin isles; so I suppose he found means to oust his rival, and resume his sovereignty; though, how an American negro, as Sam undoubtedly was, ever managed to gain such a position, remains to me an unfathomable mystery. Certainly he did not reveal any such masterful attributes as one would have expected in him, while he served as harpooner on board the *Cachalot.*

Gradually we crept south, until one morning we sighted the towering mass of Sunday Island, the principal member of the small Kermadec group, which lies nearly on the prime meridian of one hundred and eighty degrees, and but a short distance north of the extremity of New Zealand. We had long ago finished the last of our fresh provisions, fish had been very scarce, so the captain seized the opportunity to give us a run ashore, and at the same time instructed us to do such foraging as we could. It was rumoured that there were many wild pigs to be found, and certainly abundance of goats; but if both these sources of supply failed, we could fall back on fish, of which we were almost sure to get a good haul.

The island is a stupendous mass of rock, rising sheer from the waves, in some places to a height of fifteen hundred feet. These towering cliffs are clothed with verdure, large trees clinging to their precipitous sides in a marvellous way. Except at one small bight, known as Denham Bay, the place is inaccessible, not only from the steepness of its cliffs, but because, owing to its position, the gigantic swell of the South Pacific assails those immense bastions with a force and volume that would destroy instantly any vessel that unfortunately ventured too near. Denham Bay, however, is in some measure protected by reefs of scattered boulders, which break the greatest volume of the oncoming rollers. Within those protecting barriers, with certain winds, it is possible to effect a landing, with caution; but even then no tyro in boat-handling should venture to do so, as the experiment would almost certainly be fatal to boat and crew.

We hove-to off the little bay, the waters of which looked placid enough for a pleasure-party, lowered two boats well furnished with fishing gear and such other equipment as we thought would be needed, and pulled away for the landing-place. As we drew near the beach, we found that, in spite of the hindrance to the ocean swell afforded by the reefs, it broke upon the beach in rollers of immense size. In order to avoid any mishap, then, we turned the boats' heads to seaward, and gently backed towards the beach, until a larger breaker than usual came thundering in. As it rushed towards us, we pulled lustily to meet it, the lovely craft rising to its foaming crest like sea-birds. Then, as soon as we were on its outer slope, we reversed the stroke again, coming in on its mighty shoulders at racing speed. The instant our keels touched the beach we all leapt out, and, exerting every ounce of strength we possessed, ran the boats up high and dry before the next roller had time to do more than hiss harmlessly around our feet. It was a task of uncommon difficulty, for the shore was wholly composed of loose lava and pumice-stone grit, into which we sank ankle-deep at every step, besides being exceedingly steep.

We managed, however, to escape without any mishap, for the drenching was a boon to our burnt-up skins. Off we started along the level land, which, as far as I could judge, extended inland for perhaps a mile and a half by about two miles wide. From this flat shelf the cliffs rose perpendicularly, as they did from the sea. Up their sides were innumerable goat-tracks, upon some of which we could descry a few of those agile creatures climbing almost like flies. The plateau was thickly wooded, many of the trees having been fruit-bearing once, but now, much to our disappointment, barren from neglect.

A ruined house, surrounded by other vestiges of what had once been a homestead, stood in the middle of this piece of land. Feeling curious to know what the history of this isolated settlement might be, I asked the mate if he knew anything of it. He told me that an American named Halstead, with his family, lived here for years, visited only by an occasional whaler, to whom they sold such produce as they might have and be able to spare at the time. What their previous history had been, or why they thus chose to cut themselves off from the world, he did not know; but they seemed contented enough with their tiny kingdom, nor had any wish to leave it. But it came to pass that one night they felt the sure and firm-set earth trembling convulsively beneath their feet. Rushing out of their house, they saw the heavens bespread with an awful pall of smoke, the under-side of which was glowing with the reflected fires of some vast furnace. Their terror was increased by a smart shower of falling ashes and the reverberations of subterranean thunders. At first they thought of flight in their boat, not reckoning the wide stretch of sea which rolled between them and the nearest land, but the height and frequency of the breakers then prevailing made that impossible.

Their situation was pitiable in the extreme. During the years of peace and serenity they had spent here, no thought of the insecurity of their tenure had troubled them. Though they had but been dwellers on the threshold of the mountain, as it were, and any extension of their territory impossible by reason of the insurmountable barrier around them, they had led an untroubled life, all unknowing of the fearful forces beneath their feet. But now they found the foundations of the rocks beneath breaking up; that withering, incessant shower of ashes and scoriæ destroyed all their crops; the mild and delicate air changed into a heavy, sulphurous miasma; while overhead the beneficent face of the bright-blue sky had become a horrible canopy of deadly black, about which played lurid coruscations of infernal fires.

What they endured throughout those days and nights of woe, could never be told. They fled from the home they had reared with such abundance of loving labour, taking refuge in a cave; for not even the knowledge that the mountain itself seemed to be in the throes of dissolution could entirely destroy their trust in those apparently eternal fastnesses. Here their eldest son died, worried to death by incessant terror. At last a passing whaler, remembering them and seeing the condition of things, had the humanity and courage to stand in near enough to see their agonized signals of distress. All of them, except the son buried but a day or two before, were safely received and carried away, leaving the terrible mountain to its solitude.

As I listened, I almost involuntarily cast my eyes upwards; nor was I at all surprised to see far overhead a solitary patch of smoky cloud, which I believe to have been a sure indication that the volcano was still liable to commence operations at any time.

So far, we had not happened upon any pigs, or goats either, although we saw many indications of the latter odoriferous animal. There were few sea-birds to be seen, but in and out among the dense undergrowth ran many short-legged brown birds, something like a partridge—the same, I believe, as we afterwards became familiar with in Stewart's Island by the name of "Maori hens." They were so tame and inquisitive that we had no difficulty in securing a few by the simple process of knocking them over with sticks. From the main branch of a large tree hung a big honey-comb, out of which the honey was draining upon the earth. Around it buzzed a busy concourse of bees, who appeared to us so formidable that we decided to leave them to the enjoyment of their sweet store, in case we should invite an attack.

So far, our rambling had revealed nothing of any service to us; but just then, struck by the appearance of a plant which was growing profusely in a glade we were passing over, I made bold to taste one of the leaves. What the botanical name of the vegetable is, I do not know; but, under the designation of "Maori cabbage," it is well known in New Zealand. It looks like a lettuce, running to seed; but it tastes exactly like young turnip-tops, and is a splendid anti-scorbutic. What its discovery meant to us, I can hardly convey to any one who does not know what an insatiable craving for potatoes and green vegetables possesses seamen when they have for long been deprived of these humble but necessary articles of food. Under the circumstances, no "find" could have given us greater pleasure—that is, in the food line—than this did.

Taking it all round, however, the place as a foraging ground was not a success. We chased a goat of very large size, and beard voluminous as a Rabbi's, into a cave, which may have been the one the Halsteads took shelter in, for we saw no other. One of the Kanakas volunteered to go in after him with a line, and did so. The resultant encounter was the best bit of fun we had had for many a day. After a period of darksome scuffling within, the entangled pair emerged, fiercely wrestling, Billy being to all appearance much the fresher of the two. Fair play seemed to demand that we should let them fight it out; but, sad to say, the other Kanakas could not see things in that light, and Billy was soon despatched. Rather needless killing, too; for no one, except at starvation-point, could have eaten the poor remains of leathery flesh that still decorated that weather-beaten frame.

But this sort of thing was tiring and unprofitable. The interest of the place soon fizzled out, when it was found there was so little worth taking away; so, as the day was getting on, it was decided to launch off and start fishing. In a few minutes we were afloat again, and anchored, in about four fathoms, in as favourable a spot for our sport as ever I saw. Fish swarmed about us of many sorts, but principally of the "kauwhai," a kind of mullet very plentiful about Auckland, and averaging five or six pounds. Much to my annoyance, we had not been able to get any bait, except a bit of raw salt-pork, which hardly any fish but the shark tribe will look at. Had I known or thought of it, a bit of goat would have been far more attractive.

However, as there was no help for it, we baited up and started. "Nary nibble ermong 'em!" growled Sam, as we sat impatiently waiting for a bite. When we hauled up to see what was wrong, fish followed the hook up in hundreds, letting us know plainly as possible that they only wanted something tasty. It was outrageous, exasperating beyond measure! At last Samuela grew so tired of it that he seized his harpoon, and hurled it into the middle of a company of kauwhai that were calmly nosing around the bows. By the merest chance he managed to impale one of them upon the broad point. It was hardly in the boat before I had seized it, scaled it, and cut it into neat little blocks. All hands rebaited with it, and flung out again. The change was astounding. Up they came, two at a time, dozens and dozens of them—kauwhai, cavallè, yellow-tail, schnapper—lovely fish of delicious flavour and goodly size. Then one of us got a fish which made him yell, "Shark! shark!" with all his might. He had a small line of American cotton, staunch as copper wire, but dreadfully cutting to the hands. When he took a turn round the loggerhead, the friction of the running line cut right into the white oak, but the wonderful cord and hook still held their own. At last the monster yielded, coming in at first inch by inch, then more rapidly, till raised in triumph above the gunwale—a yellow-tail six feet long. I have caught this splendid fish (*Elagatis bipinnulatus*) many times before and since then, but never did I see such a grand specimen as this one—no, not by thirty or forty pounds. Then I got a giant cavallè. His broad, shield-like body blazed hither and thither as I struggled to ship him, but it was long ere he gave in to superior strength and excellence of line and hook.

Meanwhile, the others had been steadily increasing our cargo, until, feeling that we had quite as much fish as would suffice us, besides being really a good load, I suggested a move towards the ship. We were laying within about half a mile of the shore, where the extremity of the level land reached the cliffs. Up one of the well-worn tracks a fine, fat goat was slowly creeping, stopping every now and then to browse upon the short herbage that clung to the crevices of the rock. Without saying a word, Polly the Kanaka slipped over the side, and struck out with swift overhead strokes for the foot of the cliff. As soon as I saw what he was after, I shouted loudly for him to return, but he either could not or would not hear me. The fellow's seal-like ability as a swimmer was, of course, well known to me, but I must confess I trembled for his life in such a weltering whirl of rock-torn sea as boiled among the crags at the base of that precipice. He, however, evidently knew what he was going to do, and, though taking risks which would have certainly been fatal to an ordinary swimmer, was quite unafraid of the result.

We all watched him breathlessly as he apparently headed straight for the biggest outlying rock—a square, black boulder about the size of an ordinary railway car. He came up to it on the summit of a foaming wave; but just as I looked for him to be dashed to pieces against its adamantine sides, he threw his legs into the air and disappeared. A stealthy, satisfied smile glowed upon Samuela's rugged visage, and, as he caught my eye, he said jauntily, "Polly savee too much. Lookee him come ontop one time!" I looked, and sure enough there was the daring villain crawling up among the kelp far out of reach of the hungry rollers. It was a marvellous exhibition of coolness and skill.

Without waiting an instant, he began to stalk the goat, dodging amongst the bushes with feet that clung to the steep sides of the cliff as well as the animal's. Before he could reach her, she had winded him, and was off up the track. He followed, without further attempt to hide himself; but, despite his vigour and ability, would, I fancy, have stood a microscopic chance of catching her had she not been heavy with kid. As it was, he had all his work cut out for him. When he did catch her, she made so fierce a struggle for life and liberty that, in the endeavour to hold her, he missed his insecure foothold, and the pair came tumbling over and over down the cliff in a miniature avalanche of stones and dust. At the bottom they both lay quiet for a time; while I anxiously waited, fearing the rash fool was seriously injured; but in a minute or two he was on his feet again.

Lashing the goat to his body, and ignoring her struggles, he crawled out as far among the rocks as he could; then, at the approach of a big breaker, he dived to meet it, coming up outside its threatening top like a life-buoy. I pulled in, as near as I could venture, to pick him up, and in a few minutes had him safely on board again, but suffering fearfully. In his roll down the cliff he had been without his trousers, which would have been some protection to him. Consequently, his thighs were deeply cut and torn in many places, while the brine entering so many wounds, though a grand styptic, must have tortured him unspeakably. At any rate, though he was a regular stoic to bear pain, he fainted while I was "dressing him down" in the most vigorous language I could command for his foolhardy trick. Then we all realized what he must be going through, and felt that he was getting all the punishment he deserved, and more. The goat, poor thing! seemed none the worse for her rough handling.

The mate gave the signal to get back on board just as Polly revived, so there were no inconvenient questions asked, and we returned alongside in triumph, with such a cargo of fish as would have given us a good month's pay all round could we have landed them at Billingsgate. Although the mate had not succeeded as well as we, the catch of the two boats aggregated half a ton, not a fish among the lot less than five pounds weight, and one of a hundred and twenty—the yellow-tail aforesaid. As soon as we reached the ship, the boats were run up, sails filled, and away we lumbered again towards New Zealand.

As the great mass of that solitary mountain faded

away in the gathering shades of evening, it was impossible to help remembering the sufferings of that afflicted family, confined to those trembling, sulphurous, ash-bestrewn rocks, amid gloom by day, and unnatural glare by night, for all that weary while. And while I admit that there is to some people a charm in being alone with nature, it is altogether another thing when your solitude becomes compulsory, your paradise a prison from which you cannot break away. There are many such nooks scattered about the ocean, where men have hidden themselves away from the busy world, and been forgotten by it; but few of them, I fancy, offer such potentialities of terror as Sunday Island.

We had hardly lost sight of the land, when Polly's capture gave birth to a kid. This event was the most interesting thing that had happened on board for a great while, and the funny little visitor would have run great risk of being completely spoiled had he lived. But, to our universal sorrow, the mother's milk failed—from want of green food, I suppose—and we were obliged to kill the poor little chap to save him from being starved to death. He made a savoury mess for some whose appetite for flesh-meat was stronger than any sentimental considerations.

To an ordinary trader, the distance between the Kermadecs and the Bay of Islands, New Zealand, roughly represents a couple of days' sail; but to us, who were apparently incapable of hurry under any circumstances, it meant a good week's bludgeoning the protesting waves before the grim outliers of the Three Kings came into view. Even then, although the distance was a mere bagatelle, it was another two days before we arrived off that magnificent harbour where reposes the oldest township in New Zealand—Russell, where rest the mortal remains of the first really Pakeha Maori, but which, for some unaccountable reason, is still left undeveloped and neglected, visited only by the wandering whalers (in ever-decreasing numbers) and an occasional trim, business-like, and gentlemanly man-o'-war, that, like a Guardsman strolling the West End in mufti, stalks the sea with never an item of her smart rig deviating by a shade from its proper set or sheer.

CHAPTER XXIV.

THE BAY OF ISLANDS AND NEW ZEALAND COAST.

In a comparative new colony like New Zealand, where the marvellous growth of the young state can be traced within living memory, from the privations of the pioneer to the fully developed city with all the machinery of our latest luxurious civilization, it is exceedingly interesting to note how the principal towns have sprung up arbitrarily, and without any heed to the intentions of the ruling powers. The old-fashioned township of Kororarika, or Port Russell, is a case very much in point. As we sailed in between the many islets from which the magnificent bay takes its name, for all appearances to the contrary, we might have been the first discoverers. Not a house, not a sail, not a boat, broke the loneliness and primeval look of the placid waters and the adjacent shores. Not until we drew near the anchorage, and saw upon opening up the little town the straight-standing masts of three whale-ships, did anything appear to dispel the intense air of solitude overhanging the whole. As we drew nearer, and rounded-to for mooring, I looked expectantly for some sign of enterprise on the part of the inhabitants—some tradesman's boat soliciting orders; some of the population on the beach (there was no sign of a pier), watching the visitor come to an anchor. Not a bit of it. The whole place seemed a maritime sleepy hollow, the dwellers in which had lost all interest in life, and had become far less energetic than the much-maligned Kanakas in their dreamy isles of summer.

Yet this was once intended for the capital of New Zealand. When the large and splendidly-built city of Dunedin, Otago, was a barren bush, haunted only by the "morepork" and the apteryx, Russell was humming with vitality, her harbour busy with fleets of ships, principally whalers, who found it the most convenient calling-place in the southern temperate zone. Terrible scenes were enacted about its "blackguard beach," orgies of wild debauchery and bloodshed indulged in by the half-savage and utterly lawless crews of the whale-ships. But it never attained to any real importance. As a port of call for whalers, it enjoyed a certain kind of prosperity; but when the South Sea fishery dwindled, Russell shrank in immediate sympathy. It never had any vitality of its own, no manufactures or products, unless the wretched coal-mines adjacent, with their dirty output, which is scoffed at by the grimiest tug afloat, could be dignified by the name.

Remembering, as I did, the beauty, the energy, and prosperity of the great New Zealand ports, some of them with not a tithe of the natural advantages of Russell, I felt amazed, almost indignant, at its dead-and-alive appearance.

Our anchor was no sooner down than the captains of the *James Arnold, Matilda Sayer*, and *Coral* lowered and came on board, eager to hear or to tell such news as was going. As we had now grown to expect, all work was over immediately the sails were fast and decks cleared up, so that we were free to entertain our visitors.

And a high old time we had of it that afternoon! What with songs, dances, *and* yarns, the hours flew by with lightning speed. Our Kanakas, too, were overjoyed to find compatriots among the visitors, and settled down to a steady stream of talk which lasted, without intermission, the whole night through. It was a wonderful exhibition of tongue-wagging, though what it was all about puzzled me greatly.

Life on board those three ships, though described in glowing terms by the visitors, was evidently not to be mentioned for comfort in the same breath as ours. But we found that our late captain's fame as a "hard citizen" was well known to all; so that it is only ordinary justice to suppose that such a life as he led us was exceptional for even a Yankee spouter. Our friends gave us a blood-curdling account of the Solander whaling ground, which we were about to visit, the *James Arnold* and *Coral* having spent a season there that cruise. I did not, however, pay much attention to their yarns, feeling sure that, even if they were fact, it would not help to brood over coming hardships, and inclined to give liberal discount to most of their statements. The incessant chatter got wearisome at last, and I, for one, was not sorry when, at two in the morning, our visitors departed to their several ships, and left us to get what sleep still remained left to us.

A pleasant expedition was planned for the next day. Our visit being principally for wooding and watering, both of which it was necessary for us to do ourselves, Captain Count showed his usual promptitude in commencing at once. Permission having been obtained and, I suppose, paid for, we set out with two boats and a plentiful supply of axes for a well-wooded promontory to prepare a store of wood. Wood chopping is not usually looked upon as a sailor's pastime; but we had had considerable experience during the voyage, as a result of which most of us could swing an axe in fine style. But the Kanakas beat us all hollow. Delighted to get ashore again, pleased with the fine axes as children with new toys, they laid about them in grand style, the young trees falling right and left in scores. Anybody would have judged that we were working piece-work, at so much a cord, the pile grew so fast. There was such a quantity collected that, instead of lightering it off in the boats, which is very rough and dirty usage for them, I constructed a sort of raft with four large spars arranged in the form of an oblong, placing an immense quantity of the smaller stuff in between. Upright sticks were rudely lashed here and there, to keep the pile from bobbing out underneath, and thus loaded we proceeded slowly to the ship with sufficient wood for our wants brought in one journey. It was immediately hoisted on board, sawn into convenient lengths, and stowed away, the whole operation being completed, of getting between eight and ten tons of firewood cut, ferried, and stowed, in less than eight hours.

Next day was devoted to watering; but as I have elsewhere described that necessary if prosaic occupation, I will not repeat the story. Sufficient to say that the job was successfully "did" in the course of the day.

All the work being accomplished for which we had come, it only remained to give the crew "liberty." So the port watch, in their best (?) rig, were mustered aft; each man received ten shillings, and away they went in glee for the first genuine day's liberty since leaving Honolulu. For although they had been much ashore in Vau Vau, that was not looked upon in the same light as a day's freedom in a town where liquor might be procured, and the questionable privilege of getting drunk taken advantage of. Envious eyes watched their progress from the other ships, but, much to my secret satisfaction, none of their crews were allowed ashore at the same time. There were quite sufficient possibilities of a row among our own crowd, without further complications such as would almost certainly have occurred had the strangers been let loose at the same time. Unfortunately, to the ordinary sailor-man, the place presented no other forms of amusement besides drinking, and I was grieved to see almost the whole crowd, including the Kanakas, emerge from the grog-shop plentifully supplied with bottles, and, seating themselves on the beach, commence their carouse. The natives evinced the greatest eagerness to get drunk, swallowing down the horrible "square gin" as if it were water. They passed with the utmost rapidity through all the stages of drunkenness. Before they had been ashore an hour, most of them were lying like logs, in the full blaze of the sun, on the beach. Seeing this, the captain suggested the advisability of bringing them on board at once, as they were only exposed to robbery by the few prowling Maories that loafed about the beach—a curious contrast to the stately fellows met with in other parts of New Zealand.

So we set to work, and brought them on board again, handing them over to their compatriots by way of warning against similar excesses, although, it must be confessed, that they were hardly to blame, with the example of their more civilized shipmates before their eyes. Sam was energetic in his condemnation of both the Kanakas for getting drunk, and the captain for giving them any money wherewith to do so. The remainder of the watch fortunately concluded their carouse without any serious disorder. A few bruises bestowed upon one another, more in clumsy horseplay than real fighting, summed up the casualties among them. By ten o'clock that evening we had them all safely on board again, ready for sore heads and repentance in the morning.

During the day I had evolved a scheme, which I had great hopes of carrying out when our watch should be let loose on the morrow. When morning came, and the liberty men received their money, I called them together and unfolded my plan. Briefly, I proposed a sort of picnic at a beautiful spot discovered during our wooding expedition. I was surprised and very pleased at the eager way in which all, with the sole exceptions of Tui and his fellow-harpooner, a Portuguese, fell in with my suggestions. Without any solicitation on my part, my Kanakas brought me their money, begging me to expend it for them, as they did not know how, and did not want to buy gin.

Under such favourable auspices as these, we landed shortly after eight a.m., making a bee-line for the only provision shop the place boasted. Here we laid in a stock of such savouries as we had long been strangers to, both eatables and drinkables, although I vetoed fire-water altogether. Beer in bottle was substituted, at my suggestion, as being, if we must have drinks of that nature, much the least harmful to men in a hot country, besides, in the quantity that we were able to take, non-intoxicant. We also took tea, sugar, milk, and a kettle. Thus furnished, we struck for the country, merry as a group of schoolboys, making the quiet air ring again with song, shout, and laughter—all of which may seem puerile and trivial in the extreme; but having seen liberty men ashore in nearly every big port in the world, watched the helpless, dazed look with which they wander about, swinging hands, bent shoulders, and purposeless rolling gait, I have often fervently wished that some one would take a party of them for a ramble with a definite purpose, helping them to a little enjoyment, instead of them falling, from sheer lack of knowing what else to do, into some dirty, darksome gin-mill, to be besotted, befooled, and debased.

I do earnestly wish that some of the good folk in London and Liverpool, who are wringing their hands for want of something to do among their fellow-men, would pay a visit to sailor-town for the purpose of getting up a personally-conducted party of sailors to see the sights worth seeing. It is a cheap form of pleasure, even if they paid all expenses, though that would not be likely. They would have an uphill job at first, for the sailor has been so long accustomed to being preyed upon by the class he knows, and neglected by everybody else except the few good people who want to preach to him, that he would probably, in a sheepish, shame-faced sort of way, refuse to have any "truck" with you, as he calls it. If the "sailors' home" people were worth their salt, they would organize expeditions by carriage to such beautiful places as—in London, for instance—Hampton Court, Zoological Gardens, Crystal Palace, Epping Forest, and the like, with competent guides and good catering arrangements. But no; the sailor is allowed to step outside the door of the "home" into the grimy, dismal streets with nothing open to him but the dance-house and brothel on one side, and the mission hall or reading-room on the other. God forbid that I should even appear to sneer at missions to seamen; nothing is farther from my intention; but I do feel that sailors need a little healthy human interest to be taken in providing some pleasure for them, and that there are unorthodox ways of "missioning" which are well worth a trial.

I once took a party (while I was an A.B.) from Wells-street Home to the South Kensington Museum. There were six of them—a Frenchman, a Dane, a Russian Finn, two Englishmen, and an Irishman. Though continually sailing from London for years, this was the first occasion they had ever been west of Aldgate. The only mistake I made was in going too deep at one step. The journey from Shadwell to South Kensington, under the guidance of one familiar, through the hardest personal experiences, with every corner of the vast network, was quite enough for one day. So that by the time we entered the Museum they were surfeited temporarily with sight-seeing, and not able to take in the wonders of the mighty place. Seeing this, I did not persist, but, after some rest and refreshment, led them across the road among the naval models. Ah! it was a rare treat to see them there. For if there is one thing more than another which interests a sailor, it is a well-made model of a ship. Sailors are model makers almost by nature, turning out with the most meagre outfit of tools some wonderfully-finished replicas of the vessels in which they have sailed. And the collection of naval models at South Kensington is, I suppose, unsurpassed in the world for the number and finish of the miniature vessels there shown.

Our day was a great success, never to be forgotten by those poor fellows, whose only recreation previously had been to stroll listlessly up and down the gloomy, stone-flagged hall of the great barracks until sheer weariness drove them out into the turbid current of the "Highway," there to seek speedily some of the dirty haunts where the "runner" and the prostitute awaited them.

But I have wandered far from the Bay of Islands while thus chattering of the difficulties that beset the

22

path of rational enjoyment for the sailor ashore. Returning to that happy day, I remember vividly how, just after we got clear of the town, we were turning down a lane between hedgerows wonderfully like one of our own country roads, when something—I could not tell what—gripped my heart and sent a lump into my throat. Tears sprang unbidden to my eyes, and I trembled from head to foot with emotion. Whatever could it be? Bewildered for the moment, I looked around, and saw a hedge laden with white hawthorn blossom, the sweet English "may." Every Londoner knows how strongly that beautiful scent appeals to him, even when wafted from draggled branches borne slumwards by tramping urchins who have been far afield despoiling the trees of their lovely blossoms, careless of the damage they have been doing. But to me, who had not seen a bit for years, the flood of feeling, undammed by that odorous breath, was overwhelming. I could hardly tear myself away from the spot, and, when at last I did, found myself continually turning to try and catch another whiff of one of the most beautiful scents in the world.

Presently we came to a cottage flooded from ground to roof-ridge with blossoms of scarlet geranium. There must have been thousands of them, all borne by one huge stem which was rooted by the door of the house. A little in front of it grew a fuchsia, twelve or fourteen feet high, with wide-spreading branches, likewise loaded with handsome blooms; while the ground beneath was carpeted with the flowers shaken from their places by the rude wind.

So, through scenes of loveliness that appealed even to the dusky Kanakas, we trudged gaily along, arriving pretty well fagged at our destination—a great glade of tenderest green, surrounded by magnificent trees on three sides; the fourth opening on to a dazzling white beach sloping gently down to the sea. Looking seaward, amidst the dancing, sparkling wavelets, rose numerous tree-clothed islets, making a perfectly beautiful seascape. On either side of the stretch of beach fantastic masses of rock lay about, as if scattered by some tremendous explosion. Where the sea reached them, they were covered with untold myriads of oysters, ready to be eaten and of delicious flavour.

What need to say more? With oyster-feeding, fishing, bathing, tree-climbing, tea-making, song-singing, the hours fled with pitiless haste, so that, before we had half emptied the brimming cup of joys proffered us, the slanting rays of the setting sun warned us to return lest we should get "bushed" in the dark. We came on board rejoicing, laden with spoils of flowers and fish, with two-thirds of our money still in our pockets, and full of happy memories of one of the most delightful days in our whole lives.

A long night's sound sleep was rudely broken into in the morning by the cry of "Man the windlass." Having got all we wanted, we were bound away to finish, if luck were with us, the lading of our good ship from the teeming waters of the Solander grounds. I know the skipper's hopes were high, for he never tired of telling how, when in command of a new ship, he once fished the whole of his cargo—six thousand barrels of sperm oil—from the neighbourhood to which we were now bound. He always admitted, though, that the weather he experienced was unprecedented. Still, nothing could shake his belief in the wonderful numbers of sperm whales to be found on the south coasts of New Zealand, which faith was well warranted, since he had there won from the waves, not only the value of his new ship, but a handsome profit in addition, all in one season.

Hearing this kind of thing every day made me feel quite hungry to reach the battle-field; but, for reasons which doubtless were excellent, although I cannot pretend to explain them, we started north about, which not only added nearly one hundred miles to the distance we had to go, but involved us in a gale which effectually stopped our progress for a week. It was our first taste of the gentle zephyrs which waft their sweetness over New Zealand, after sweeping over the vast, bleak, iceberg-studded expanse of the Antarctic Ocean. Our poor Kanakas were terribly frightened, for the weather of their experience, except on the rare occasions when they are visited by the devastating hurricane, is always fine, steady, and warm. For the first time in their lives they saw hail, and their wonder was too great for words. But the cold was very trying, not only to them, but to us, who had been so long in the tropics that our blood was almost turned to water. The change was nearly as abrupt as that so often experienced by our seamen, who at the rate of sixteen knots an hour plunge from a temperature of eighty degrees to one of thirty degrees in about three days.

We, with the ready adaptability of seamen, soon got accustomed to the bleak, bitter weather, but the Kanakas wilted like hothouse plants under its influence. They were well fed and well clothed, yet they seemed to shrivel up, looking thinner every day, several of them getting deep coughs strongly suggestive of a cemetery. It was no easy task to get them to work, or even move, never a one of them lumbering aloft but I expected him to come down by the run. This was by no means cheering, when it was remembered what kind of a campaign lay before us. Captain Count seemed to be quite easy in his mind, however, and as we had implicit confidence in his wisdom and judgment, we were somewhat reassured.

The gale at last blew itself out, the wind veering to the northward again, with beautiful, spring-like weather, just cool enough to be pleasant, and, withal, favourable for getting to our destination. We soon made the land again about New Plymouth, jogging along near enough to the coast to admire the splendid rugged scenery of the Britain of the south. All hands were kept busily employed preparing for stormy weather—reeving new running-gear, bending the strongest suit of sails, and looking well to all the whaling gear.

In this active exercise of real sailor-work, the time, though long for an ordinary passage, passed quickly and pleasantly away, so that when we hauled round the massive promontory guarding the western entrance to Foveaux Straits, we were almost surprised to find ourselves there so soon.

This, then, was the famous and dreaded Solander whaling ground. Almost in the centre of the wide stretch of sea between Preservation Inlet, on the Middle Island, and the western end of the South, or Stewart's Island, rose a majestic mass of wave-beaten rock some two thousand feet high, like a grim sentinel guarding the Straits. The extent of the fishing grounds was not more than a hundred and fifty square miles, and it was rarely that the vessels cruised over the whole of it. The most likely area for finding whales was said to be well within sight of the Solander Rock itself, but keeping on the western side of it.

It was a lovely day when we first entered upon our cruising ground, a gentle north-east wind blowing, the sky a deep, cloudless blue, so that the rugged outline of Stewart's Island was distinctly seen at its extreme distance from us. To the eastward the Straits narrowed rapidly, the passage at the other end being scarcely five miles wide between the well-known harbour of the Bluff, the port of Invercargill, and a long rocky island which almost blocked the strait. This passage, though cutting off a big corner, not only shortening the distance from the westward considerably, but oftentimes saving outward bounders a great deal of heavy weather off the Snares to the south of Stewart's Island, is rarely used by sailing-ships, except coasters; but steamers regularly avail themselves of it, being independent of its conflicting currents and baffling winds.

CHAPTER XXV.

ON THE SOLANDER GROUNDS.

OUR opening day was an auspicious one. We had not been within the cruising radius more than four hours before the long-silent cry of "Blo-o-o-w!" resounded from the mainmast head. It was a lone whale, apparently of large size, though spouting almost as feebly as a calf. But that, I was told by the skipper, was nothing to go by down here. He believed right firmly that there were no small whales to be found in these waters at all. He averred that in all his experience he had never seen a cow-cachalot anywhere around Stewart's Island, although, as usual, he did no theorizing as to the reason why.

Eagerly we took to the boats and made for our first fish, getting alongside of him in less than half an hour from our first glimpse of his bushy breath. As the irons sank into his blubber, he raised himself a little, and exposed a back like a big ship bottom up. Verily, the skipper's words were justified, for we had seen nothing bigger of the whale-kind that voyage. His manner puzzled us not a little. He had not a kick in him. Complacently, as though only anxious to oblige, he laid quietly while we cleared for action, nor did he show any signs of resentment or pain while he was being lanced with all the vigour we possessed. He just took all our assaults with perfect quietude and exemplary patience, so that we could hardly help regarding him with great suspicion, suspecting some deep scheme of deviltry hidden by this abnormally sheep-like demeanour. But nothing happened. In the same peaceful way he died, without the slightest struggle sufficient to raise even an eddy on the almost smooth sea.

Leaving the mate by the carcass, we returned on board, the skipper hailing us immediately on our arrival to know what was the matter with him. We, of course, did not know, neither did the question trouble us. All we were concerned about was the magnanimous way in which he, so to speak, made us a present of himself, giving us no more trouble to secure his treasure than as if he had been a lifeless thing. We soon had him alongside, finding, upon ranging him by the ship, that he was over seventy feet long, with a breadth of bulk quite in proportion to such a vast length.

Cutting in commenced at once, for fine weather there was by no means to be wasted, being of rare occurrence and liable at the shortest notice to be succeeded by a howling gale. Our latest acquisition, however, was of such gigantic proportions that the decapitation alone bade fair to take us all night. A nasty cross swell began to get up, too—a combination of north-westerly and south-westerly which, meeting at an angle where the Straits began, raised a curious "jobble," making the vessel behave in a drunken, uncertain manner. Sailors do not mind a ship rolling or pitching, any more than a rider minds the motion of his horse; but when she does both at once, with no approach to regularity in her movements, it makes them feel angry with her. What, then, must our feelings have been under such trying conditions, with that mountain of matter alongside to which so much sheer hard labour had to be done, while the sky was getting greasy and the wind beginning to whine in that doleful key which is the certain prelude to a gale?

Everybody worked like Chinamen on a contract, as if there was no such feeling as fatigue. Little was said, but we all realized that unless this job was got over before what was brooding burst upon us, we should certainly lose some portion of our hard-won whale. Still, our utmost possible was all we could do; and when at daylight the head was hauled alongside for cutting up, the imminent possibility of losing it, though grievous to think of, worried nobody, for all had done their best. The gale had commenced in business-like fashion, but the sea was horrible. It was almost impossible to keep one's footing on the stage. At times the whole mass of the head would be sucked down by the lee roll of the ship, and go right under her keel, the fluke-chain which held it grinding and straining as if it would tear the bows out of her. Then when she rolled back again the head would rebound to the surface right away from the ship, where we could not reach it to cut. Once or twice it bounced up beneath our feet, striking the stage and lifting it with its living load several inches, letting it fall again with a jerk that made us all cling for dear life to our precarious perch.

In spite of these capers, we managed to get the junk off the head. It was a tremendous lift for us; I hardly think we had ever raised such a weight before. The skipper himself estimated it at fifteen tons, which was no small load for the tackles in fine weather, but with the ship tumbling about in her present fashion, it threatened to rip the mainmast out by the roots—not, of course, the dead-weight strain; but when it was nearly aboard, her sudden lee wallow sometimes floated the whole mass, which the next instant, on the return roll, would be torn out of water, with all the force of the ship suddenly rolling the other way. Every splinter, every rope-yarn of her groaned again under this savage treatment; but so splendid was her construction that she never made a drop of water more than just sufficient to sweeten the limbers.

It was with great and genuine satisfaction that we saw it at last safely lowered on deck and secured. But when we turned our attention to the case, which, still attached to the skull, battered alongside, any chance of saving it was at once seen to be hopeless. Indeed, as the old man said, it was time for us to "up stick" and run for shelter. We had been too fully occupied to notice the gradual increase of the wind; but when we did, there was no gainsaying the fact that it was blowing a very stiff breeze (*Anglice*, a violent gale). Fortunately for us, it was from the westward, fair for the harbour of Port William, on the Stewart's Island side of the Straits, so that we were free from the apprehension of being blown out to sea or on a jagged lee shore.

While we were thus thinking during a brief pause to take breath, the old packet herself solved our last difficulty in emphatic fashion. She gave a tremendous lee lurch, which would inevitably have destroyed the cutting stage if we had not hoisted it, driving right over the head, which actually rose to the surface to windward, having passed under her bottom. The weather roll immediately following was swift and sudden. From the nature of things, it was evident that something must give way this time. It did. For the first and only time in my experience, the fluke-chain was actually torn through the piece to which it was fast—two feet of solid gristle ripped asunder. Away went the head with its £150 to £200 worth of pure spermaceti, disappearing from view almost immediately.

It had no sooner gone than more sail was set, the yards were squared, and the vessel kept away up the Straits for shelter. It was a big improvement, for she certainly had begun to make dirty weather of it, and no wonder. Now, however, running almost dead before the gale, getting into smoother water at every fathom, she was steady as a rock, allowing us to pursue our greasy avocation in comparative comfort. The gale was still increasing, although now blowing with great fury; but, to our satisfaction, it was dry and not too cold. Running before it, too, lessened our appreciation of its force; besides which, we were exceedingly busy clearing away the enormous mass of the junk, which, draining continually, kept the decks running with oil.

We started to run up the Straits at about ten a.m. At two p.m. we suddenly looked up from our toil, our attention called by a sudden lull in the wind. We had rounded Saddle Point, a prominent headland, which shut off from us temporarily the violence of the gale. Two hours later we found ourselves hauling up into the pretty little harbour of Port William, where, without taking more than a couple of hands off the work, the vessel was rounded-to and anchored with quite as little fuss as bringing a boat alongside a ship. It was the perfection of seamanship.

Once inside the bay, a vessel was sheltered from all winds, the land being high and the entrance intricate. The water was smooth as a mill-pond, though the leaden masses of cloud flying overhead and the muffled roar of the gale told eloquently of the unpleasant state of affairs prevailing outside. Two whale-ships lay here—the *Tamerlane*, of New Bedford, and the *Chance*, of Bluff Harbour. I am bound to confess that there was a great difference in appearance between the Yankee and the colonial—very much in favour of the former. She was neat, smart, and seaworthy, looking as if just launched; but the *Chance* looked like some poor old relic of a bygone day, whose owners, unable to sell her, and too poor to keep her in repair, were just letting her go while keeping up the insurance, praying fervently each day that she might come to grief, and bring them a little profit at last.

But although it is much safer to trust appearances in ships than in men, any one who summed up the *Chance* from her generally outworn and poverty-stricken looks would have been, as I was, "way off." Old she was, with an indefinite antiquity, carelessly rigged, and vilely unkempt as to her gear, while outside she did not seem to have had a coat of paint for a generation. She looked what she really was—the sole survivor of the once great whaling industry of New Zealand. For although struggling bay whaling stations did exist in a few sheltered places far away from the general run of traffic, the trade itself might truthfully be said to be practically extinct. The old *Chance* alone, like some shadow of the past, haunted Foveaux Straits, and made a better income for her fortunate owners than any of the showy, swift coasting steamers that rushed contemptuously past her on their eager way.

In many of the preceding pages I have, though possessing all an Englishman's pride in the prowess of mine own people, been compelled to bear witness to the wonderful smartness and courage shown by the

American whalemen, to whom their perilous calling seems to have become a second nature. And on other occasions I have lamented that our own whalers, either at home or in the colonies, never seemed to take so kindly to the sperm whale fishery as the hardy "down Easters," who first taught them the business; carried it on with increasing success, in spite of their competition and the depredations of the *Alabama;* flourished long after the English fishery was dead; and even now muster a fleet of ships engaged in the same bold and hazardous calling. Therefore, it is the more pleasant to me to be able to chronicle some of the doings of Captain Gilroy, familiarly known as "Paddy," the master of the *Chance*, who was unsurpassed as a whale-fisher or a seaman by any Yankee that ever sailed from Martha's Vineyard.

He was a queer little figure of a man—short, tubby, with scanty red hair, and a brogue thick as pea-soup. Eccentric in most things, he was especially so in his dress, which he seemed to select on the principle of finding the most unfitting things to wear. Rumour credited him with a numerous half-breed progeny—certainly he was greatly mixed up with the Maories, half his crew being made up of his dusky friends and relations by *marriage*. Overflowing with kindliness and good temper, his ship was a veritable ark of refuge for any unfortunate who needed help, which accounted for the numerous deserters from Yankee whalers who were to be found among his crew. Such whaling skippers as our late commander hated him with ferocious intensity; and but for his Maori and half-breed bodyguard, I have little doubt he would have long before been killed. Living as he had for many years on that storm-beaten coast, he had become, like his Maories, familiar with every rock and tree in fog or clear, by night or day; he knew them, one might almost say, as the seal knows them, and feared them as little. His men adored him. They believed him capable of anything in the way of whaling, and would as soon have thought of questioning the reality of daylight as the wisdom of his decisions.

I went on board the evening of our arrival, hearing some rumours of the doings of the old *Chance* and her crew, also with the idea that perhaps I might find some countrymen among his very mixed crowd. The first man I spoke to was Whitechapel to the backbone, plainly to be spotted as such as if it had been tattooed on his forehead. Making myself at home with him, I desired to know what brought him so far from the "big smoke," and on board a whaler of all places in the world. He told me he had been a Pickford's van-driver, but had emigrated to New Zealand, finding that he did not at all like himself in the new country. Trying to pick and choose instead of manfully choosing a pick and shovel for a beginning, he got hard up. During one of Captain Gilroy's visits to the Bluff, he came across my ex-drayman, looking hungry and woe-begone. Invited on board to have a feed, he begged to be allowed to remain; nor, although his assistance was not needed, was he refused. "An nar," he said, his face glowing with conscious pride, "y'ort ter see me in a bloomin' bowt. I ain't a-gowin' ter say as I kin fling wun o' them 'ere bloomin' 'arpoones like ar bowt-steerers kin; but I kin do my bit o' grawft wiv enny on 'em—don'tchu make no bloomin' herror." The glorious incongruity of the thing tickled me immensely; but I laughed more heartily still when on going below I was hailed as "Wot cher, chummy; 'ow yer hoppin' up?" by another barbarian from the wilds of Spitalfields, who, from the secure shelter of his cats'-meat round in 'Oxton, had got adrift, and, after being severely buffeted by tempestuous ill-fortune, had finally found himself in the comfortable old *Chance*, a haven of rest in the midst of storms. There were sixteen white men on board the *Chance*, including the skipper, drawn as usual from various European and American sources, the rest of her large crew of over forty all told being made up of Maories and half-breeds. One common interest united them, making them the jolliest crowd I ever saw—their devotion to their commander. There was here to be found no jealousy of the Maories being officers and harpooners, no black looks or discontented murmuring; all hands seemed particularly well satisfied with their lot in all its bearings; so that, although the old tub was malodorous enough to turn even a pretty strong stomach, it was a pleasure to visit her cheerful crowd for the sake of their enlivening society.

Of course, under our present circumstances, with the *débris* of our late enormous catch filling every available space and loudly demanding attention, we had little time to spare for ship visiting. Some boat or other from the two ships was continually alongside of us, though, for until the gale abated they could not get out to the grounds again, and time hung heavy on their hands. The *Tamerlane's* captain avoided Paddy as if he were a leper—hated the sight of him, in fact, as did most of his *confrères;* but our genial skipper, whose crew were every whit as well treated and contented as the *Chance's*, and who therefore needed not to dread losing them, met the little philanthropist on the most friendly terms.

The first fine weather, which came four days after our arrival, both our harbour mates cleared out.

Characteristically, the *Chance* was away first, before daylight had quite asserted itself, and while the bases of the cliffs and tops of the rocks were as yet hidden in dense wreaths of white haze. Paddy lolled on the taffrail near the wheel, which was held by an immense half-breed, who leant back and carried on a desultory, familiar conversation with his skipper; the rest of the crew were scattered about the decks, apparently doing what they liked in any manner they chose. The anchor was being catted, sails going up, and yards being trimmed; but, to observers like us, no guiding spirit was noticeable. It seemed to work all right, and the old ark herself looked as if she was as intelligent as any of them; but the sight was not an agreeable one to men accustomed to discipline. The contrast when the *Tamerlane* came along an hour or so after was emphatic. Every man at his post; every order carried out with the precision of clockwork; the captain pacing the quarter-deck as if she were a line-of-battle ship—here the airs put on were almost ludicrous in the other direction. Although she was only "a good jump" long, as we say, whenever an order was given, it was thundered out as if the men were a mile away, each officer appearing to vie with the others as to who could bellow the loudest. That was carrying things to the opposite extreme, and almost equally objectionable to merchant seamen.

We were thus left alone to finish our trying-out, except for such company as was afforded by the only resident's little schooner, in which he went oyster-dredging. It was exceedingly comfortable in the small harbour, and the fishing something to remember all one's life. That part of New Zealand is famous for a fish something like a bream, but with a longer snout, and striped longitudinally with black and yellow. I am ignorant of any polysyllabic prefix for it, only knowing it by its trivial and local appellation of the "trumpeter," from the peculiar sound it makes when out of water. But no other fish out of the innumerable varieties which I have sampled in all parts of the world could compare with the trumpeter for flavour and delicacy. These qualities are well known to the inhabitants of the large towns, who willingly pay high prices for the scanty supply of these delicious fish which they are able to obtain. Of other succulent fish there was a great variety, from the majestic "grouper," running up to over a hundredweight, down to the familiar flounder. Very little fishing could be done at night. Just as day was dawning was the ideal time for this enticing sport. As soon as the first few streaks of delicate light enlivened the dull horizon, a stray nibble or two gladdened the patient fishermen; then as the light strengthened the fun became general, and in about an hour enough fish would be caught to provide all hands with for the day.

One morning, when a stark calm left the surface of the bay as smooth as a mirror, I was watching a few stealthily-gliding barracouta sneaking about over the plainly visible bottom, though at a depth of seven or eight fathoms. Ordinarily, these fish must be taken with a live bait; but, remembering my experience with the dolphin, I determined to try a carefully-arranged strip of fish from one recently caught. In precisely the same way as the dolphin, these long, snaky rascals carefully tested the bait, lying still for sometimes as long as two minutes with the bait in their mouths, ready to drop it out on the first intimation that it was not a detached morsel. After these periods of waiting the artful creature would turn to go, and a sudden jerk of the line then reminded him that he was no longer a free agent, but mounting at headlong speed to a strange bourne whence he never returned to tell the tale. My catch that lovely morning scaled over a hundredweight in less than an hour, none of the fish being less than ten pounds in weight.

The Maories have quite an original way of catching barracouta. They prepare a piece of "rimu" (red pine) about three inches long, by an inch broad, and a quarter of an inch thick. Through one end of this they drive an inch nail bent upwards, and filed to a sharp point. The other end is fastened to about a fathom of stout fishing-line, which is in turn secured to the end of a five-foot pole. Seated in a boat with sail set, they slip along until a school of barracouta is happened upon. Then the peak of the sail is dropped, so as to deaden the boat's way, while the fishermen ply their poles with a sidelong sweep that threshes the bit of shining red through the water, making it irresistibly attractive to a struggling horde of ravenous fish. One by one, as swiftly as the rod can be wielded, the lithe forms drop off the barbless hook into the boat, till the vigorous arm can no longer respond to the will of the fisherman, or the vessel will hold no more.

Such were the goodly proportions of this first Solander whale of ours that, in spite of the serious loss of the case, we made thirteen and a half tuns of oil. When the fifteen huge casks containing it were stowed in their final positions, they made an imposing show, inspiring all of us with visions of soon being homeward bound. For the present we were, perforce, idle; for the wind had set in to blow steadily and strongly right up the Straits, preventing any attempts to get out while it lasted. The time did not hang heavy on our hands, for the surrounding country offered many attractions, which we were allowed to take full advantage of. Spearing eels and flounders at night by means of a cresset hung out over the boat's bow, as she was slowly sculled up the long, shallow creeks, was a favourite form of amusement. Mr. Cross, the resident, kindly allowed us to raid his garden, where the ripe fruit was rotting by the bushel for want of consumers. We needed no pressing; for fruit, since we left Vau Vau, of any kind had not come in our way; besides, these were "homey"—currants, gooseberries, strawberries—delightful to see, smell, and taste. So it came to pass that we had a high old time, unmarred by a single regrettable incident, until, after an enforced detention of twenty days, we were able to get to sea again.

Halfway down the Straits we sighted the *Chance*, all hands ripping the blubber off a sizeable whale in the same "anyhow" fashion as they handled their ship. They were in high glee, giving us a rousing cheer as we passed them on our westward course. Arriving on the ground, we found a goodly company of fine ships, which I could not help thinking too many for so small an area. During our absence the *Tamerlane* had been joined by the *Eliza Adams*, the *Matilda Sayer*, the *Coral*, and the *Rainbow;* and it was evident that no whale venturing within the radius of the Solander in the daytime would stand much chance of escaping such a battery of eager eyes. Only three days elapsed after our arrival when whales were seen. For the first time, I realized how numerous those gigantic denizens of the sea really are. As far as the eye could reach, extending all round one-half of the horizon, the sea appeared to be alive with spouts—all sperm whales, all bulls of great size. The value of this incredible school must have been incalculable. Subsequent experience satisfied me that such a sight was by no means uncommon here; in fact, "lone whales" or small "pods" were quite the exception.

Well, we all "waded in," getting, some two, some one whale apiece, according to the ability of the crews or the fortune of war. Only one fell to our lot in the *Cachalot*, but it was just as well. We had hardly got him fast by the fluke alongside when it began to pipe up from the north-east. In less than one watch the sea was fairly smoking with the fierceness of the wind. We were unable to get in anywhere, being, with a whale alongside, about as handy as a barge loaded with a haystack; while those unfortunate beggars that had two whales fast to them were utterly helpless as far as independent locomotion went, unless they could run dead before the wind. Every ship made all snug aloft, and hoisted the boats to the top notch of the cranes, fully anticipating a long, hard struggle with the elements before they got back to the cruising ground again. Cutting-in was out of the question in such weather; the only thing possible was to hope for a shift of wind before she got too far out, or a break in the weather. Neither of these events was probable, as all frequenters of South New Zealand know, bad weather having there an unhappy knack of being as persistent as fine weather is brief.

Night drew on as our forlorn and heavily-handicapped little fleet bore steadily seaward with their burdens, the angry, ever-increasing sea battering at us vengefully, while the huge carcasses alongside tore and strained at their fastenings as if they would rend the ships asunder. Slowly our companions faded from sight as the murky sky shut down on us, until in lonely helplessness we drifted on our weary way out into the vast, inhospitable Southern Ocean. Throughout the dark and stormy night our brave old ship held on her unwilling way right gallantly, making no water, in spite of the fearful strain to which she was subjected, nor taking any heavy sea over all. Morning broke cheerlessly enough. No abatement in the gale or change in its direction; indeed, it looked like lasting a month. Only one ship was visible far to leeward of us, and she was hull down. Our whale was beginning to swell rapidly, already floating at least three feet above the surface instead of just awash, as when newly killed. The skipper eyed it gloomily, seeing the near prospect of its entire loss, but he said nothing. In fact, very little was said; but the stories we had heard in the Bay of Islands came back to us with significant force now that their justification was so apparent.

Hour after hour went by without any change whatever, except in the whale, which, like some gradually-filling balloon, rose higher and higher, till at nightfall its bulk was appalling. All through the night those on deck did little else but stare at its increasing size, which, when morning dawned again, was so great that the animal's bilge rode level with the ship's rail, while in her lee rolls it towered above the deck like a mountain. The final scene with it was now a question of minutes only, so most of us, fascinated by the strange spectacle, watched and waited. Suddenly, with a roar like the bursting of a dam, the pent-up gases tore their furious way out of the distended carcass, hurling the entrails in one horrible entanglement widespread over the sea. It was well for us that it was to leeward and a strong gale howling; for even then the unutterable fœtor wrought its poisonous way back through that fierce, pure blast, permeating every nook of the ship with its filthy vapour till the stoutest stomach there protested in unmistakable terms against such vile treatment. Knowing too well that the blubber was now worthless, the skipper gave orders to cut the corrupt mass adrift. This was speedily effected by a few strokes of a spade through the small. Away went eight hundred pounds' worth of oil—another sacrifice to the exigencies of the Solander, such as had gained for it so evil a reputation.

Doubtless a similar experience had befallen all the other ships, so that the aggregate loss must have run into thousands of pounds, every penny of which might have been saved had steam been available.

That gale lasted, with a few short lulls, for five days longer. When at last it took off, and was succeeded by fine weather, we were so far to the southward that we might have fetched the Aucklands in another twenty-four hours. But, to our great relief, a strong southerly breeze set in, before which, under every rag of canvas, we sped north again.

Steady and reliable as ever, that good south wind carried us back to our old cruising ground ere it blew itself out, and we resumed our usual tactics as if nothing had happened, being none the worse as regards equipment for our adventures. Not so fortunate our companions, who at the same time as ourselves were thrust out into the vast Southern Ocean, helplessly burdened and exposed defenceless to all the ferocity of that devouring gale. Two of them were here prowling about, showing evident signs of their conflict in the battered state of their hulls. The glaring whiteness of new planking in many places along the bulwarks told an eloquent story of seas bursting on board carrying all before them, while empty cranes testified to the loss of a boat in both of them. As soon as we came near enough, "gamming" commenced, for all of us were anxious to know how each other had fared.

As we anticipated, every whale was lost that had been caught that day. The disappointment was in nowise lessened by the knowledge that, with his usual good fortune, Captain Gilroy had not only escaped all the bad weather, but while we were being threshed within an inch of our lives down in the bitter south, he was calmly trying-out his whale (which we had seen him with on our outward journey) in the sheltered haven of Port William. Many and deep were the curses bestowed upon him by the infuriated crews of those two ships, although he had certainly done them no harm. But the sight of other people's good fortune is gall and wormwood to a vast number of people, who seem to take it as a personal injury done to themselves.

Only two days elapsed, however, before we again saw an immense school of sperm whales, and each ship succeeded in securing one. We made no attempt to get more this time, nor do I think either of the others did; at any rate, one each was the result of the day's work. They were, as usual, of huge size and apparently very fat. At the time we secured our fish alongside, a fresh north-westerly wind was blowing, the weather being clear and beautiful as heart could wish. But instead of commencing at once to cut-in, Captain Count gave orders to pile on all sail and keep her away up the Straits. He was evidently determined to take no more chances, but, whenever opportunity offered, to follow the example set by the wily old skipper of the *Chance*. The other ships both started to cut-in at once, tempted, doubtless, by the settled appearance of the weather, and also perhaps from their hardly concealed dislike of going into port. We bowled along at a fine rate, towing our prize, that plunged and rolled by our side in eccentric style, almost as if still alive. Along about midnight we reached Saddle Point, where there was some shelter from the sea which rolled up the wide open strait, and there we anchored.

Leaving me and a couple of Kanakas on watch, the captain, and all hands besides, went below for a little sleep. My instructions were to call the captain if the weather got at all ugly-looking, so that we might run in to Port William at once, but he did not wish to do so if our present position proved sufficiently sheltered. He had not been below an hour before there was a change for the worse. That greasy, filmy haze was again drawn over the clear blue of the sky, and the light scud began to fly overhead at an alarmingly rapid rate. So at four bells I called him again. He came on deck at once, and after one look round ordered the hands up to man the windlass. By eight bells (four a.m.) we were rounding the frowning rocks at the entrance of Port William, and threading our way between the closely-set, kelp-hidden dangers as if it were broadest, clearest daylight. At 4.30 we let go the anchor again, and all hands, except the regular "anchor-watch," bolted below to their bunks again like so many rabbits.

It was very comfortable, cutting-in a sperm whale in harbour, after the dire difficulty of performing the same operation in a seaway. And, although it may seem strange, this was the first occasion that voyage that I had had a really good opportunity of closely studying the whale's anatomy. Consequently the work was exceedingly interesting, and, in spite of the labour involved, I was almost sorry when the job was done. Under the present favourable circumstances we were ready to cut the carcass adrift shortly after midday, the head, of course, having been taken off first. Just after we started to cut in a boat appeared alongside with six Maories and half-breeds on board. Their leader came up and civilly asked the skipper whether he intended doing anything with the carcass. Upon being promptly answered in the negative, he said that he and his companions proposed hooking on to the great mass when we cut it adrift, towing it ashore, and getting out of it what oil we had been unable to extract, which at sea is always lost to the ship. He also suggested that he would be prepared to take reasonable terms for such oil, which we should be able to mingle with ours to our advantage. An arrangement was speedily arrived at to give him £20 per tun for whatever oil he made. They parted on the best of terms with each other, and as soon as we cut the carcass loose the Maories made fast to it, speedily beaching it in a convenient spot near where they had previously erected a most primitive try-works.

That afternoon, after the head was inboard, the skipper thought he would go ashore and see how they were getting on. I was so fortunate as to be able to accompany him. When we arrived at the spot, we found them working as I have never seen men work, except perhaps the small riggers that at home take a job—three or four of them—to bend or unbend a big ship's sails for a lump sum to be paid when the work is done. They attacked the carcass furiously, as if they had a personal enmity against it, chopping through the massive bones and rending off huge lumps of the flesh with marvellous speed. They had already laid open the enormous cavity of the abdomen, and were stripping the interminable intestines of their rich coating of fat. In the maw there were, besides a large quantity of dismembered squid of great size, a number of fish, such as rock-cod, barracouta, schnapper, and the like, whose presence there was a revelation to me. How in the name of wonder so huge and unwieldly a creature as the cachalot could manage to catch those nimble members of the finny tribe, I could not for the life of me divine! Unless—and after much cogitation it was the only feasible explanation that I could see—as the cachalot swims about with his lower jaw hanging down in its normal position, and his huge gullet gaping like some submarine cavern, the fish unwittingly glide down it, to find egress impossible. This may or may not be the case; but I, at any rate, can find no more reasonable theory, for it is manifestly absurd to suppose the whale capable of *catching* fish in the ordinary sense, indicating pursuit.

Every part of the animal yielded oil. Even the bones, broken up into pieces capable of entering the pot, were boiled; and by the time we had finished our trying-out, the result of the Maories' labour was ready for us. Less than a week had sufficed to yield them a net sum of six guineas each, even at the very low rate for which they sold us the oil. Except that it was a little darker in colour, a defect that would disappear when mixed with our store, there was no difference between the products that could be readily detected. And at the price we paid for it, there was a clear profit of cent per cent, even had we kept it separate and sold it for what it was. But I suppose it was worth the Maories' while thus to dispose of it and quickly realize their hard earnings.

So far, our last excursion had been entirely satisfactory. We had not suffered any loss or endured any hardship; and if only such comfortable proceedings were more frequent, the Solander ground would not have any terrors for us at least. But one afternoon there crept in around the eastern horn of the harbour three forlorn and half-dismantled vessels, whose weather-worn crews looked wistfully at us engaged in clearing up decks and putting away gear upon the finishing of our trying-out. Poor fellows! they had seen rough times since that unforgettable evening when we parted from them at the other end of the island, and watched them slowly fade into the night. Two of them were so badly damaged that no further fishing was possible for them until they had undergone a thorough refit, such as they could not manage there. One was leaking badly, the tremendous strain put upon her hull in the vain attempt to hold on to the two whales she had during the gale having racked her almost all to pieces. The third one was still capable of taking the ground again, with sundry repairs such as could be effected by her crew. But the general feeling among all three crews was that there was more loss than gain to be expected here, in spite of the multitude of whales visiting the place.

As if to fill up their cup, in came the old *Chance* again, this time with a whale on each side. Captain Gilroy was on the house aft, his chubby red face in a ruddy glow of delight, and his crew exuberant. When he passed the American ships, as he was bound to do very closely, the sight of their scowling faces seemed to afford him the most exquisite amusement, and he laughed loud and long. His crew, on the impulse of the moment, sprang to the rail and cheered with might and main. No one could gainsay that they had good reason, but I really feared for a time that we should have "ructions." As Paddy said, it was not wise or dignified for those officers to be so angry with him on account of his success, which he frankly owned was due almost entirely to the local knowledge he possessed, gained in many years' study of the immediate neighbourhood. He declared that, as far as the technical duties of whale-fishing went, all the Americans could beat him hollow; but they ought to realize that something else was needed here which no man could hope to have unless he were content to remain on the coast altogether. With which words of wisdom our skipper cordially agreed, bearing in mind his own exploits in the bygone time around those rugged shores.

The strong breeze which brought Paddy and his whales home died down that night, enabling us to start for the grounds again—a concession gratefully received, for not the least of the hindrances felt there was the liability to be "wind-bound" for a long time, while fine weather was prevailing at the fishing grounds.

We made a fine passage down the Straits with a leading wind, finding our two late companions still cruising, having managed to get their whales aboard without mishap, and being somewhat inclined to chaff our old man for running in. He gave a wink full of wisdom, as he replied, "I'm pretty ole whale myself naouw; but I guess I ain't too old to learn; 'n wut I learn I'm goin' ter use. See?" Of course the fine weather did not last long—it never does; and seeing the gloomy masses of violet-edged cumuli piling up on the southern horizon, we hugged the Solander Rock itself pretty close, nor ventured far to seaward. Our two consorts, on the contrary, kept well out and on the northern verge, as if they intended the next gale that blew to get north, *if* they could. The old man's object in thus keeping in was solely in order that he might be able to run for shelter; but, much to his delight and certainly surprise, as we passed about a mile to the southward of the lonely, towering crags of the great rock, there came from aloft the welcome cry of "Sperm whale!"

There was only one, and he was uncomfortably near the rock; but such a splendid chance was not to be missed, if our previous training was of any avail. There was some speculation as to what he could be doing so close inshore, contrary to the habit of this animal, who seems to be only comfortable when in deep waters; but except a suggestion that perhaps he had come in to scrape off an extra accumulation of barnacles, nobody could arrive at any definite conclusion. When we reached him, we found a frightful blind swell rolling, and it needed all our seamanship to handle the boats so that they should not be capsized. Fortunately, the huge rollers did not break, or we should hardly have got back safely, whale or no whale.

Two irons were planted in him, of which he took not the slightest notice. We had taken in sail before closing in to him on account of the swell, so that we had only to go in and finish him at once, if he would let us. Accordingly, we went in with a will, but for all sign of life he showed he might as well have been stuffed. There he lay, lazily spouting, the blood pouring, or rather spirting, from his numerous wounds, allowing us to add to their number at our pleasure, and never moving his vast body, which was gently swayed by the rolling sea. Seeing him thus quiescent, the mate sent the other two boats back to the ship with the good news, which the captain received with a grave smile of content, proceeding at once to bring the ship as near as might be consistent with her safety. We were now thoroughly sheltered from sight of the other ships by the enormous mass of the island, so that they had no idea of our proceedings.

Finding that it was not wise to take the ship in any closer, while we were yet some distance from our prize, a boat was sent to Mr. Cruce with the instructions that he was to run his line from the whale back to the ship, if the creature was dead. He (the mate) replied that the whale died as quietly as he had taken his wounds, and immediately started for the ship. When he had paid out all his line, another boat bent on, until we got the end on board. Then we merrily walked him up alongside, while sufficient sail was kept drawing to prevent her being set in any nearer. When he was fast, we crowded on all canvas to get away; for although the sea was deep close up to the cliff, that swell was a very ugly feature, and one which has been responsible for the loss of a great number of ships in such places all over the world. Notwithstanding all our efforts, we did get so near that every detail of the rock was clearly visible to the naked eye, and we had some anxious minutes while the old ship, rolling tremendously, crawled inch after inch along the awful side of that sea-encircled pyramid.

At one point there was quite a cave, the floor of which would be some twenty feet above high-water mark, and its roof about the same distance higher. It appeared to penetrate some distance into the bowels of the mountain, and was wide and roomy. Sea-birds in great numbers hovered around its entrance, finding it, no doubt, an ideal nesting-place. It appeared quite inaccessible, for even with a perfect calm the swell dashed against the perpendicular face of the cliff beneath with a force that would have instantly destroyed any vessel unfortunate enough to get within its influence.

Slowly, slowly we forged past the danger; but the moment we opened out the extremity of the island, a fresh breeze, like a saving hand, swept across the bows, filling the head-sails and swinging the old vessel away from the island in grand style. Another minute, and the other sails filled also. We were safe, all hands breathing freely once more.

Now the wind hung far round to the eastward—far enough to frustrate any design we might have had of going up the Straits again. The old man, however, was too deeply impressed with the paramount necessity of shelter to lightly give up the idea of getting in somewhere; so he pointed her for Preservation Inlet, which was only some thirty miles under her lee. We crowded all sail upon her in the endeavour to get in before nightfall, this unusual proceeding bringing our two friends up from to leeward with a run to see what we were after. Burdened as we were, they sailed nearly two knots to our one, and consequently intercepted us some while before we neared our port. Great was their surprise to find we had a whale, and very anxious their queries as to where the rest of the school had gone. Reassured that they had lost nothing by not being nearer, it being a "lone" whale, off they went again.

With all our efforts, evening was fast closing in when we entered the majestic portals of Preservation Inlet, and gazed with deepest interest upon its heavily-wooded shores.

CHAPTER XXVI.

PADDY'S LATEST EXPLOIT.

NEW ZEALAND is pre-eminently a country of grand harbours; but I think those that are least used easily bear the palm for grandeur of scenery and facility of access. The wonderful harbour, or rather series of harbours, into which we were now entering for the first time, greatly resembled in appearance a Norwegian fjord, not only in the character of its scenery, but from the interesting, if disconcerting, fact that the cliffs were so steep-to that in some places no anchorage is found alongside the very land itself. There are, however, many places where the best possible anchorage can be obtained, so securely sheltered that a howling south-wester may be tearing the sea up by the roots outside, and you will know nothing of it within, except what may be surmised from the motion of the clouds overhead. It was an ideal place for a whaling station, being right on the Solander.

We found it exceedingly convenient, and much nearer than Port William, but, from the prevailing winds, difficult of access in nine cases out of ten, especially when hampered with a whale. Upon cutting-in our latest catch, an easy explanation of his passive attitude was at once forthcoming. He had been attacked by some whale-ship, whose irons had drawn, leaving deep traces of their presence; but during the battle he had received *seven* bombs, all of which had entered around his small, but had not exploded. Their general effect had been, I should think, to paralyze the great muscles of his flukes, rendering him unable to travel; yet this could not have taken place until some time after he had made good his escape from those aggressors. It was instructive, as demonstrating what amount of injury these colossi really can survive, and I have no doubt that, if he had been left alone, he would have recovered his normal energy, and been as well as ever. From our point of view, of course, what had happened was the best possible thing, for he came almost as a gift—the second capture we had made on those grounds of a like nature.

At the close of our operations the welcome news was made public that four more fish like the present one would fill us bung-up, and that we should then, after a brief visit to the Bluff, start direct for home. This announcement, though expected for some time past, gave an amazing fillip to everybody's interest in the work. The strange spectacle was witnessed of all hands being anxious to quit a snug harbour for the sea, where stern, hard wrestling with the elements was the rule. The captain, well pleased with the eagerness manifested, had his boat manned for a trip to the entrance of the harbour, to see what the weather was like outside, since it was not possible to judge from where the ship lay. On his return, he reported the weather rough, but moderating, and announced his intention of weighing at daylight next morning. Satisfied that our days in the southern hemisphere were numbered, and all anxiety to point her head for home, this news was most pleasing, putting all of us in the best of humours, and provoking quite an entertainment of song and dance until nearly four bells.

During the grey of dawn the anchor was weighed. There was no breath of wind from any quarter, so that it was necessary to lower boats and tow the old girl out to her field of duty. Before she was fairly clear of the harbour, though, there came a "snifter" from the hills that caught her unprepared, making her reel again, and giving us a desperate few minutes to scramble on board and hoist our boats up. As we drew out from the land, we found that a moderate gale was blowing, but the sky was clear, fathomless blue, the sun rose kindly, a heavenly dream of soft delicate colour preceding him; so that, in spite of the strong breeze, all looked promising for a good campaign. At first no sign could be seen of any of the other ships, though we looked long and eagerly for them. At last we saw them, four in all, nearly hull down to seaward, but evidently coming in under press of sail. So slow, however, was their approach that we had made one "leg" across the ground and halfway back before they were near enough for us to descry the reason of their want of speed. They had each got a whale alongside, and were carrying every rag of canvas they could spread, in order to get in with their prizes.

Our old acquaintance, the *Chance*, was there, the three others being her former competitors, except those who were disabled, still lying in Port William. Slowly, painfully they laboured along, until well within the mouth of the Straits, when, without any warning, the wind which had been bringing them in suddenly flew round into the northward, putting them at once in a most perilous position. Too far within the Straits to "up helm" and run for it out to sea; not far enough to get anywhere that an anchor might hold; and there to leeward, within less than a dozen miles, loomed grim and gloomy one of the most terrific rock-bound coasts in the world. The shift of wind had placed the *Chance* farther to leeward than all the rest, a good mile and a half nearer the shore; and we could well imagine how anxiously her movements were being watched by the others, who, in spite of their jealousy of his good luck, knew well and appreciated fully Paddy's marvellous seamanship, as well as his unparalleled knowledge of the coast.

Having no whale to hamper our movements, besides being well to windward of them all, we were perfectly comfortable as long as we kept to seaward of a certain line and the gale was not too fierce, so for the present all our attention was concentrated upon the labouring ships to leeward. The intervention of the land to windward kept the sea from rising to the awful height it attains under the pressure of a westerly, or a south-westerly gale, when, gathering momentum over an area extending right round the globe, it hurls itself upon those rugged shores. Still, it was bad enough. The fact of the gale striking across the regular set of the swell and current had the effect of making the sea irregular, short, and broken, which state of things is considered worse, as far as handling the ship goes, than a much heavier, longer, but more regular succession of waves.

As the devoted craft drifted helplessly down upon that frowning barrier, our excitement grew intense. Their inability to do anything but drift was only too well known by experience to every one of us, nor would it be possible for them to escape at all if they persisted in holding on much longer. But it was easy to see why they did so. While Paddy held on so far to leeward of them, and consequently in so much more imminent danger than they were, it would be derogatory in the highest degree to their reputation for seamanship and courage were they to slip and run before he did. He, however, showed no sign of doing so, although they all neared, with an accelerated drift, that point from whence no seamanship could deliver them, and where death inevitable, cruel, awaited them without hope of escape. The part of the coast upon which they were apparently driving was about as dangerous and impracticable as any in the world. A gigantic barrier of black, naked rock, extending for several hundred yards, rose sheer from the sea beneath, like the side of an ironclad, up to a height of seven or eight hundred feet. No outlying spurs of submerged fragments broke the immeasurable landward rush of the majestic waves towards the frowning face of this world-fragment. Fresh from their source, with all the impetus accumulated in their thousand-mile journey, they came apparently irresistible. Against this perpendicular barrier they hurled themselves with a shock that vibrated far inland, and a roar that rose in a dominating diapason over the continuous thunder of the tempest-riven sea. High as was the summit of the cliff, the spray, hurled upwards by the tremendous impact, rose higher, so that the whole front of the great rock was veiled in filmy wreaths of foam, hiding its solidity from the seaward view. At either end of this vast rampart nothing could be seen but a waste of breakers seething, hissing, like the foot of Niagara, and effectually concealing the *chevaux de frise* of rocks which produced such a vortex of tormented waters.

Towards this dreadful spot, then, the four vessels were being resistlessly driven, every moment seeing their chances of escape lessening to vanishing-point. Suddenly, as if panic-stricken, the ship nearest to the *Chance* gave a great sweep round on to the other tack, a few fluttering gleams aloft showing that even in that storm they were daring to set some sail. What the manœuvre meant we knew very well—they had cut adrift from their whale, terrified at last beyond endurance into the belief that Paddy was going to sacrifice himself and his crew in the attempt to lure them with him to inevitable destruction. The other two did not hesitate longer. The example once set, they immediately followed; but it was for some time doubtful in the extreme whether their resolve was not taken too late to save them from destruction. We watched them with breathless interest, unable for a long time to satisfy ourselves that they were out of danger. But at last we saw them shortening sail again—a sure sign that they considered themselves, while the wind held in the same quarter, safe from going ashore at any rate, although there was still before them the prospect of a long struggle with the unrelenting ferocity of the weather down south.

Meanwhile, what of the daring Irishman and his old barrel of a ship? The fugitives once safe off the land, all our interest centred in the *Chance*. We watched her until she drew in so closely to the seething cauldron of breakers that it was only occasionally we could distinguish her outline; and the weather was becoming so thick and dirty, the light so bad, that we were reluctantly compelled to lose sight of her, although the skipper believed that he saw her in the midst of the turmoil of broken water at the western end of the mighty mass of perpendicular cliff before described. Happily for us, the wind veered to the westward, releasing us from the prospect of another enforced visit to the wild regions south of the island. It blew harder than ever; but being now a fair wind up the Straits, we fled before it, anchoring again in Port William before midnight. Here we were compelled to remain for a week; for after the gale blew itself out, the wind still hung in the same quarter, refusing to allow us to get back again to our cruising station.

But on the second day of our enforced detention a ship poked her jibboom round the west end of the little bay. No words could describe our condition of spell-bound astonishment when she rounded-to, cumbrously as befitting a ship towing a whale, and revealed to us the well-remembered outlines of the old *Chance*. It was like welcoming the first-fruits of the resurrection; for who among sailor men, having seen a vessel disappear from their sight, as we had, under such terrible conditions, would ever have expected to see her again? She was hardly anchored before our skipper was alongside, thirsting to satisfy his unbounded curiosity as to the unheard-of means whereby she had escaped such apparently inevitable destruction. I was fortunate enough to accompany him, and hear the story at first-hand.

It appeared that none of the white men on board, except the redoubtable Paddy himself, had ever been placed in so seemingly hopeless and desperate a position before. Yet when they saw how calm and free from anxiety their commander was, how cool and business-like the attitude of all their dusky shipmates, their confidence in his ability and resourcefulness kept its usual high level. It must be admitted that the test such feelings were then subjected to was of the severest, for to their eyes no possible avenue of escape was open. Along that glaring line of raging, foaming water not a break occurred, not the faintest indication of an opening anywhere wherein even so experienced a pilot as Paddy might thrust a ship. The great black wall of rock loomed up by their side, grim and pitiless as doom—a very door of adamant closed against all hope. Nearer and nearer they drew, until the roar of the baffled Pacific was deafening, maddening, in its overwhelming volume of chaotic sound. All hands stood motionless, with eyes fixed in horrible fascination upon the indescribable vortex to which they were being irresistibly driven.

At last, just as the fringes of the back-beaten billows hissed up to greet them, they felt her motion ease. Instinctively looking aft, they saw the skipper coolly wave his hand, signing to them to trim the yards. As they hauled on the weather braces, she plunged through the maelström of breakers, and before they had got the yards right round they were on the other side of that enormous barrier, the anchor was dropped, and all was still. The vessel rested, like a bird on her nest, in a deep, still tarn, shut in, to all appearance, on every side by huge rock barriers. Of the furious storm but a moment before howling and raging all around them, nothing remained but an all-pervading, thunderous hum, causing the deck to vibrate beneath them, and high overhead the jagged, leaden remnants of twisted, tortured cloud whirling past their tiny oblong of sky. Just a minute's suspension of all faculties but wonder, then, in one spontaneous, heartfelt note of genuine admiration, all hands burst into a cheer that even overtopped the mighty rumble of the baffled sea.

Here they lay, perfectly secure, and cut in their whale as if in dock; then at the first opportunity they ran out, with fearful difficulty, a kedge with a whale-line attached, by which means they warped the vessel out of her hiding-place—a far more arduous operation than getting in had been. But even this did not exhaust the wonders of that occasion. They had hardly got way upon her, beginning to draw out from the land, when the eagle-eye of one of the Maories detected the carcass of a whale rolling among the breakers about half a mile to the westward. Immediately a boat was lowered, a double allowance of line put into her, and off they went to the valuable flotsam. Dangerous in the highest degree was the task of getting near enough to drive harpoons into the body; but it was successfully accomplished, the line run on board, and the prize hauled triumphantly alongside. This was the whale they had now brought in. We shrewdly suspected that it must have been one of those abandoned by the unfortunate vessels who had fled, but etiquette forbade us saying anything about it. Even had it been, another day would have seen it valueless to any one, for it was by no means otto of roses to sniff at now, while they had certainly salved it at the peril of their lives.

When we returned on board and repeated the story, great was the amazement. Such a feat of seamanship was almost beyond belief; but we were shut up to believing, since in no other way could the vessel's miraculous escape be accounted for. The little, dumpy, red-faced figure, rigged like any scarecrow, that now stood on his cutting-stage, punching away vigorously at the fetid mass of blubber beneath him, bore no outward visible sign of a hero about him; but in our eyes he was transfigured—a being to be thought of reverently, as one who in all those qualities that go to the making of a man had proved himself of the seed royal, a king of men, all the more kingly because unconscious that his deeds were of so exalted an order.

I am afraid that, to a landsman, my panegyric may smack strongly of gush, for no one but a seaman can rightly appraise such doings as these; but I may be permitted to say that, when I think of men whom I feel glad to have lived to know, foremost among them rises the queer little figure of Paddy Gilroy.

CHAPTER XXVII.

PORT PEGASUS.

THE wind still holding steadily in the old quarter, our skipper got very restless. He recalled his former exploits, and, firing at the thought, decided then and there to have a trip round to Port Pegasus, in the hope that he might meet with some of his former good luck in the vicinity of that magnificent bay. With the greatest alacrity we obeyed his summons, handling the old barky as if she were a small boat, and the same morning, for the first time, ran out of the Straits to the eastward past Ruapuke Island. Beautiful weather prevailed, making our trip a delightful one, the wonderful scenery of that coast appealing to even the most callous or indifferent among us. We hugged the land closely, the skipper being familiar with all of it in a general way, so that none of its beauties were lost to us. The breeze holding good, by nightfall we had reached our destination, anchoring in the north arm near a tumbling cascade of glittering water that looked like a long feather laid on the dark-green slope of the steep hill from which it gushed.

We had not been long at anchor before we had visitors—half-breed Maories, who, like the Finns and Canadians, are farmers, fishermen, sailors, and shipwrights, as necessity arises. They brought us potatoes—most welcome of all fruit to the sailor—cabbages, onions, and "mutton birds." This latter delicacy is a great staple of their flesh food, but is one of the strangest dishes imaginable. When it is being cooked in the usual way, *i.e.* by grilling, it smells exactly like a piece of roasting mutton; but it tastes, to my mind, like nothing else in the world so much as a kippered herring. There is a gastronomical paradox, if you like. Only the young birds are taken for eating. They are found, when unfledged, in holes of the rocks, and weigh sometimes treble as much as their parents. They are exceedingly fat; but this substance is nearly all removed from their bodies before they are hung up in the smoke-houses. They are split open like a haddock, and carefully smoked, after being steeped in brine. Baskets, something like exaggerated strawberry pottles of the old conical shape, are prepared, to hold each about a dozen birds. They are lined with leaves, then packed with the birds, the melted fat being run into all the interstices until the basket is full. The top is then neatly tied up with more leaves, and, thus preserved, the contents will keep in cool weather an indefinite length of time.

Captain Count was soon recognized by some of his old friends, who were delighted to welcome him again. Their faces fell, however, when he told them that his stay was to be very brief, and that he only required four good-sized fish to fill up. Inquiry as to the prevalence of sperm whales in the vicinity elicited the news that they were as plentiful as they had ever been—if anything, more so, since the visits of the whalers had become fewer. There were a couple of "bay" whaling stations existing; but, of course, their success could not be expected to be great among the cachalots, who usually keep a respectful distance from harbours, while they had driven the right whales away almost entirely.

No one could help being struck by the manly bearing, splendid physique, and simple manners of the inhabitants. If ever it falls to the lot of any one, as I hope it will, to establish a sperm whale fishery in these regions, there need be no lack of workers while such grand specimens of manhood abound there as we saw—all, moreover, fishermen and whalers from their earliest days.

We did not go far afield, but hovered within ten or fifteen miles of the various entrances, so as not to be blown off the land in case of sudden bad weather. Even with that timid offing, we were only there two days, when an enormous school of sperm whales hove in sight. I dare not say how many I believe there were, and my estimate really might be biassed; but this I know, that in no given direction could one look to seaward and not see many spouts.

We got among them and had a good time, being more hampered by the curiosity of the unattached fish than by the pugnacity of those under our immediate attention. So we killed three, and by preconcerted signal warned the watchers on the lofty points ashore of our success. As speedily as possible off came four boats from the shore stations, and hooked on to two of our fish, while we were busy with the third. The wind being off shore, what there was of it, no time was to be lost, in view of the well-known untrustworthiness of the weather; so we started to cut-in at once, while the shore people worked like giants to tow the other two in. Considering the weakness of their forces, they made marvellous progress; but seeing how terribly exhausting the toil was, one could not help wishing them one of the small London tugs, familiarly known as "jackals," which would have snaked those monsters along at three or four knots an hour.

However, all went well; the usual gale did blow, but not till we had got the last piece aboard and a good "slant" to run in, arriving at our previous moorings at midnight. In the morning the skipper went down in his boat to visit the stations, and see how they had fared. Old hand as he was, I think he was astonished to see what progress those fellows had made with the fish. They did not reach the stations till after midnight, but already they had the whales half flenched, and, by the way they were working, it looked as if they would be through with their task as soon as we were with ours. Their agreement with the skipper was to yield us half the oil they made, and, if agreeable to them, we would take their moiety at £40 per tun. Consequently they had something to work for, even though there were twenty of them to share the spoil. They were a merry party, eminently good tempered, and working as though one spirit animated them all. If there was a leader of the band, he did his office with great subtilty, for all seemed equal, nor did any appear to need directing what to do. Fired by their example, we all worked our hardest; but they beat us by half a day, mainly, I think, by dint of working nearly all the time with scarce any interval for sleep. True, they were bound to take advantage of low water when their huge prize was high and dry—to get at him easily all round. Their method was of the simplest. With gaff-hooks to haul back the pieces, and short-handled spades for cutting, they worked in pairs, taking off square slabs of blubber about a hundredweight each. As soon as a piece was cut off, the pair tackled on to it, dragging it up to the pots, where the cooks hastily sliced it for boiling, interspersing their labours with attention to the simmering cauldrons.

Their efforts realized twenty-four tuns of clear oil

and spermaceti, of which, according to bargain, we took twelve, the captain buying the other twelve for £480, as previously arranged. This latter portion, however, was his private venture, and not on ship's account, as he proposed selling it at the Bluff, when we should call there on our way *home*. So that we were still two whales short of our quantity. What a little space it did seem to fill up! Our patience was sorely tested, when, during a whole week following our last haul, we were unable to put to sea. In vain we tried all the old amusements of fishing, rambling, bathing, etc.; they had lost their "bite;" we wanted to get home. At last the longed-for shift of wind came and set us free. We had hardly got well clear of the heads before wo saw a school of cachalots away on the horizon, some twelve miles off the land to the southward. We made all possible sail in chase, but found, to our dismay, that they were "making a passage," going at such a rate that unless the wind freshened we could hardly hope to come up with them. Fortunately, we had all day before us, having quitted our moorings soon after daylight; and unless some unforeseen occurrence prevented us from keeping up our rate of speed, the chances were that some time before dark they would ease up and allow us to approach them. They were heading to the westward, perhaps somewhat to the northward withal, to all appearance making for the Solander. Hour after hour crawled by, while we still seemed to preserve our relative distance, until we had skirted the southern shore of the island and entered the area of our old fishing ground. Two vessels were cruising thereon, well to the northward, and we thought with glee of the excitement that would seize them did they but gain an inkling of our chase.

To our great delight, what we had hoped, but hardly

dared expect, came to pass. The school, as if with one impulse, hauled up on their course four points, which made them head direct for the western verge of the Solander ground, and—what was more important to us—made our coming up with them a matter of a short time. We made the customary signals with the upper sails to our friends to the northward, who recognized them immediately, and bore down towards us. Not only had the school shifted their course, but they had slackened speed; so that by four o'clock we were able to lower for them at less than a mile distance.

It was an ideal whaling day—smooth water, a brisk breeze, a brilliant sun, and plenty of whales. I was, as became my position, in the rear when we went into action, and hardly hoped for an opportunity of doing much but dance attendance upon my seniors. But fortune favoured me. Before I had any idea whether the chief was fast or not, all other considerations were driven clean out of my head by the unexpected apparition of a colossal head, not a ship's length away, coming straight for us, throwing up a swell in front of him like an ironclad. There was barely time to sheer to one side, when the giant surged past us in a roar of foaming sea, the flying flakes of which went right over us. Samuela was "all there," though, and as the great beast passed he plunged a harpoon into him with such force and vigour that the very socket entered the blubber. It needed all the strength I could muster, even with such an aid as the nineteen feet steer-oar, to swing the boat right round in his wake, and prevent her being capsized by his headlong rush.

For, contrary to the usual practice, he paused not an instant, but rather quickened his space, as if spurred. Heavens, how he went! The mast and sail had to come down—and they did, but I hardly know how. The spray was blinding, coming in sheets over the bows, so that I could hardly see how to steer in the monster's wake. He headed straight for the ship, which lay-to almost motionless, filling me with apprehension lest he should in his blind flight dash that immense mass of solid matter into her broadside, and so put an inglorious end to all our hopes. What their feelings on board must have been, I can only imagine, when they saw the undeviating rush of the gigantic creature straight for them. On he went, until I held my breath for the crash, when at the last moment, and within a few feet of the ship's side, he dived, passing beneath the vessel. We let go line immediately, as may be supposed; but although we had been towing with quite fifty fathoms drift, our speed had been so great that we came up against the old ship with a crash that very nearly finished us. He did not run any farther just then, but sounded for about two hundred and fifty fathoms, rising to the surface in quite another mood. No more running away from him. I cannot say I felt any of the fierce joy of battle at the prospect before me. I had a profound respect for the fighting qualities of the sperm whale, and, to tell the truth, would much rather have run twenty miles behind him than have him turn to bay in his present parlous humour. It was, perhaps, fortunate for me that there was a crowd of witnesses, the other ships being now quite near enough to see all that was going on, since the feeling that my doings were full in view of many experts and veterans gave me a determination that I would not disgrace either myself or my ship; besides, I felt that this would probably be our last whale this voyage, if I did not fail, and that was no small thing to look forward to.

All these things, so tedious in the telling, flashed

through my mind, while, with my eyes glued to the huge bulk of my antagonist or the hissing vortices above him when he settled, I manœuvred my pretty craft with all the skill I could summon. For what seemed a period of about twenty minutes we dodged him as he made the ugliest rushes at us. I had not yet changed ends with Samuela, as customary, for I felt it imperative to keep the helm while this game was being played. My trusty Kanaka, however, had a lance ready, and I knew, if he only got the ghost of a chance, no man living would or could make better use of it.

The whole affair was growing monotonous as well as extremely wearying. Perhaps I was a little off my guard; at any rate, my heart almost leaped into my mouth when just after an ugly rush past us, which I thought had carried him to a safe distance, he stopped dead, lifted his flukes, and brought them down edgeways with a vicious sweep that only just missed the boat's gunwale, and shore off the two oars on that side as if they had been carrots. This serious disablement would certainly have led to disaster but for Samuela. Prompt and vigorous, he seized the opportune moment when the whale's side was presented just after the blow, sending his lance quivering home all its length into the most vital part of the leviathan's anatomy. Turning his happy face to me, he shouted exultingly, "How's dat fer high?"—a bit of slang he had picked up, and his use of which never failed to make me smile. "High" it was indeed—a master-stroke. It must have pierced the creature's heart, for he immediately began to spout blood in masses, and without another wound went into his flurry and died.

Then came the reaction. I must have exerted myself beyond what I had any idea of, for to Samuela I was obliged to delegate the task of fluke-boring, while I rested a little. The ship was soon alongside, though, and the whale secured. There was more yet to be done before we could rest, in spite of our fatigue. The other boats had been so successful that they had got two big fish, and what we were to do with them was a problem not easily solvable. By dint of great exertion, we managed to get another whale alongside, but were fain to come to some arrangement with the *Eliza Adams*, one of the ships that had been unsuccessful, to take over our other whale on an agreement to render us one-third of the product either in Port William or at home, if she should not find us in the former place.

Behold us, then, in the gathering dusk with a whale on either side, every stitch of canvas we could show set and drawing, straining every nerve to get into the little port again, with the pleasant thought that we were bringing with us all that was needed to complete our well-earned cargo. Nobody wanted to go below; all hands felt that it was rest enough to hang over the rail on either side and watch the black masses as they surged through the gleaming sea. They represented so much to us. Very little was said, but all hearts were filled with a deep content, a sense of a long season of toil fitly crowned with complete success; nor was any depression felt at the long, long stretch of stormy ocean between us and our home port far away in the United States. That would doubtless come by-and-by, when within less than a thousand miles of New Bedford; but at present all sense of distance from home was lost in the overmastering thought that soon it would be our only business to get there as quickly as possible, without any avoidable loitering on the road.

We made an amazing disturbance in the darkness of

the sea with our double burthen, so much so that one of the coasting steamers changed her course a bit to range up by our side in curiosity. We were scarcely going two and a half knots, in spite of the row we made, and there was hardly room for wonder at the steamboat captain's hail, "Want any assistance?" "No, thank you," was promptly returned, although there was little doubt that all hands would have subscribed towards a tow into port, in case the treacherous weather should, after all, play us a dirty trick. But it looked as if our troubles were over. No hitch occurred in our steady progress, slow though it necessarily was, and as morning lifted the heavy veil from the face of the land, we arrived at our pretty little haven, and quietly came to an anchor. The *Chance* was in port wind-bound, looking, like ourselves, pretty low in the water. No sooner did Paddy hear the news of our arrival in such fine trim than he lowered his boat and hurried on board of us, his face beaming with delight. Long and loud were his congratulations, especially when he heard that we should now be full. Moreover, he offered—nor would he take any denial—to come with the whole of his crew and help us finish.

For the next four days and nights, during which the wind prevented the *Chance* from leaving us, our old ship was a scene of wild revelry, that ceased not through the twenty-four hours—revelry entirely unassisted by strong waters, too, the natural ebullient gaiety of men who were free from anxiety on any account whatever, rejoicing over the glad consummation of more than two years' toil, on the one hand; on the other, a splendid sympathy in joy manifested by the satisfied crew under the genial command of Captain Gilroy. With their cheerful help we made wonderful progress; and when at last the wind hauled into a favourable quarter, and they were compelled to leave us, the back of our work was broken, only the tedious task of boiling being left to finish.

Never, I am sure, did two ships' companies part with more hearty good-will than ours. As the ungainly old tub surged slowly out of the little harbour, her worn-out and generally used-up appearance would have given a Board of Trade inspector the nightmare; the piratical looks of her crowd were enough to frighten a shipload of passengers into fits; but to us who had seen their performances in all weathers, and under all circumstances, accidental externals had no weight in biassing our high opinion of them all. Good-bye, old ship; farewell, jolly captain and sturdy crew; you will never be forgotten any more by us while life lasts, and in far other and more conventional scenes we shall regretfully remember the free-and-easy time we shared with you. So she slipped away round the point and out of our lives for ever.

By dint of steady hard work we managed to get the last of our greasy work done in four days more, then faced with a will the job of stowing afresh the upper tiers of casks, in view of our long journey home. The oil bought by the skipper on private venture was left on deck, secured to the lash-rail, for discharging at the Bluff, while our stock of water casks were carefully overhauled and recoopered prior to being stowed in their places below. Of course, we had plenty of room in the hold, since no ship would carry herself full of casks of oil; but I doubt whether, if we had borne a "Plimsoll's mark," it would not have been totally submerged, so deep did we lie. Wooding and watering came next—a different affair to our casual exercises in those directions before.

Provision had to be made now for a possible four or five months' passage, during which we hoped to avoid any further calls, so that the accumulation of firewood alone was no small matter. We cleared the surrounding neighbourhood of potatoes at a good price, those useful tubers being all they could supply us with for sea-stock, much to their sorrow.

Then came the most unpleasant part of the whole business—for me. It had been a part of the agreement made with the Kanakas that they were not to be taken home with us, but returned to their island upon the termination of the whaling. Now, the time had arrived when we were to part, and I must confess that I felt very sorry to leave them. They had proved docile, useful, and cheerful; while as for my harpooner and his mate Polly, no man could have wished for smarter, better, or more faithful helpers than they were. Strong as their desire was to return to their homes, they too felt keenly the parting with us; for although they had unavoidably suffered much from the inclemency of the weather—so different from anything they had ever previously experienced—they had been kindly treated, and had moved on precisely the same footing as the rest of the crew. They wept like little children when the time arrived for them to leave us, declaring that if ever we came to their island again they would use all their endeavours to compel us to remain, assuring us that we should want for nothing during the rest of our lives, if we would but take up our abode with them. The one exception to all this cordiality was Sam. His ideas were running in quite other channels. To regain his lost status as ruler of the island, with all the opportunities for indulging his animal propensities which such a position gave him, was the problem he had set himself, and to the realization of these wishes he had determinedly bent all his efforts.

Thus he firmly declined the offer of a passage back in the *Eliza Adams*, which our captain secured for all the Kanakas; preferring to be landed at the Bluff, with the goodly sum of money to which he was entitled, saying that he had important business to transact in Sydney before he returned. This business, he privately informed me, was the procuring of arms and ammunition wherewith to make war upon his rival. Of course we could not prevent him, although it did seem an abominable thing to let loose the spirit of slaughter among those light-hearted natives just to satisfy the ambition of an unscrupulous negro. But, as I have before noticed, from information received many years after I learned that he had been successful in his efforts, though at what cost to life I do not know.

So our dusky friends left us, with a good word from every one, and went on board the *Eliza Adams*, whose captain promised to land them at Futuna within six months. How he carried out his promise, I do not know; but, for the poor fellows' sakes, I trust he kept his word.

CHAPTER XXVIII.

TO THE BLUFF, AND HOME.

AND now the cruise of the good old whaling barque *Cachalot*, as far as whaling is concerned, comes to an end. For all practical purposes she now becomes a humdrum merchantman in haste to reach her final port of discharge, and get rid of her cargo. No more will she loiter and pry around anything and everything, from an island to a balk of drift-wood, that comes in her way, knowing not the meaning of "waste of time." The "crow's-nests" are dismantled, taunt topgallant-masts sent up, and royal yards crossed. As soon as we get to sea we shall turn-to and heave that ancient fabric of bricks and mortar—always a queer-looking erection to be cumbering a ship's deck—piecemeal over the side. It has long been shaky and weather-beaten; it will soon obstruct our movements no more. Our rigging has all been set up and tarred down; we have painted hull and spars, and scraped wherever the wood-work is kept bright. All gear belonging to whaling has been taken out of the boats, carefully cleaned, oiled, and stowed away for a "full due." Two of the boats have been taken inboard, and stowed bottom-up upon the gallows aft, as any other merchantman carries them. At last, our multifarious preparations completed, we ride ready for sea.

It was quite in accordance with the fitness of things that, when all things were now ready for our departure, there should come a change of wind that threatened to hold us prisoners for some days longer. But our "old man" was hard to beat, and he reckoned that, if we could only get out of the "pond," he would work her across to the Bluff somehow or other. So we ran out a kedge with a couple of lines to it, and warped her out of the weather side of the harbour, finding, when at last we got her clear, that she would lay her course across the Straits to clear Ruapukè—nearly; but the current had to be reckoned with. Before we reached that obstructing island we were down at the eastern end of it, and obliged to anchor promptly to save ourselves from being swept down the coast many miles to leeward of our port.

But the skipper was quite equal to the occasion. Ordering his boat, he sped away into Bluff harbour, only a matter of six or seven miles, returning soon with a tug, who for a pound or two placed us, without further trouble, alongside the wharf, amongst some magnificent clipper ships of Messrs. Henderson's and the New Zealand Shipping Co.'s, who seemed to turn up their splendid noses at the squat, dumpy, antiquated old serving-mallet that dared to mingle with so august a crowd. There had been a time, not so very far back, when I should have shared their apparent contempt for our homely old tub; but my voyage had taught me, among other things, that, as far as true comfort went at sea, not a "three-skysail-yarder" among them could compare with the *Cachalot*. And I was extremely glad that my passage round the Horn was to be in my own ship, and not in a long, snaky tank that, in the language of the sailor, takes a header when she gets outside the harbour, and only comes up two or three times to blow before she gets home.

Our only reason for visiting this place being to discharge Captain Count's oil, and procure a sea-stock of salt provisions and hard bread, those duties were taken in hand at once. The skipper sold his venture of oil to good advantage, being so pleased with his success that he gave us all a good feed on the strength of it.

As soon as the stores were embarked and everything ready for sea, leave was given to all hands for twenty-four hours, upon the distinct understanding that the privilege was not to be abused, to the detriment of everybody, who, as might be supposed, were anxious to start for home. In order that there might be less temptation to go on the spree generally, a grand picnic was organized to a beautiful valley some distance from the town. Carriages were chartered, an enormous quantity of eatables and drinkables provided, and away we went, a regular wayzgoose or bean-feast party. It was such a huge success, that I have ever since wondered why such outings cannot become usual among sailors on liberty abroad, instead of the senseless, vicious waste of health, time, and hard-earned wages which is general. But I must not let myself loose upon this theme again, or we shall never get to sea.

Liberty over without any trouble arising, and all hands comfortably on board again, the news ran round that we were to sail in the morning. So, after a good night's rest, we cast loose from the wharf, and, with a little assistance from the same useful tug that brought us in, got fairly out to sea. All sail was set to a strong, steady north-wester, and with yards canted the least bit in the world on the port tack, so that every stitch was drawing, we began our long easterly stretch to the Horn, homeward bound at last.

Favoured by wind and weather, we made an average run of one hundred and eighty miles per day for many days, paying no attention to "great circle sailing," since in such a slow ship the net gain to be secured by going to a high latitude was very small, but dodging comfortably along on about the parallel of 48° S., until it became necessary to draw down towards "Cape Stiff," as that dreaded extremity of South America, Cape Horn, is familiarly called by seamen. As we did so, icebergs became numerous, at one time over seventy being in sight at once. Some of them were of immense size—one, indeed, that could hardly be fitly described as an iceberg, but more properly an ice-field, with many bergs rising out of it, being over sixty miles long, while some of its towering peaks were estimated at from five hundred to one thousand feet high. Happily, the weather kept clear; for icebergs and fog make a combination truly appalling to the sailor, especially if there be much wind blowing.

Needless, perhaps, to say, our look-out was of the best, for all hands had a double interest in the safety of the ship. Perhaps it may be thought that any man would have so much regard for the safety of his life that he would not think of sleeping on his look-out; but I can assure my readers that, strange as it may seem, such is not the case. I have known men who could never be trusted not to go to sleep, no matter how great the danger. This is so well recognized in merchant ships that nearly every officer acts as if there was no look-out at all forward, in case his supposed watchman should be having a surreptitious doze.

Stronger and stronger blew the brave west wind; dirtier, gloomier, and colder grew the weather, until, reduced to two topsails and a reefed foresail, we were scudding dead before the gale for all we were worth. This was a novel experience for us in the *Cachalot*, and I was curious to see how she would behave. To my mind, the supreme test of a ship's sea-kindliness is the length of time she will scud before a gale without "pooping" a sea or taking such heavy water on board over her sides as to do serious damage. Some ships are very dangerous to run at all. Endeavouring to make the best use of the gale which is blowing in the right direction, the captain "hangs on" to all the sail he can carry, until she ships a mighty mass of water over all, so that the decks are filled with wreckage, or, worse still, "poops" a sea. The latter experience is a terrible one, even to a trained seaman. You are running before the wind and waves, sometimes deep in the valley between two liquid mountains, sometimes high on the rolling ridge of one. You watch anxiously the speed of the sea, trying to decide whether it or you are going the faster, when suddenly there seems to be a hush, almost a lull, in the uproar. You look astern, and see a wall of water rising majestically higher and higher, at the same time drawing nearer and nearer. Instinctively you clutch at something firm, and hold your breath. Then that mighty green barrier leans forward, the ship's stern seems to settle at the same time, and, with a thundering noise as of an avalanche descending, it overwhelms you. Of course the ship's way is deadened; she seems like a living thing overburdened, yet struggling to be free; and well it is for all hands if the helmsman be able to keep his post and his wits about him. For if he be hurt, or have fled from the terrible wave, it is an even chance that she "broaches to;" that is to say, swings round broadside on to the next great wave that follows relentlessly its predecessor. Then, helpless and vulnerable, she will most probably be smashed up and founder. Many a good ship has gone with all hands to the bottom just as simply as that.

In order to avoid such a catastrophe, the proper procedure is to "heave-to" before the sea has attained so dangerous a height; but even a landsman can understand how reluctant a shipmaster may be to lie like a log just drifting, while a more seaworthy ship is flying along at the rate of, perhaps, three hundred miles a day in the desired direction. Ships of the *Cachalot's* bluff build are peculiarly liable to delays of this kind from their slowness, which, if allied to want of buoyancy, makes it necessary to heave-to in good time, if safety is at all cared for.

To my great astonishment and delight, however, our grand old vessel nobly sustained her character, running on without shipping any heavy water, although sometimes hedged in on either side by gigantic waves that seemed to tower as high as her lowermast-heads. Again and again we were caught up and passed by the splendid homeward-bound colonial packets, some of them carrying an appalling press of canvas, under which the long, snaky hulls, often overwhelmed by the foaming seas, were hardly visible, so insignificant did they appear by comparision with the snowy mountain of swelling sail above.

So we fared eastward and ever southward, until in due time up rose the gloomy, storm-scarred crags of the Diego Ramirez rocks, grim outposts of the New World. To us, though, they bore no terrific aspect; for were they not the turning-point from which we could steer north, our head pointed for home? Immediately upon rounding them we hauled up four points, and, with daily improving weather, climbed the southern slopes towards the line.

Very humdrum and quiet the life appeared to all of us, and had it not been for the saving routine of work by day, and watch by night, kept up with all our old discipline, the tedium would have been insupportable after the incessant excitement of expectation to which we had so long been accustomed. Still, our passage was by no means a bad one for a slow ship, being favoured by more than ordinarily steadfast winds until we reached the zone of the south-east trades again, where the usual mild, settled wind and lovely weather awaited us. On and on, unhasting but unresting, we stolidly jogged, by great good fortune slipping across the "doldrums"—that hateful belt of calms about the line so much detested by all sailor-men—without losing the south-east wind.

Not one day of calm delayed us, the north-east trades meeting us like a friend sent to extend a welcoming hand and lend us his assistance on our homeward way. They hung so far to the eastward, too—sometimes actually at east-by-north—that we were able to steer north on the starboard tack—a slice of luck not usually met with. This "slant" put all hands in the best of humours, and already the date of our arrival was settled by the more sanguine ones, as well as excellent plans made for spending the long voyage's earnings.

For my part, having been, in spite of my youth, accustomed to so many cruel disappointments and slips between the cup and lip, I was afraid to dwell too hopefully upon the pleasures (?) of getting ashore. And after the incident which I have now to record occurred.

I felt more nervous distrust than I had ever felt before at sea since first I began to experience the many vicissitudes of a sailor's life.

We had reached the northern verge of the tropics in a very short time, owing to the favourable cant in the usual direction of the north-east trades before noted, and had been met with north-westerly winds and thick, dirty weather, which was somewhat unusual in so low a latitude. Our look-outs redoubled their vigilance, one being posted on each bow always at night, and relieved every hour, as we were so well manned. We were now on the port tack, of course, heading about north-east-by-north, and right in the track of outward-bound vessels from both the United Kingdom and the States. One morning, about three a.m.—that fateful time in the middle watch when more collisions occur than at any other—suddenly out of the darkness a huge ship seemed to leap right at us. She must have come up in a squall, of which there were many about, at the rate of some twelve knots an hour, having a fair wind, and every rag of sail set. Not a gleam of light was visible anywhere on board of her, and, to judge from all appearances, the only man awake on board was the helmsman.

We, being "on the wind, close-hauled," were bound by the "rule of the road at sea" to keep our course when meeting a ship running free. The penalty for doing *anything* under such circumstances is a severe one. First of all, you do not *know* that the other ship's crew are asleep or negligent, even though they carry no lights; for, by a truly infernal parsimony, many vessels actually do not carry oil enough to keep their lamps burning all the voyage, and must therefore economize in this unspeakably dangerous fashion. And it may be that just as you alter your course, daring no longer to hold on, and, as you have every reason to believe, be run down, the other man alters his. Then a few breathless moments ensue, an awful crash, and the two vessels tear each other to pieces, spilling the life that they contain over the hungry sea. Even if you escape, *you* are to blame for not keeping your course, unless it can be proved that you were not seen by the running ship.

Well, we kept our course until, I verily believe, another plunge would have cut us sheer in two halves. At the last moment our helm was put hard down, bringing our vessel right up into the wind at the same moment as the helmsman on board the other vessel caught sight of us, and instinctively put his helm down too. The two vessels swung side by side amidst a thunderous roar of flapping canvas, crackling of fallen spars, and rending of wood as the shrouds tore away the bulwarks. All our davits were ripped from the starboard side, and most of our bulwarks too; but, strangely enough, we lost no spars nor any important gear. There seemed to be a good deal of damage done on board the stranger, where, in addition, all hands were at their wits' end. Well they might be, aroused from so criminal a sleep as theirs. Fortunately, the third mate had a powerful bull's-eye lantern, which in his watch on deck he always kept lighted. Turning it on the stern of the delinquent vessel as she slowly forged clear of us, we easily read her name, which, for shame's sake as well as for prudential reasons, I withhold. She was a London ship, and a pretty fine time of it I had for the next day or two, listening to the jeers and sarcasms on the quality of British seamanship.

Repairing damages kept us busy for a few days; but whatever of thankfulness we were capable of feeling was aroused by this hairbreadth escape from death through the wicked neglect of the most elementary duty of any man calling himself a seaman.

Then a period of regular Western-ocean weather set in. It was early spring in the third year since our departure from this part of the world, and the north-easter blew with bitter severity, making even the seasoned old captain wince again; but, as he jovially said, "it smelt homey, n' *he* warn't a-goin' ter growl at thet." Neither were any of us, although we could have done with less of a sharp edge to it all the same.

Steadily we battled northward, until at last, with full hearts, we made Cape Navesink ("Ole Neversunk"), and on the next day took a tug and towed into New Bedford with every flag we could scare up flying, the centre of admiration—a full whale-ship safe back from her long, long fishing round the world.

My pleasant talk is done. I wish from my heart it were better performed; but, having done my best, I must perforce be content. If in some small measure I have been able to make you, my friendly reader, acquainted with a little-known or appreciated side of life, and in any wise made that life a real matter to you, giving you a fresh interest in the toilers of the sea, my work has not been wholly in vain. And with that fond hope I give you the sailor's valedictory—

SO LONG!

Lightning Source UK Ltd.
Milton Keynes UK
UKHW010223220219
337758UK00004B/95/P

9 780343 529444